Steered
by the
Falling
Stars

A Father's Journey

Steered by

the Falling Stars

Daniel Spurr

Ragged Mountain Press

CAMDEN, MAINE

Published by Ragged Mountain Press, an imprint of
McGraw-Hill, Inc.

Questions regarding the content of this book should be
addressed to:

Ragged Mountain Press
P.O. Box 220
Camden, ME 04843

For every book sold, Ragged Mountain Press will make a
contribution to an environmental cause.

Steered by the Falling Stars is printed on 60-pound Renew
Opaque Vellum, which contains 50 percent waste paper
(preconsumer) and 10 percent postconsumer waste paper.

Edited by Jonathan Eaton and Pamela Benner.
Production by Molly Mulhern.
Text design by James F. Brisson.

Library of Congress Cataloging-in-Publication Data
Spurr, Daniel, 1947–
Steered by the Falling Stars : a father's journey /
Daniel Spurr.
p.   cm.
ISBN 0-87742-332-6
1. Spurr, Daniel, 1947 –   . 2. Spurr, Daniel, 1947 –
— Journeys — United States — Atlantic Coast.   3. Fathers
and sons —
United States — Biography.   4. Sailing — Atlantic
Ocean.   5.
Atlantic Coast (U.S.) — Description and travel.   6. Sail-
boat
living. I. Title.
CT275.S6295A3   1992
910'.9163 — dc20   92-13055
CIP
10 9 8 7 6 5 4 3 2 1

For Peter Josiah Spurr

CONTENTS

viii

PROLOGUE

A sailboat cruise is a singularly impractical means of getting somewhere. The "rooms" are small, the "ceilings" low, the "yard" is an obstacle course of rigging, winches, awkward ledges of uncertain footing, and there is rope everywhere underfoot. Even on the best of days, the time is always slow, the way always long.

Most of the drawbacks, however, are directly related to bad weather. When the wind blows, the seas kick; the roll, pitch, and yaw of the boat conspire to turn even the strongest stomach inside out. And when the weather is balmy, time stands still, the other world ceases to exist, and the plainness of the seascape seems to mirror the sedated interior of your mind.

Vulnerability to the elements is part of the appeal. A boat is no wall of concrete footed in the earth. It is more like an egg, round and buoyant, each part fragile, yet in its sum profoundly seaworthy. There are those who love a boat for the thing itself—this crafted, precisely functional, sometimes beautiful collection of wood, plastic, and metal. Who can run his finger over the grain of oiled ash without tactile pleasure, or behold a polished brass fitting and not admire its gleaming finish?

But the essence of sailing is not adoration of an inanimate object but the spiritual awakening of the man or woman who steers it.

I

In one hand the sailor holds the wind, in the other the sea. The only sound is of the waves spinning off the hull, bubbling like chimes. The colors of the water stretch as far as the eye can see—blue, white, steel-gray, aqua, green. How alive and changeable it is!

The sailor is alone. Not even the mountaineer, lost in the scrub pine and granite outcroppings, feels the same alienation from his surroundings. For the sailor trespasses in an environment for which he is poorly equipped: He swims not much better than a dog.

Like a spaceman hurtling in orbit around a distant moon, the offshore sailor depends entirely upon his boat, his preparations, and his skill.

Living on a sailboat for an extended period is an ascetic exercise in which the comforts of hot showers, three-course meals and twenty-four-hour contact with the world are forsaken. No TVs, no telephones, no Federal Express overnight letters. The acquisition of material goods—man's (and woman's) first addiction—is a credo rejected. Convention is a god forsworn. It is also a good way to do penance for one's excesses. Like the holy man who worships his god through abstinence and denial, I rid myself of most worldly possessions and crawled into the tiny cave of my boat.

My plan to go cruising began as a strike against the "quiet desperation" of the humdrum life so earnestly scorned by Henry Thoreau. Through remarriage and the learning of a new trade, it wove itself like a Colombian mola tapestry, bursting with color, ingenious in its design, the story full of surprise. It ended, quite unpredictably, as a metaphor of life, plotting its own alpha and omega, scoring the music of our laughter and tears, a pictograph blocked with symbols of light and darkness, sowing and harvesting, prophesying our gifts and losses—the bountiful corn and the black, ominous crow.

The objective was partly met. No venture ever proceeds exactly as planned. Ours certainly didn't. We left on the scheduled day, and that is about where the plan fell apart. My wife, Andra, and I never made it around the world, nor even to the Caribbean on which I'd set my sights early. There would be good days ahead, blessed with sunshine and happiness, and others of unspeakable sadness. We ended the cruise a year later. Yet in that interregnum my wife and I came to know each other in ways never imagined, and the children, ah, the children . . . well, therein lies the story.

I

Lists

Every trip must begin somewhere, and ours began in a boatyard. It was April, and I was sitting in the cockpit of *Adriana,* the thirty-three-foot sailboat my wife and I were outfitting for a cruise of the East Coast and Bahamas. Winter had lingered in Rhode Island, the ground thawed grudgingly, and the buds of the forsythia bushes along the shore road trembled in the spring breeze. Like a bull at the gate, I was anxious to begin final preparations.

Each day I awoke to the dizzying details of disconnecting ourselves from the structures of ordinary living: buying and installing boat gear, storing household effects, arranging mail forwarding, banking, and answering all our friends' questions. But it was the questions we asked of ourselves—about destinations and timetables, occupations, family, and faith . . . faith that we wouldn't drown, drive each other to divorce, or return penniless and unemployable—that made us realize the significance of our decision.

We had a small savings, plus a stipend from *Cruising World,* a magazine for wanderlust sailors. For eight years I had been its senior editor, vicariously living the lives of its authors, who sailed the far corners of the globe to dive on Byzantine ruins in Turkey, discover the rare double coconut on a beach in the Seychelles, and photograph the last flower on Earth in a rare patch of soil on Antarctica's Palmer peninsula. Our ambition was far more modest: Head north to Canada, then turn south and see what might happen. Still, the yearning to drop all and follow the sun was compelling. If there is a voice in each of us that must be obeyed, mine said: "Quit work and go sailing."

I had never gotten around to covering the boat for the winter, and so the decks were a cake of dirt, bird droppings, and the more recent strata of epoxy, sawdust, and engine oil. No matter—if this were the makeup she was fated to wear, she would wear it proudly, and like orphans we would run away together, bonded by our stains and poverty.

We roosted high above the weeds and tangled rubble of Tiny Clark's boatyard in Jamestown, on the eastern shore of Conanicut Island. The boat sat on her keel, stern to a weathered shed, held upright by a series of screw jacks, or *poppets* as they are called in New England. A pair of tired old birds we were, looking out over Narragansett Bay, rich and glitzy Newport opposite. The bay bridge spanning the blue canvas between the two islands was a rainbow of promise. A few boats were tacking through the inshore currents, and I was jealous that our launch was weeks, perhaps months, away. My consolation was the uncertain plan of leaving Newport and the workaday world for a year's cruise; come fall I'd be lying on some fine-sand beach in the Exumas while these early-bird sailors unstepped spars, wrapped their boats in plastic, and hibernated. Though I tried to anticipate the leavetaking with equanimity, the event was momentous. For I saw the cruise as an escape from routine and boredom, an affirmative action against a dull and ordinary life, the fulfillment of a dream born in the bowels of a Michigan prison when I was twenty years old.

I learned to sail when I was fifteen, struggling on the stumpridden manmade waters of Barton Pond in my father's wooden Snipe. The small, open daysailer was keenly sensitive to the mistakes of the helmsman, and so it was a good trainer. I was mostly self-taught, though I received several important lessons from the cranky and agile Mrs. Stewart, whose invalid husband had forced her to shanghai the family collie for crew. One day as I was lazing around the placid waters, unable to make the boat move, she pulled alongside in her own Snipe and boarded, glaring beneath a Chinese garden hat with eyes no less bloody than those of the pirate Anne Bonney. While the dog gripped the mainsheet in its teeth, she remonstrated me for hoisting the jib upside down. Whereupon she set it right and warned me never again to commit such a sin.

But the lust didn't fix there in Ann Arbor; it was five years later, one night in C Block, when I went to visit my friend Lennie Zazzarino. He was from New Jersey, a streetwise Italian with a five o'clock shadow from jaw to jaw and a round head that was prematurely balding. He was doing time for selling marijuana; I was, by comparison, a country bumpkin, though my crime of bank embezzlement made me think of myself as much more worldly than that. I learned the hard way that eighteen-year-old bank tellers are too young to be dressed up in linen suits and confined to a basement counting barrels of coins.

The greed and foolery cost me two years of my life. I was an embarrassment to my young wife, Margaret, and to my family, and I was ashamed.

I spent two months in the Wayne County Jail during the Detroit race riots. In August 1967, federal marshals drove me in manacles and leg irons to a prison in Kentucky; later, in the winter, I was transferred to the federal correctional institution in Milan, Michigan. The Mafia stool pigeon Joe Valachi was serving his sentence there, and each evening we watched through barred windows as the guards led him around the courtyard in a weary parade of supposed exercise. After a few Michigan winters, in exchange for a transfer, he agreed to testify again before Congress on organized crime. He was, to that date, the highest-ranking gangster to turn stoolie against his own kind. What television and the newspapers didn't print, the world learned from the book, *The Valachi Papers.* By the end of my first year he'd been shipped to another prison in Arizona, where, ironically, he soon died of natural causes. He had complained bitterly of Michigan. His last line was, "I hate the cold."

I labored frenetically in the parole office typing casework reports on blue mimeograph paper, which stained our shirts and fingertips like an indelible brand of guilt. Still, it was a welcome

6

promotion from my first assignment in the steamy laundry, where the inmates yelled and roughhoused and the guards beat the bars with billy clubs. It was George Raft versus Bull Nelson, the crazy con trying to win the unwinnable battle of minds against an overweight, neckless corrections officer who'd survived the Bataan Death March only to end his life watching thieves.

My comrade typists were two: Robertson from Rock Island, Illinois, a car thief and bearer of that ignominious label "habitual offender," and Hubbard, from a tarpapered home in northern Michigan, a Jehovah's Witness and conscientious objector to the Vietnam War. Each day we donned headphones and transcribed the monotonic caseworker evaluations of an inmate's progress (or distinct lack thereof), then hung the perforated stencils on a large metal drum, inked the well, and hand-cranked copies; to the subject of the report (often containing sensitive recommendations concerning parole), an extra copy smuggled in your pants was worth a "box" of cigarettes.

Lennie worked down the hall in the record office taking mug shots of incoming prisoners. "Zazz" and I became fast friends, but on this night, as I rattled the steel door to his cinderblock cell, he didn't answer, not at first. I pushed into the cramped, dark space. The air smelled like a soap shop. When my eyes adjusted I saw that he was standing on his chair in the middle of the cell, rocking gently as he alternated his weight from one foot to the other. "Sshh!" he admonished. I stood and listened. A few minutes later he whispered, "I'm sailing, maannn! Can't you hear the rigging hum in the wind, the waves lapping the bow, the creak of old timbers giving to the sea?"

"Yeahhh, try it," Lennie ordered. I climbed onto the chair and closed my eyes, imagining myself on the deck of a square rigger, easing along a smooth sea under a Polynesian moon. He put his hands on my ankles to show me how to shift my weight. The seat creaked. When he spoke, his voice was hushed and nasal, his enunciation sinisterly precise. "Are you *there,* maannn?"

Later, with the light on, we sat and talked before the guards came to perform the evening count. I asked him what was the sweet smell. "Talcum powder," he answered, staring at me as if I were incredibly naive. "Covers the smell of the Mary Jane."

The seventies were here, and I didn't even know it: Hippies were preaching love not war (all I knew about Vietnam was from the Smothers Brothers variety show), and Dr. Timothy Leary was saying that drugs could enlighten you. (I'd smoked a joint once, a crushed straw of paper mailed from a hood in Chicago to a friend of mine in Michigan—it gave me a headache.) All I knew now was the calendar, whose pages fell as slowly as needles from a pine tree.

In the visiting room I told Margaret how some con had smuggled Lennie's marijuana in a baggie inserted into his rectum. Neither of us could believe it.

Our departure date was August 1, and I was working fast. The hull needed painting, the mast new stainless steel rigging stays, the crazed Plexiglas windows replacement with bulletproof Lexan, the Loran C navigation receiver and electronic autopilot delicate installation. And a hundred other items on a list so long that for every job I added I forgot another.

Novelist Jim Harrison once wrote in *Cruising World* that he is so fond of lists, he sometimes writes down things he has already done just for the satisfaction of crossing them out. While I appreciated Harrison's cuteness, my dependency on lists was such that I began to chafe under their tyranny. They lost themselves in my backpack, added entries without permission, scribbled incorrect dimensions in the margins, and worst of all, they were never one-hundred-percent finished. But I had the singlemindedness of a dream chaser and persevered, eventually coming to regard my grease-stained lists as just another set of tools whose job was to help me get to some magical place where lists were no longer necessary. Surely, I told myself, the West Indians know nothing about the psychological dictatorship of lists.

The trick for me was to know when to stop being anal and just go.

This day, however, I had hit some sort of black hole, and I didn't like it. I was revved for work but going nowhere. I paced about the boat, my feet like propellers out of water. Various ongoing projects had arrived simultaneously at a crossroads with a broken traffic light; there was nothing further to be done without a trip to the hardware store and phone calls to factory experts: Is Mercury's new corrosion-proof grease suitable for lubing seacocks? Will a four-degree misalignment of the self-steering wind vane affect its performance? Can the Loran be grounded to the boat's lightning system? What is the diameter of a number five screw? How many beers will it take to get the yard personnel to launch us on time?

Some people only talk about going cruising; Andra and I were doing it, at least taking the first infantile steps. And thus far all I had to show for our efforts were long days and nights ravaged by anxious dreams.

Looking out at the other boats sailing by, it was hard not to be discouraged, hard not to believe that somehow the whole plan was unraveling, that the boat and I had passed through a weird warp in space and were frozen on a facsimile planet where a lifetime of labor produced nothing.

For Clifford Springston, the fifty-one-year-old New York architect-cum-builder/renovator ("Nobody *builds* in New York") who was restoring an old wooden schooner on the other side of Tiny Clark's shed, time had ceased to exist altogether. Every fair weekend for six years he had driven his Audi out of "the City," along the insane, narrow-laned Connecticut turnpike, where stressed-out commuters drive like there's no tomorrow, and the truck drivers in their black-and-chrome Kenworths bash Japanese compacts into Long Island Sound.

Springston was drawn between this Scylla and Charybdis to the serenity of Clark's yard, as if Tiny were Circe and the relic hulls all that was left of the men whose lists had grown too long. There, amid the wild roses and rocky outcroppings, Springston, bespectacled with amber frames, puttering in a golf hat and nylon slicker, cut out rotten pieces of *Vanguard*'s skeletal remains. The object of his love was a fifty-five-foot William Hand–designed schooner he had bought for one dollar. The previous owner had hauled her during the hurricane of '54 and she hadn't felt the water since. Someday, Springston said, he would like to spend a winter in the Caribbean, perhaps a summer in the Med.

Some days, when I couldn't stand my own boat any longer and felt I might turn mute for lack of company, I sat in a pile of his woodchips and visited.

"It doesn't look like it," he said, "but I'm well over the hump. The cabin is off—some kids burned half of it on the rocks there. The spar? Gave it away; didn't want it. Too old for a main gaff boom anyway. I figure four more years. With any luck I'll have the hull sealed by winter. Difference between boats and buildings is there's no plumb and no square. You could build this entire hull new in a fraction of the time it's taking me, given the materials. You can't win all the battles, but I think this one can be licked."

I asked him if he was a list keeper. "I'm a list *maker*, not a list keeper," he replied. "Too many facets; if you don't record everything you can't keep it in your mind." He picked up a stick and heaved it down the yard for Darcy, the German shepherd who, as far as I could tell, was his only companion in this mind-numbing project. Turned out later he had a wife, "the best boat painter I know; but I won't tell you who taught her or the incident that made her." He winked.

She stayed at a nearby bed-and-breakfast, and I never saw her. It seemed he was married only to a dream, a dream with room for no other person and the attendant obligations, outcries, and of course, the dread ultimatum, "Me or the boat."

Recreation, said Murray Davis, founder of *Cruising World,* is an important part of contemporary living and should not be dismissed as trivial or bourgeois. And voyaging under sail, as many of our readers believed, is more than recreation, it is a way of life.

At my desk I worked inside a pleasure dome, an imaginary bubble full of books, stories, clacking typewriters, and phone calls from Walter Mittys who wanted to know how to sell it all and escape to the good life. On Friday afternoons there were wine parties, and reggae music played on the turntable under my desk. I traveled the world, honed my writing skills, and learned as much as I could about boats, gear, navigation, and seamanship.

After several years, I gave up my apartment and moved aboard a twenty-eight-foot fiberglass sloop. And with the money saved, in two years I traded up.

Adriana was a 1967 auxiliary sloop built by the Pearson company in Bristol, Rhode Island. She was laid up with fiberglass, which some would say forfeits the soul. I disagree. Her lines were gainly and fair, and there was good wood on her for warmth and dress-up. She measured almost 33 feet overall, less than 23 on the waterline, about 9½ at the beam, and would plow the bottom in anything less than 5 feet. The keel was deep enough for ocean sailing and marginally suitable for the shallow waters of the Chesapeake, Florida Keys, and Bahama Islands. Her documented displacement was six tons, moderately heavy for her length, which gave her a seakindly motion. There were permanent berths for four, a three-burner stove with oven, a toilet compartment, and a small table. It was compact living but civilized. Those unfamiliar with small boats, however, would call it primitive, and Andra was one of them.

At the time of purchase the boat appeared supremely well equipped for cruising. Indeed, she had been sailed in the Caribbean by a former owner, but how soon the jewel tarnished! The aging diesel engine suffered an embolism in the oil cooler and required replacement, the sails were so thin you could see through them, and much of the metal gear was crystallized by years of exposure to salt air.

I set about a protracted period of upgrading. The boat was repowered with a new Yanmar diesel and new sails built by Newport's Aaron Jasper, the cushions were reupholstered, rigging wires replaced, the interior teak varnished, the electrical system rewired, and the hull painted. For cruising comfort, a simple but efficient shower was fitted to the head compartment using an instantaneous propane water heater. It was fed in turn by a flexible water tank and a deck fill that collected free rainwater. The poorly insulated icebox was ripped out, and in its place a 2½-cubic-foot propane refrigerator fitted; it was small, designed for a Winnebago, but still had room for essential perishables such as milk, eggs, juice, and meats. Most importantly, it made a cute little tray of ice in just over an hour, so we never feared having to make gin and tonics with clear marbles that we would clink and chink to fool ourselves.

The summer of '87 arrived, and we found ourselves racing to make all the final preparations in spite of nagging obstacles (read: time and money). But when we lay awake at night thinking of the alternatives, we realized there really were none. Newport had changed during the past eight years. The navy had left, and the "touroids" arrived—a human assault that made the Chinese Red Army look like a Girl Scout clean-up troop. Local government had sold the waterfront to the highest bidders—developers from just about anywhere but Newport who bought out the Irish barkeeps and Italian fishmongers and on their memories built highrise condominiums, clapboard and cedar-shaked shopping emporiums. The public accesses to the water were routinely lost to private interests, and now there was scarcely a place to dock a dinghy. Ironically, the only effort at expansion that failed to pass the muster of zoning and environmental agencies was the city's own project to extend its public Ann Street pier.

The tax base soared, and the locals cursed and toiled. On summer weekends pink-and-green Izod "watermelons" from Massachusetts and Connecticut filled the discos and fudge shops. Kids named Vinny from Fall River raced down Aquidneck Island in baby-blue Trans Ams to "rinse" beers in the Dockside Saloon and One Pelham East; girls named Muffy, with short foreheads and large trust funds, lithely cut through traffic on their mopeds; and fat families from Ohio stopped you on the street wondering where they could find the America's Cup, though it, and our humor, had been lost years ago.

Parking was nonexistent, the overtaxed sewer system dumped raw excrement into the harbor, and a glass of tap water was a cloudy diorama of suspended particles. The only honest man who profited from this rape was Ian Scott, whose family owns the Crystal Spring Water Company. The magic aquifer welled beneath their ancestral home like black gold, and even the poor people, tired of boiling out alleged carcinogens, were happy to pay for bottled water.

Once this wild scene had appealed to me, probably because I was younger then and single. Now I was almost forty and remarried, to a second-generation Swedish girl I'd met at *Cruising World.* Andra had grown up in Rhode Island but lived nine years in Colorado. She too longed for a change of scenery, never hesitating to say what she felt, often with just the right touch of comic cynicism. With the vow of escape a strong bond between us, and the understanding that my days as a diaper-changer were over, we eloped to Mexico, with Peter and Adriana—my children by Margaret—as our underage "testigos." We said "si" to the Oficial de Matrimonio and astonished our friends on our return when we announced our marriage at a party in Newport's Hibernian Hall.

Andra, however, was not a sailor, and I suspect she would have been just as happy to hop in a van and drive west. In late June she enrolled in Bing Murray's Adventurer Sailing School, taught on Narragansett Bay in a forty-two-foot cutter. Bing was a big, strapping man with a kindly Fred MacMurray face. He was a fighter pilot in the Korean War, shot down and held prisoner. I don't know how this changed him, but, like my time in prison, at the least it must have taught him patience. During three days in June he made Andra plot courses in the fog, jibe in thirty-knot winds, and back out of tight slips with million-dollar yachts choking either side. Before the class, she worried about my falling overboard; now, for the first time, she showed signs of confidence in dealing with such emergencies. But her most important attribute was a total immunity to seasickness, a quality that would stand her in good stead in the months to come. More than one Newport romance had failed on that count, and I was quietly encouraged.

Soon Peter and Adriana would arrive to sail with us on the first leg north to Maine. They had flown out each summer since my leaving Michigan, and on weekends we made short cruises to Block Island, Cuttyhunk, and Martha's Vineyard. These were inauspicious first steps toward the boundless, tree-ripened life I imagined just the other side of the cutline between sea and sky, but at least I was moving in the right direction. Early on I had seen how sailing—or more accurately, travel—had opened their eyes to the wondrous world around them. And I was convinced that the best way to prevent them from becoming narrow-minded adults, handicapped by ignorance and bigotry, was to expose them to the varying cultures of the peoples of the globe. Setting out beyond home waters, which for them were the Great Lakes—its shores populated with Icelanders, Swedes, and Germans—and New England, that Puritan bastion of straight-backed chairs, starched collars, and stiff upper lips, would broaden their view and deepen their understanding of life. It is easy to say I did it for their education. . . . I did. But I also was trying to pay a debt, trying to make up for all the track meets, proms, and parent conferences I'd missed.

They learned how to row the dinghy, raise sails, drop anchor, find the nearest dock in a fog, tell the difference between a mussel and a clam, and to name the constellations of the stars that revolve above us. Adria took a class in watercolors and demonstrated the talent that would later lead her to the Rhode Island School of Design. And Peter, despite having cerebral palsy, and being too weak to swim, said he wanted, when he grew up, to live on a boat next to mine (but bigger, of course). They had, from all appearances, accepted the consequences of their father's choices. They prospered.

As launch day approached, I spent long hours in the yard scraping the boat's bottom, puttying cracks, and wielding a vast array of disposable brushes. One day Andra came by and announced she was going to clean and oil the teak trim. I was rather surprised as she was usually busy with her own work. She gave it a few hours, and when I looked again she was seated below at the dinette writing something in my small notepad—probably, I surmised, performing obeisance to her own demon list.

Mine shrank, grew again, then lapsed into temporary remission under press of time. Will Tuttle, my neighbor refurbishing his father's ninety-eight-year-old wooden sloop, said he envied me. *Me?* After all the hours I watched him drop his sander to go windsurfing? After all the times his friend in the Saab Turbo picked him up for mysterious "intermissions?" In truth, progress is inevitable, Will said, as long as you put in the grunt time—Rome wasn't built in a day and Hannibal didn't cross the Alps on half-tracks.

In *Adriana's* cockpit at day's end there was plenty of time to examine my life. Like Thoreau, I did not want to find myself on my deathbed with regrets, believing I had not lived. I wanted to see America, get to know the people who live and work on her waters, to travel those waters on my own boat simply and without ostentation. For the birds don't preen for the loud motor-yacht, and the local folks don't talk to loud people. In this window in our lives the planets were aligned about as close as they would ever be for us. This would be my job for a year, with only the wind and the waves and the gulls as my writing muses. And a goal would be realized that I had promised myself long ago, in 1967, in Lennie Zazzarino's prison cell.

On a hazy Saturday in June, *Adriana* slid down the railway at the Jamestown Boat Yard into a light north wind. I stood at the helm, and on cue from Dean, the yard supervisor, started the engine and backed her out, stern to the rocky islands called the Dumplings, and Cling Stone, the strange, isolated house built upon them.

As I motored out into the bay, aiming for my mooring in Newport Harbor, I reached into my pocket for my pipe. My latest list, interrupted by the fury of launching, fluttered into the wind. The sheet hovered in front of me for an instant as if stayed by an invisible hand. I glimpsed, "install wind indicator," "new engine stop cable," and, in a strange hand, "kiss your wife."

Kiss my wife? And then it was gone, swirling into the updrafts, lost against a milk-white sky.

2

Bishop Berkeley's Rock

The work on *Adriana* continued on our mooring in Newport Harbor. The pace was hellish, every errand hampered by the tourists who swarmed the wharves to shop in "boatiques" and eat baked stuffed seafood with a harbor view.

Driving through downtown was as futile as trying to find a public urinal. Feeling like a traitor to the working class, I bit the bullet and bought a moped, which are despised in tourist towns everywhere. They are, however, efficient. Laden with bags of rope, caulking, and wires and bolts, I dipped and weaved around the gridlocked cars. In my eyes and fingers was all the urgency of the messenger from Marathon.

Still, there was much to be said for Newport when you looked beneath the veneer. There is the Redwood Library, the country's oldest, a fine place to sit on a rainy day and read obscure periodicals. Ride a bike around Ocean Drive and climb out to Spouting Rock when a good sou'wester is blowing. In autumn, when the city has fallen into its equinoctial slumber, Gary Kilroy kindles the first fire of fall in his Franklin stove at One Pelham East, and one finds old friends stirring hot buttered rums with cinnamon sticks.

Long interested in philosophy, I sometimes slipped out of town into the lanes and pastures between Middletown and the Sakonnet River for a visit to White Hall. There, between 1728 and 1731, the

16

great Trinity philosopher George Berkeley lived while preaching at Newport's First Congregational Church (also the country's oldest). His school was subjective idealism. There is no existence of matter, he wrote, that is independent of the mind. *Esse est percipi.*

Berkeley's arguments were vexing. Does a tree falling in the forest make a noise, even when no one hears? The question is easy to dismiss as a problem of semantics, but I was willing to grant Berkeley this: If existence is predicated on cognition, one can escape reality—the pain of consciousness when one is sad or depressed—only by ceasing to think. Unfortunately, there is no main power switch in the brain that, during times of grief, can be shut down to standby mode. Short of suicide or a lobotomy, we are all prisoners of our minds, irrevocably chained to our senses.

I had long felt a prisoner of the past. The strange thing about this cruise was I now felt like a prisoner of the future as well. I had set in motion a series of irreversible events. Jobs were quit and money spent.

In July Peter and Adriana arrived from Michigan. The prospect of sailing to Maine with us before returning to school delighted them. The boat was their second home, and they knew the ropes well.

Adria, blond-haired and blue-eyed, was a good-natured girl, full of enthusiasm for travel, reading, art, and the revelations of Nature that greeted her on the ocean. At sweet sixteen she possessed remarkable maturity and grace. At times the only clues to her real age were her stereo cassette tapes—English Beat, the Church, and the cacophonous B-52s, the only group that sounded anything like its name. Mercifully, some wise relative had given her a Walkman, so that as she sat in the cockpit drawing, her inspiration was purely private. She loved her summers in Newport, never visibly affected by the divorce. She had learned to sail, swim, paint, and make friends with the old geezers at the Aquidneck Lobster Company. I enjoyed her companionship as much as any adult's, and of her future I had few doubts.

Peter was a precious twelve-year-old, skinny as a mizzenmast, his long eyelashes the envy of all the girls. His cerebral palsy made him tipsy as a drunk. His knees were scab on scab, but he had a stoic attitude about his frequent falls. He was afraid of the water but loved boats. Sometimes he faded into a mysterious silence and seemed almost autistic. At those times I wondered if he harbored feelings of anger toward me and was just waiting to give me a good licking when he was at last old and strong enough. But these moods never lasted long; soon his big smile brightened the darkest room, and we were the best of buddies.

As July slipped away, Andra gutted the apartment, loaning out our major furniture (i.e., a couch) and scrubbing two years of pipe and cigarette smoke off the ceilings. Meanwhile, Adria and Peter helped me build a three-piece nesting dinghy in Ned Reynolds's boatshop. This unusual craft was designed by Danny Greene, a naval architect and contributing editor to *Cruising World.* He'd profited nicely selling plans for an earlier plywood pram named Two Bits. Besides giving him funds to cruise, I believe it established him as the inventor of small "nesting" boats, whose subsections stack inside each other like Chinese boxes.

Tryst, as he called his newest design, represented a third or fourth generation of thinking on the "dinghy problem." *Reductio ad simplicitas*: How does one design the largest possible dinghy to fit in the smallest possible space so it may be carried on the deck of a small cruising sailboat? And how does one engineer it so simply that a fisherman in the Third World can construct it on a beach?

Odd as it may seem to non-sailors, these are the questions that have haunted Danny Greene during the dozen or so years he has sailed between New England and the Caribbean. He has no use for fashionable inflatables, subject as they are to puncture, leaks, and theft; further, they won't tow straight and row like an egg.

Danny is the supreme pragmatist, and his designs derive from the dictum that function always precedes form. At the Webb Institute on Long Island he studied the science of hull design and fluid dynamics. Disdaining the strict regulations of the dormitory, he slept, along with all his belongings, in a metal wardrobe laid flat on the floor of his room. When he awoke, à la Bela Lugosi, he "cleaned up" by closing the doors coffin-style. He rejected ordinary furniture as extraneous and therefore an intolerable nuisance. The student judiciary challenged his unorthodoxy. No doubt its attitude was exacerbated by his aboriginal hairstyle and antisocial habit of going to bed immediately after dinner, then arising at 3 A.M. to study. But he won his case and graduated with honors.

Tryst was the distillation of a natural philosophy that would have made Thoreau's days at Walden Pond seem like a vacation in Aspen. She is 16 feet long fully assembled, but when the sections are stacked inside one another, the package is just 6½ feet. The hull is double-ended for easy construction on a simple jig, the seams are stitched with wire and "taped" with fiberglass so that errors in lofting (the transferring of lines from the plans to full-size patterns) are unnoticeable and irrelevant. The exterior is crudely faired with a jamlike mixture of epoxy and a fine purple powder called microballoons. Half-inch bolts with wingnuts fasten the hull sections together. Assembly and disassembly is quick. Danny justifies his caveman engineering with the premise that rocks, pilings, and the rigors of cruising undo in seconds the torturous hours spent sanding bumps and filling voids. Those are hours better spent with a book on a beach.

George Day, my editor at *Cruising World*, helped install a new electric windlass on the foredeck. The handsome bronze gear was a wedding gift from Andra's oldest friend, Cliff Raymond at Ideal Windlass Company. "When you cruise you really should anchor with chain, and the only way to haul chain is with an electric windlass. I won't have your cruise ruined by hauling anchors by hand," he told her. And in a comic footnote, he supplied us with a spare white foot-pad switch in case the standard black pad got too hot for her bare foot.

One day Andra presented me with a Texas flag to fly from the spreaders. Why, I'm not sure. Perhaps because the marine store in Austin, where we had spent Christmas with my parents, stocked neither of the two burgee-size flags we first needed—a yellow quarantine flag, to be flown on entering a foreign country, and the national flag of the Bahamas. In any case, I am fond of the Lone Star State and was happy to carry a little piece of Texas on our journey.

I unpacked the flag and prepared to hoist it in the rigging. But which was rightside up? The flag has three sections: The left third is a vertical blue bar with a white star in the middle, and the two-thirds to the right consists of two horizontal stripes of equal size, one white and one red. Because there was no obvious rightside up, I hoisted the flag with the red stripe up and forgot about it.

As summer slipped away, the clock and calendar became our greatest enemies. In order to reach Canada before cold weather set in, it was essential that we leave Newport by early August. And that date was upon us. At last the dinghy was ready for launching. Andra and several friends were invited to a christening party after work; all that remained was to screw on the rubber-and-canvas gunwale guard. Late that afternoon I slammed my foot into a drill bit and punctured an artery. Blood burbled from my arch as if from some low-pressure city-park drinking fountain with the stained chromium you dread putting your lips to. Adria fainted in the ensuing hysteria, and Peter hid in the dinghy. The launching party had been derailed by a trip to the hospital and a tetanus shot. And Andra, seemingly stood-up, a bottle of champagne in hand, was later found at Cafe Zelda wondering why on Earth she had married a sailor.

Until now, Andra hadn't been sure whether she would leave with us or meet up en route. Not surprisingly, she cited unfinished business and decided to rendezvous with us in Portland, Maine, a week later.

The day before the designated departure, our friend Danny Keirns, an intemperate, barrel-chested, redheaded handyman, gave us a bountiful cornucopia of food, a bottle of rum, and a Rag Mop fishing lure to troll for bluefish. He drank the entire bottle of Mount Gay while fashioning an outboard motor bracket on *Adriana*'s stern pulpit. We worked with a fever, for Keirns doesn't fool around when he's driving nails or mixing drinks. The day ended when our mutual friend Herb McCormick, another *Cruising World* editor, sped by in his new J/24 racing sloop. Keirns leaped aboard barefoot and never returned.

The next morning, August 3, the kids and I hoisted sail and grooved into Narragansett Bay with the magazine's photo boat escorting us bravely under leaden skies.

We towed the new dinghy on a long line, riding the cross seas smartly. Because the sailboat was named for Adria, we called the dinghy *For Pete's Sake.* Peter was mighty proud of her. From the cockpit he craned his neck over the side to watch nervously as it rode our stern wave, its chin high, obedient to the course of its mothership.

It began to rain as we sailed past Hammersmith Farm (Jackie Kennedy Onassis's childhood summer home), and near Castle Hill Light at the mouth of the bay our friends and colleagues turned back, heads tucked ducklike into the armpits of their slickers. Andra was there, waving sadly, though I am sure confident of her decision. And so was Keirns, whom she'd found wandering shoeless outside the *Cruising World* office that morning. He had the look of an all-nighter slapped like an insult on his rosy, hangdog face.

"Check the bolts on the bracket!" he hollered, grinning across the water. "I forgot to tighten them!"

Of course, it was a joke, and so were his paint-spackled boots, which I tossed to him; only then did the others realize he was barefoot.

Adriana thundered into building seas. When we reached the Brenton Reef tower we tacked for Cuttyhunk, one of the Elizabeth Islands nestled in the southern crotch of Cape Cod. The rain came in torrents, and the land disappeared. Adria threw up, and the refrigerator door broke off, spilling its carefully packed contents about the cabin.

Peter whispered, "Dad, I'll keep you company." Then he stretched out under the cockpit pillows and fell fast asleep.

Later the rain and wind gave way to fog. Whiteout. My eyes

couldn't focus. As Herman Melville discoursed in *Moby Dick,* white is infinitely more evil than black, because it disguises the devil in lamb's clothing. In the darkest night you can see the faintest light; in fog, your eyes see nothing and your imagination everything—black-hulled freighters, towering cliffs, oil rigs, and skyscrapers looming behind the mist, never quite materializing.

On reflection, it was stupid to have left in such miserable weather, but the only thing I feared more than rain and fog was another night in Newport. It was time to escape, and we had.

The next day dawned bright and beautiful, a seeming miracle. I awoke at six, and while the children slept I raised the anchor and began motoring toward the Cape Cod Canal. Buzzards Bay was flat enough to serve as a shaving mirror, and the trees of Massachusetts were a brilliant green. It was as if we had snuck through some purgatorial passage into a newer, better world beyond.

Peter woke and joined me in the cockpit for a breakfast of orange juice and apples. Adria slumbered until midmorning, but with her first open eye she was into her bathing suit and basking on a sail bag.

Later that day I found she had written the following message in the log:

> Last night I woke about 3 A.M. and felt compelled to come out on deck. I saw a light approaching, but it was dim and had a faint limish glow that made it recognizably different from the anchor lights of the other boats. As I watched, it began to come closer. Listening carefully for clues, I heard a clink-clong, clink-clong sound at short-spaced intervals. Entranced, I realized this object was coming right for our boat and would hit us broadside.
>
> Within moments an old man in a skiff had pulled up and given me his line. He was bearded, and his eyebrows nearly covered his eyes, and I watched them as he told me of his nocturnal adventure. In his boat were ten large fish. Atop his rod was a glowing object, which he said he had used to catch them. Although I'm not a good fisher, I knew the mass of slime couldn't have been bought at a bait shop. Its wrinkled surface had many cavities.

He said he must be going, and I felt a pull come over me. My head nodded and the water seemed closer.

With my super incredible wonton noodle shoes I slid back on deck and kicked the old man in the ear, and said, "It's late, I don't want to go fishing."

As I watched him row away, I noticed two eyes on his bait and two large buck teeth protruding from one cavity, echoing and singing:

> *"I've heard a hundred tales,*
> *And I've caught a thousand more,*
> *And next time we will score,*
> *With a head that I adore!"*

During the 1970s, the controversial Reverend Moon raised the ire of Gloucester fishermen when he established his own fishing fleet in the harbor. A bitter range war ensued, but the persecution only hardened the Moonies' resolve. They have survived the deportation of their master and outlasted their critics. As we sailed in, we were passed by dozens of their deep-sea runabouts, all named *One Hope*. The two-man crews were young, clean-shaven Occidentals and Anglos with beatific grins. What security there must be in the feeling of absolute righteousness!

In contrast, against the commercial piers rust-stained draggers were stacked three- and four-deep. The booms were raised like telephone poles, the green-and-white nets rolled up on huge aluminum drums, the generators rumbling night and day.

A good percentage of fish sticks come from Gloucester, and I remembered sadly Newport's once-active fleet. In Gloucester, at least, a great seafaring tradition is preserved without subsidy. These rust-stained rigs are descendants of the beautiful schooners my great-grandfather once captained. A popular family story claims he was the inspiration for Rudyard Kipling's novel *Captains Courageous*. The tale may be apocryphal, but I felt proud to be descended from blood that ran away to sea. Like Jack London, my great-grandfather was a lad eager for man's work.

Commercial fishing has been called the country's most dangerous profession. Watching a trawler heading out to sea in the face of a January gale, you cannot help but wonder if it will return. But with the banks depleted of their once-great schools of fish and increased competition from Russia, Japan, and other countries, the weather is a secondary concern: You can't catch fish without a hook in the water, and soon all the hooks in the world won't pay the mortgage, as songwriter Archie Fisher suggests in "The Final Trawl":

Now it's three long years since we made her pay,
Sing haul away, my laddie-o,
And we can't get by on the subsidy,
Sing haul away, my laddie-o.

Then heave away for the final trawl,
Sing haul away, my laddie-o,
It's an easy pull for the catch is small,
Sing haul away, my laddie-o.

So stow your gear lads and batten down,
Sing haul away, my laddie-o,
And I'll take the wheel lads and turn her 'round,
Sing haul away, my laddie-o.

And we'll join the Venture *and the* Morning Star,
Sing haul away, my laddie-o,
Riding high and empty toward the bar,
Sing haul away, my laddie-o.

For I'd rather beach her on the skerry rock,
Sing haul away, my laddie-o,
Than to see her torched in the breakers' dock,
Sing haul away, my laddie-o.

And when I die you could stow me down,
Sing haul away, my laddie-o,

In her rusty hold where the breakers sound,
Sing haul away, my laddie-o.

And I'd make my haven the fiddler's green,
Sing haul away, my laddie-o,
Where the grub is good and the bunks are clean,
Sing haul away, my laddie-o.

For I've fished a lifetime, boy and man,
Sing haul away, my laddie-o,
And the final trawl scarcely nets a cran,
Sing haul away, my laddie-o.

On we sailed for the strange and desolate rocks called the Isles of Shoals. By far they are the most interesting feature of New Hampshire's thirteen-mile coastline. Stark, treeless, and vulnerable, they are fit only for gulls, a brief walk through whose nesting grounds proves indisputably that they indeed own these islands. A hundred yards in we were divebombed and forced to retreat.

The list of humans here is few: a handful of lobstermen, scientists and students assigned to the biological research station, and Unitarian Universalists who make periodic retreats to the Star Hotel.

A hundred years ago these barren rocks were witness to a grisly murder. An immigrant (and possibly retarded) laborer, indentured to a fishing family, left a bar one night on the mainland, rowed the dozen miles to the Isles of Shoals, axed them all, and rowed back to the saloon before last call.

As I related the tale, Peter peered around the canvas dodger protecting the cockpit at the white and gray rocks growing on the horizon. He shivered and said softly, "Stop talking, Dad. I don't like legends."

Lennie and I had envisioned a more perfect world when we contemplated our escape to the South Seas. But there were risks in such reveries, and these were made dramatically and poignantly clear whenever an inmate "hit the wall."

After a time in prison, you begin to wonder what really keeps you from simply scaling the wall to freedom. The outer yard at Milan, accessible to inmates with minimum-security clearance, is cordoned by two high steel fences with trip lines and rolls of concertina wire. In between is a no-man's-land. There are guard-houses at each corner of the yard, and you can see the silhouettes of men armed with M-16s moving silently back and forth. They are mostly ex-army, putting in a few more years toward federal pensions; the others are former cops and rent-a-cops who in their everyday dreams stalk The Greatest Game.

You know their fingers are itchy, that despite their almost-pleasant demeanor in the cell blocks, silently they are goading you to run rabbit: "C'mon son, give me a try. Bet you don't make the second fence." Would they really shoot you? Never know until you try. The Dale Carnegie courses urge you, "Dare to be great!" Want to live a life of quiet desperation with Thoreau sneering at you? Want to be a sheep in a pen all your life? Up and over!

You think about it and bide your time. You read the anecdote in which Bishop Berkeley walks with a skeptical friend down a country road. As they near a rock on the roadside, the friend closes his eyes, slams his foot into the rock, and falls.

"There!" he cries defiantly. "I refute you thus!"

"Ah," the bishop smirks, "but the rock still exists in *God's* mind!"

Does God keep his thoughts on prison walls? You are about to take the gamble. You've had it here. The food is so bad your teeth rot. Yesterday you saw a guy get stabbed with a pair of scissors in the laundry line, two holes in his chest. He was a bank robber who had snitched on his partner, then through a bureaucratic oversight was transferred to the same prison. His partner took one look at him, grabbed the shears, and vaulted the counter into his chest.

Yes, perhaps it is time to leave this place. Maybe, just maybe, the walls and fences and M-16s aren't real. After all, you don't believe in God, and if the bricks and wires don't exist in your mind. . . .

You don't dare discuss your plans with other inmates, because they don't want to hear crazy talk, or if they do, you fear they might snitch. A tunnel would be a classy way out—you've seen it work in the movies. Clinging to the underside of a delivery truck might succeed too, or disguising yourself as the milkman, but you doubt you could pull it off. No, the easiest way is simply up and over the fence. One in ten makes it. Wear heavy clothes in case the concertina wire is real. Try not to hit the trip line, which lights two red bulbs to either side of the break point and gives the head-hunters in the towers a target area to spray until the searchlights pick you out.

While you are waiting for your moment one sunny afternoon, staring through the sallygate into the outer yard where a softball game is in progress, you hear a popping noise. No one else seems to notice at first. The pitcher winds up, then balks. The left-fielder has bolted. Your eyes burn. A pair of brown khakis hangs on the first fence. You want to take a closer look, but a siren sounds and you are herded back to your cell. Later you learn Machevsky took a shot in his arm and a tracer burn between his thigh and left testicle. Lucky, they all say.

You wait another six months and are about to go again. You are sitting one night in the visiting room with your mother when a body falls from the roof into the floodlights illuminating the main entrance. They nailed some sap climbing over the fence on top of the administration building. A week passes before the guards remove the icy gloves frozen in the barbed wire.

You are back in Lennie's cell with that awful smell of talcum powder hanging in the air, as thick as the dust in a cement factory. He turns out the light and climbs on top of his chair. There once again is the creaking of the rigging, the waves lapping the hull, a soft breeze overdubbing the faint noise of the machines in the bowels of the prison. Not even Randle Patrick McMurphy can beat the Combine or make you big again. But you can dream, and you dream of sailing. Maybe not to the Isles of Shoals and down east to Maine, but you dream nonetheless. You dream of the high seas, where they will never catch you. And when you awake twenty years later, what you did then and what you are doing now are no more real than Bishop Berkeley's rock.

3
Fish Stories

Nowhere do the boundaries between states and countries seem more arbitrary than on the water. There are no signs to mark passage from one sovereignty to another, no discount liquor stores or slot machines at the roadside to give impact and meaning to your crossing over. Your only proof is the dotted line on a chart.

It is no wonder fishermen intrude on the territorial waters of neighboring nations without conscience. The seaman has always felt that the risks he endures entitle him to come and go as he pleases, because the extension of political boundaries into the ocean is to him a violation of Nature, a fabrication of old men in distant parliaments, easy to ignore.

Our first stop in Maine was Cape Porpoise, a small harbor with a handful of lobsterboats and a few yachts. Peter expected to see the water boil with the namesake mammals, but this was not to be.

Yet here, for the cruiser heading east, is the first hint of the pristine wilderness that lies in the vaporous netherland ahead. And the tides, ah the tides, whose rise and fall accelerate from three feet below Cape Cod to ten, twenty, and thirty feet as easting is made into the Bay of Fundy.

Squeezed by the mainlands of the United States and Canada to the west, and Nova Scotia to the east, the Atlantic is whipped into every bay and river, creating unimaginable tides, tumbling overfalls where winds and currents collide, and whirlpools that are capable of swallowing small craft.

The entrance to Cape Porpoise is tricky, first because the appearance of surrounding shoals and islands changes dramatically with the tide. When you anchor in the channel at high tide there is good protection, though you wonder why you hug the markers when there are acres of open water to either side. You must have faith in the charts, because a few hours later you peep out the window and are startled by vast mud flats, brown and gelatinous in the late sunlight. Were it not for the current, which keeps the boats weathervaned upstream or down, a crosswind, you fear, would entrench the hull in mud, fossilizing the rudder.

The second cause for wariness is the astounding number of lobster traps strewn about the channel like so many candy-colored beads. The traps are also called pots, a nomenclature that seemingly swings with the tide; it is said they are called traps east of Penobscot Bay and pots to the west.

About ten years ago, the U.S. Coast Guard ordered the fairway cleared. As it happened, the position of town harbormaster was vacant, and there was no one to enforce the edict. Applications were solicited, offers were tendered—thanks but no thanks. The lobsterman, of course, owns the water; it is his workplace, his livelihood, and no black-shoed politician is going to tell him where to drop his traps. The elders of Dodge City had no easier time hiring a sheriff when Billy the Kid was shooting out saloon mirrors.

After several years, a harbormaster was hired, negotiations were conducted, and eventually some of the traps were removed. The channel was further defined by moving the buoys closer together, thereby exempting many of the traps. All seemed settled . . . for a time. The next season the traps were back, and they remain there today, as they no doubt will until the cows come home or the lobsters move to Missouri.

At high tide we clamped the outboard to the dinghy's transom and motored past the fishermen's co-op to the harbor head. There, a couple of old fellahs reconditioning a pier allowed as how we could tie up to do some shopping.

"Over heah," one said, motioning to the deep-water side of the float, "less you want t'dig clams when you come back."

We rounded Cape Elizabeth with the genoa poled out in a southwesterly breeze. Adria wrote in the log: "We left Cape Porpoise with a purpose."

Suddenly we were in the thick of the Round Monhegan Race, with a big Portland fleet barreling upwind. The white sails drove around us, overlapping each other in a confusing melee for the mark. In this situation, you can forget the Rules of the Road. We were a slug among snakes, and the only call that counts is "We're racing!" It is a warning delivered with the desperation and indignity of a man rushing his pregnant wife to the hospital, usually bellowed by some fair-complected jughead on the windward rail who thinks he can intimidate you with Henri Lloyd foul-weather gear and Ray-Ban racing shades. At times like these you wish for a steel boat and a sawbill the size of the battering ram on Captain Nemo's *Nautilus*.

Adria hauled in the Rag Mop, which had eluded the racers as well as the fish, and added a perfunctory note in the log: "The fish aren't biting yet."

Andra and her sister Linnea sauntered down the dock as we anchored off the fashionable Portland suburb of Falmouth Foreside. The anchorage, we were to learn on the return leg, is exposed to the north and south but a great place to jump off into the islands of Casco Bay.

Jewell Island, a scant six miles east, is just that — a piece of broken jade dropped on a blue tablecloth — with good holding for the anchor in a tight cleft hewn from brown stone. With Andra aboard at last, we entered the jagged cleft with a thin fog clinging to the damp cliffs, and a solitary gull, its white body sharp and distinct against the tall, dark firs, appearing strangely beautiful and foreboding in this antediluvian harbor.

Adria spotted our first seal in Robinhood Cove, a carefully concealed waypoint on the Sheepscot River. The spotted creature surprised us, surfacing a few feet from the dinghy as we rowed along the densely wooded shore. Immediately it sounded and another appeared. Later, from the boat, we saw many more, pushing their inquisitive noses through the calm waters like Labrador retrievers sniffing for a bird in the bush.

That evening the mosquitoes came in swarms, driving us below, with just two screened hatches for ventilation. The air grew stale, and the smell of the kerosene lamp was faintly nauseating. Andra, Adria, and I relegated ourselves to a game of Scrabble. Peter's learning disability made spelling and phonetics about as comprehensible to him as hieroglyphics. Growing antsy and bored, he decided it was safe to open the unscreened portlights.

"Don't you dare!" Adria threatened.

"But the mosquitoes are gone," Peter protested.

"No they're not!" she shot back. "Open that window and I'll break your arm."

Quietly, he opened it anyway, then innocently sat down beside me. Adria slapped a mosquito on her cheek. Then another. Soon the air was full of them.

"Peter!" Adria screamed. "There are too mosquitoes!"

Peter shrugged and smiled. "So I was wrong."

Boothbay reminded us too much of Newport, and we moved on into Muscongus Bay, sailing at the leisurely pace of ten to twenty miles a day. When the wind wasn't on the nose it was on vacation; the log shows we motored sixty percent of the time, building a good case for the ungainly motorsailer with a big diesel, flat hull sections aft, and a shaded pilothouse with racks for charts and coffee mugs.

Though Rockland has an excellent Mexican restaurant and one of the last picture shows on the coast, at the time it was also home to one of the few remaining factories to process fish waste into farm-animal feed. The town was reputed to smell like a crime committed somewhere between a stockyard and a sewer, but most of the locals called it the smell of jobs. Fortunately, what little olfactory sensitivity I inherited from my father has been numbed by pipe smoke, nasal spray, and cauterization; I liked the town. Four years later the processing plant has closed, putting 150 people out of work, and Rockland is floundering in the depths of a recession as it tries to transform its large deep-water harbor into the next Boothbay or Newport. With the odor gone, the waterfront is safe for condominiums, but will the quality of life be better, and for whom?

In the heart of Penobscot Bay we found chaste and lovely Pulpit Harbor, its narrow entrance camouflaged among the hardwoods on the west side of North Haven. Large lawns roll down to the water on one side, tempering the uneven hand of Nature, who in other corners carelessly juxtaposes maples and pines, jumbles of rocks and mud flats, daisies and wild roses.

We chose the quietest of three coves, a sure spot for fish, Andra declared. But an hour of casting with smelly clam bait proved futile. We had been given the damaged mollusks by a clerk in a Boothbay fish market, who advised (with a shrug): "Use just about anything to catch the first 'un, then chop him up to get t'others." When we could stand the smell no longer, Andra tried turkey bologna.

An elderly couple, anchored nearby on a twenty-seven-foot sailboat, hailed us. Homeport: Dallas, Texas. Later they invited us over for drinks, in part, I suppose, so we could account for the Texas flag on a Rhode Island boat. I explained that my parents lived in Texas. "But," I concluded, "I'm not sure whether the red or the white stripe is supposed to be up."

Drucella Sheldon smiled and responded sweetly, "Well, in Texas we have a saying that blood is thicker than water."

So much for my knowledge of Texas trivia. Not wanting to offend anyone, that evening I turned the flag so that the red side was down. You never know when you'll run across a Longhorn.

"Mainiacs" (an erroneous tag if ever there was one) find "citified" people too educated, too full of themselves, too stultified by an unnecessarily complex world to understand the most obvious facts of Nature. So dumb, it's surprising they know how to propagate. In Maine, where the mythology of outsider ignorance and "born-here" wisdom has found its quintessential expression in Bert & I humor, the city slicker supplants the ignominious Pole, Black, and Jew as the butt. Every culture chides what it fears.

Listen: There is the story of the Buckeye chatting up a local man digging clams at low tide.

"What are you looking for?" he asks.

No answer.

The city man, anxious to be cordial, shuffles nervously, sees his feet in the mud, and tries again. "Does the water do this every day?"

No answer. Just a trace of a sneer.

And then a final, desperate attempt.

"Have you lived here all your life?"

"Not yet."

Eleven days and 275 miles after leaving Newport, we reached my cousin Sophie's house on the backwaters of Horseshoe Cove. We slid in on a dying breeze, ghosting past Cape Rosier where for half a century Helen and Scott Nearing popularized self-sufficiency with such books as *Living the Good Life.*

Keeping two privately maintained spars to port and a homemade daymark to starboard, we threaded the submerged outcroppings and picked up one of the Seal Cove Boatyard moorings, buoyed by a large log with a hole drilled in one end for reeving the pendant.

Sophie's husband, Peter Chase, motored out to meet us in *Sweet Pea,* a scabby green motorboat powered by a Chrysler car engine. A boatbuilder by trade, Pete is an affable Huckleberry Finn sort: fair-faced, clomping about in heavy boots, tangled wisps of thinning hair combed only before weddings and funerals. Like any boatbuilder worth his salt, he has a corncob pipe that is more a thinking tool than a smoking piece—a smooth, tactile thing to be rubbed and turned over in the hand like a good-luck stone. When there is a problem to noodle, he puffs thoughtfully. Then his girls, Karina and Rosie, hound him mercilessly until he shrugs and stuffs it in a shirt pocket.

At the house, a simple passive-solar affair Pete built within earshot of the reversing falls at the cove's head, he collects derelict boats the way hillbillies keep junked cars. In the yard sits the venerable *An Remon,* a turn-of-the-century Galway hooker they bought in Ireland and shipped to Halifax. It had acquired a cover since my last visit, while losing a few strakes where the keel had been opened for repairs, promised some time before its centenary or the Second Flood—Pete is hard to pin down. And the engineless lobsterboat, at last observation withering at the edge of the drive, had been cut in half with a chainsaw and hauled to a nearby field, where the cabin reposes as a stoop for two pigs.

If the good life means giving up pork and poultry for whole grains and wild rice, Sophie and Pete haven't been reading the right books. But like most Maine transplants, they enjoy life at a pace that would anesthetize most of us. The nearest town is Blue Hill, where Sophie maintains a law office, and that's thirty minutes to nowhere. No pubs, no movies (you drive to Ellsworth or Bangor for that recreation), no auditoriums, and except for the summer population of bluehairs and watercolor artists, very few people.

That weekend, the eight of us rambled out in *Sweet Pea* for a picnic at Pickering Island, towing our dinghy, a small burgundy sailboat of Peter's design, and toting inboard one of the fiberglass Puddle Dipper kayaks he built at Dirigo Boatbuilding Company. Midway we passed Scott Island and the verandaed cottage of author/illustrator Robert McCloskey, the man who for generations has painted in the child's mind the most accurate pictures of Maine. *Time of Wonder, One Morning in Maine,* and *Blueberries for Sal,* first published in the 1940s, are still in print.

A rendezvous was planned with Billy and Sally Tomkins. Billy is a Brooksville lobsterman, operating *Kokadjo,* a thirty-five-footer with the trademark high, plumb bow and sweeping sheer.

When a lobsterman isn't hauling traps, there's still much to be done, and one of the constants is the procurement of bait. He spends several thousand dollars a year baiting his traps: herring cuttings bought from sardine factories, a long drive in the pickup for alewives when they run in some neighboring bay, nighttime seining for pogies, or store-bought fish meal wrapped in perforated polyethylene.

So Billy stayed on the beach for just two beers, then itched back to *Kokadjo* with the kids for some fishing. After an hour and a half he had helped the kids hook nine dogfish, also called sand sharks. No good for lobsters, he said, but the crabs will take them. So will Arthur Treacher and McDonalds, who reputedly buy the vicious little bottom feeders to make fish-and-chips.

Billy chummed the water with herring and no sooner was one brought aboard, his body pinned with a heavy foot and the hook rudely yanked with pliers, than the next one bit. He had created a feeding frenzy, which in the vernacular of television might have been called "Blue Water, Dog Breath."

Billy swore when a dogfish suddenly broke away with the hook, sinker, and bait.

"He's gonna die," lamented his daughter, eight-year-old Kate.

"Of what?" Billy retorted. "Lead poisoning?"

Meanwhile, Peter discovered that he was able to propel and maneuver the lightweight Puddle Dipper kayak. We fitted him with a life jacket and spray skirt and watched, with no little trepidation, as he paddled to and from shore, more often than not helplessly spinning in circles. The solid, wooden oars of even our smallest dinghy were too heavy for his frail arms to lift and pull, and this was the first time he'd been able to handle a boat by himself. He was thrilled. Only the setting sun and the chill, evening air persuaded him to at last grind ashore and let us pull his hunched and shivering body from the kayak. "Dad," he whispered proudly, "I did it!"

Soon after, we borrowed Sophie's car and drove Pete and Adria back to Portland, covering in three hours the distance we had labored over in one week under sail. But on the freeway there is nothing to see, and we arrived dazed, feeling as though we'd spent the day with a jackhammer in our hands.

Adria burst into tears. "I had a great time, Dad."

And I believed her, promising to fly her to the Bahamas for semester break. Pete, as usual, was all smiles, ready to head home.

"I love you," I said.

"Me too, Dad." He lurched up the ramp and was gone.

Andra and I stayed at the airport until the plane took off, crossing our fingers and trying to forget the grim news of the Northwest flight that had crashed in Detroit the day before, killing all passengers except a four-year-old girl.

If I ever have to go back to prison, the man I'd choose for my rap partner would be Gunnar Hansen. When I say this forty-year-old native of Reykjavík, Iceland, is big, you have no idea, and I will not embarrass him by guessing. Suffice it to say that he fills a doorway the way a key fills a lock — and he is not fat.

A more pleasant man you will never meet, though this is not at all evident from distant impressions. His black hair and beard are flecked with gray, the thick eyebrows jump when he drops a punch line, and his hands could pop basketballs for exercise. When he enters a room, heads turn, the sun is blotted. If he were a priest (say Rasputin), his very flesh would suck out the sins and fevers of his penitents.

If you think you recognize him, your first thought would be a big-time wrestler. Then, if you have seen the movie *Texas Chainsaw Massacre,* it would dawn on you that Gunnar Hansen was none other than . . . Leatherface! The Sultan of Splattermania!

This nonverbal performance is his one claim to movie stardom (until recently, when he traveled to Los Angeles to make *Hollywood Chainsaw Hookers*), but what a singular distinction! If you could star in only one movie in your lifetime, and another person had already grabbed Rhett Butler in *Gone with the Wind,* what better role than the Mad McCullough of the rottenest B flick of our time?

Andra and I met Gunnar one winter in Newport. Except for a stint in Austin, Texas, where he went to college as well as stumbled into the movie business (October 1974), he has lived in Maine. We promised to look him up at his Northeast Harbor home, and did so after leaving Horseshoe Cove.

Northeast Harbor is one of several popular anchorages on Mt. Desert Island, the others being Southwest Harbor (home of the Henry R. Hinckley company, builder of America's finest sailboats since World War II), and Somes Sound, the only natural fjord on the East Coast. Acadia National Park covers most of the island with enough mountains and hiking trails to keep a backpacker busy all summer.

We met Gunnar at his second-floor office, above the Crackers kiddy store. The room was Spartan. On one wall was an old map of Baxter State Park, two bare oak desks with a phone on one and a word processor (IBM knockoff) on the other, a bookshelf at angles to the bay window (a good place to stand with a mug of coffee on a rainy day), and two stereo floor speakers built from the seats of a '59 Dodge.

The brass nameplate in the hall says he's in; yes, there in the corner, Sasquatch at the green CRT screen. How do the tips of his fingers work the little buttons? Won't frustration drive him to pick up the dumb machine and smash it?

No, there is work to be done: a script for a film on the Maine coast, a free-lance article for *The Yacht,* and letters, many letters concerning the *Oiseau Blanc.*

In the spring of 1977, Gunnar read about Anson Berry, an old hermit who claimed that fifty years earlier, while fishing in a canoe on Round Lake near Machias, he heard an airplane pass in the clouds overhead.

"He heard it stop," Gunnar said, "then crash."

Gunnar has plotted the track of this and sixteen Newfoundland sightings; he believes it charts the final hours of the French aviators Charles Nungesser and Francois Coli. Presumably they crashed on the afternoon of May 9, 1927, just twelve days before Charles Lindbergh flew into history with a record solo flight. Nungesser and Coli were World War I heroes attempting the first nonstop flight connecting New York and Paris. At stake was the Oteig Prize, worth twenty-five thousand dollars. The *White Bird* never arrived. The North American coast was blanketed by fog, and rain and light snow fell in the north. A massive sea search proved luckless.

Since 1977 Gunnar has made annual excursions into the woods to search for the remains of *White Bird,* though he says now only the engine may be left. And if that were toted away by some rat-pack farmer, his last hope is using sophisticated detection devices to pinpoint the radium instrument dials.

His *White Bird* Search Group, which includes adventure novelist Clive Cussler (*Raise the Titanic*), is well organized but basically "just a bunch of guys who went into the woods."

Gunnar settled back in his chair. "Each year," he said, "we feel more convinced it's here and less convinced we're going to find it."

The three of us had dinner in *Adriana's* cockpit that evening. The varnished Hinckleys glistened in the moonlight, Malcolm Forbes's bagpiper welcomed guests aboard his fabulous *Highlander* motoryacht, and the lights and sounds of the Asticou Inn on dance night made you think sentimentally of your own summer of '42, first kisses, drinking beers in some rich kid's mahogany runabout, and a lot of other nostalgic things that never really happened, but you wish had.

The next morning we found Gunnar at the office eating donuts with a lobsterman friend from the Cranberry Isles. He gave us a trail map for Acadia and his car keys, then sent us off to Sargent Mountain for the day. At the edge of the alpine, where the trees give way to scrub, we picked blueberries. It had been dry, the season was late, and there were few of them.

The wind blew, and from the summit we watched low, dark storm clouds move in from the southwest. Gradually they obscured the islands of Jericho Bay—Swan's, Great Gott, and Placentia. At 1,300 feet the air grew cold, and it began to rain. There was no shelter, and we descended quickly. The harbor was swallowed in the turbulence. We climbed down into the valleys, then up Gilmore, Peck, and Bald peaks. Down again, cautiously taking granite footholds from the creek to Parkman Mountain, glimpses of Somesville to the west, coming and going in the clouds as if we were Nungesser and Coli, plunging earthward, the air silent in those last tranquil seconds.

In the morning Andra's cousin Cathy came aboard for breakfast. She brought fresh butter and pastries from the Asticou kitchen, where she worked as a summer chef. And she witnessed the catching of our first fish, a herring I jagged in the side quite by accident (or so the fish would say). I marinated the meager fillets in a mayonnaise jar according to the guidance offered in *Joy of Cooking* — vinegar, sugar, onion, and lemon strips.

Weeks later, the meat fiber had all but disintegrated into a diarrheic brown fluid. Andra, in courteous asides, told friends I had pickled a pogie. I told myself, you're okay Spurr, you know a pogie is some kind of herring, and you know the ocean rises and falls every day.

4

East of Schoodic

Yech! Gross!" Andra grimaced.

I watched her recoil from the rusty can of fruit cocktail I had just opened for dessert. The black ooze suppurating through the lid should have been a good clue, but being stubborn (and cheap), I needed convincing that the canned food in our bilge had in fact spoiled. I peered inside; the little squares and rhomboids of peaches and pears and half-rounds of cherries had all turned black and settled to the bottom in an inky mulch. Obviously a fertile compost for culturing botulism.

"Okay," I admitted glumly. "Over the side it goes."

The problem was we were bound east of Schoodic. This small point of land about two-thirds of the way up the coast of Maine (or east as the magnetic needle on the compass bears) is the unofficial demarcation of Down East and down-and-out.

Consider: There is only one city between Mt. Desert and Canada—Eastport, with a population of two thousand—and you first have to straddle the international boundary before provisioning here at the doorstep of Passamaquoddy Bay.

Also, water is unavailable on the crooked, daddy longleg piers, and even if you fill a jerry jug from someone's garden hose, how will you descend one-handed the moss-covered ladders? The tides in these Bay of Fundy waters, after all, rise and fall twenty feet. A mile's walk from the lobsterman's pier in, say, Bunkers Harbor or Cape Split, you may find a small grocery where the selection is limited, the prices high, and the age of the goods about the same as those fermenting in your bilge.

Beyond Schoodic Peninsula, the land and sea are a little wilder. Gone are the Wall Street dropouts-cum-gentleman farmers. Gone are the leftover sixties flower children. Gone are the organic disciples of Scott Nearing and Euell Gibbons. After Mt. Desert and the wealthy "summer people" of Bar Harbor and Northeast Harbor, who loiter in the ubiquitous arts-and-craft galleries and preen like puffins on the decks of fancy yachts, villages such as Jonesport and Bucks Harbor are a rude, welcome throwback to a simpler place and time. There is no animosity between sail and power (every lobsterman gave us a long, slow wave like the Santa Claus in Macy's window), anchorages are private and secluded, there is no loom of city lights to spoil the nightly vista of stars, and wildlife crawls on every rock, every tidal pool, even in the dark waters beneath your keel.

Peter and Adria were home readying for the new school year, and I, like a monk seeking solace in the cloistered life, sought from the territory east of Schoodic a curative for the emptiness they left behind.

It was easy imagining their daily routine: Adria collecting leaves for some montage, jogging around the nearby lakes in training for cross-country, and huddling in her room with her girlfriends, whispering things as teenage girls do.

I saw Peter loping around the large yard with bent knees and pigeon toes, chucking black walnut shells for his dog Lucy, setting up his interstellar army of Transformers, so absorbed he'd barely look up as the daily Amtrak roared by on the ridge across Huron River Drive.

The first few weeks of school would be tough, despite his enrollment in a special education program. Every summer he forgot much of what he had learned the previous year, seemingly fated to suffer the frustration of studying the same material again and again.

I reread excerpts from his Multidisciplinary Evaluation Team reports:

> Peter is an eleven-year-old male with cerebral palsy and resultant mild spasticity. . . . His speed and accuracy in fine motor skills are impaired, greater on the right side than the left. Gross motor coordination is delayed. . . . Peter has had heel cord releases bilaterally but continues to have some tightness in that area. . . . Articulation impairment, involving substitutions and distortions of sounds persisting beyond the age at which maturation alone might be expected to correct the deviation. . . . He does not have the addition and subtraction math facts memorized even after extensive work on this last year. He is able to accurately answer the facts using his fingers. . . . In reading, Peter is currently working in the end of a first-grade basal series . . . is very sensitive to the needs of others and likes to help his fellow students . . . gets along well with everyone.

Yes, school was a worry. Last fall I'd flown to Michigan to attend a team meeting with all of his instructors at the New Horizons Educational Center. Margaret was there, too, always extremely active in Peter's care and development. After an hour of recitations that I found demoralizing, I said, "Excuse me. I know you've had many meetings such as this one without me, and I apologize if I don't quite understand. But what I'm hearing is not encouraging. You people are experienced working with CP, and I'd like to know what your prognosis is for Peter. Will he ever finish school? Will he ever hold a job?"

A hush fell over the group. They looked at one another, at a loss for words, as if to say, "Doesn't he *know?*" Margaret began some answer about the importance of progress. Clearly, the teachers had not expected to be confronted so directly. One made a remark about the program plan. Hands folded in front of me, I stared at them. At last the occupational therapist, bless her, leaned forward and said, "Peter is able to dress himself and perform personal hygiene. That's a plus. Many of our clients can't even brush their teeth. But it is doubtful he'll ever achieve a high-school equivalency or hold a job that would be meaningful to you or me.

There are some things he could probably do. I see him living in a structured residential environment. . . ."

At last, an honest evaluation of Peter's future. And it wasn't pretty. Expected perhaps, but you always hope against hope that there will be some sudden surge, a quantum leap in cognitive powers, a breakthrough. For Pete, there wouldn't be. It was hard to understand why these things happen to some of us and not to others. In Peter's case, I thought I knew, but I didn't like to think about it—that desperate frantic moment in the labor room. As I left the school all I could think of was wanting Pete to live with me, even as a thirty-year-old adult busing tables or polishing cars, even if he knew he'd been cheated, even if his ebullient face turned sad and cynical and he began over the years to look for some way out.

We rounded Schoodic Head on a clear day with a feisty sou'wester blowing us eastward. There are few good anchorages between the head and the shoal, bony finger of the Petit Manan peninsula, and the several boats we saw were headed for Prospect Harbor. To save miles the next day, however, and to find the solitude for which we had come to Maine, we snugged into Bunkers Harbor. The entrance is tricky, best approached at midtide to avoid the rocks encroaching on the narrow pass. Inside the water was calm, and only a slight surge from the near-gale outside reminded us we were not hard aground in some campsite. This was the first anchorage where we were the only recreational boat. (In the most literal sense, I suppose you could call ours a workboat, but the fishermen would object, and rightly so.) And, with the strong tidal currents, it also was the first time we found the boat lying head to a current with the wind and waves hitting from abeam. There are several clever methods of rigging breastlines from the middle of the boat to the anchor rode to hold the bow into the wind, but we didn't find them necessary.

At the head of the harbor was a dam forming a lobster pound, empty now. A local lobsterman told us it would soon be filled with "shedders," recently molted lobsters that would be held back from market until their new shells hardened. Less involved

43

sources, however, said the pounds are a convenient way for the lobstermen to hold a catch until prices rise.

For several days the wind continued to blow hard out of the southwest. From Schoodic one must decide whether to cross the two-mile bar that extends between the mainland and Petit Manan Island, or take the longer route around. The various guide books advise taking the shorter inside route over the bar in a narrow, carefully marked channel only in the best of weather. Taking heed, we left the mainsail furled, hoisted the midsize genoa, and scooted round the ninety-foot Petit Manan Lighthouse at better than six knots, putting in at Cape Split.

Harbor-hopping, as we were, is considerably more time-consuming than the offshore route paralleling the coast, but the most entrancing islands are invariably inshore, dotting the many bays and rivers. This was well illustrated at Jonesport, where boats with mast heights of less than forty-seven feet can take the Moosabec Reach through Jonesport, threading their way among the dozens of rocky, uninhabited islands that are home to ospreys, the occasional eagle, and curious seals that prefer protected waters.

Before leaving Cape Split I wanted to be certain we would clear the Beals Island bridge at Jonesport, so I hooked a tape measure to the main halyard and determined that our masthead was forty-two feet above the waterline. The bridge has just thirty-seven feet of clearance at high water, but forty-seven at low water, which that morning occurred at 6 A.M. Anxiously I used the rule of twelfths, which says that the tide rises $\frac{1}{12}$ of its total height the first hour after low, $\frac{2}{12}$ the second, $\frac{3}{12}$ the third and fourth hours, $\frac{2}{12}$ the fifth, and $\frac{1}{12}$ the sixth. We would have to make the bridge by nine.

The morning dawned bright and clear, and we left Cape Split with the dew still wet on the seats, motorsailing in a faint breeze. Half an hour before the decisive midtide we approached the bridge, and not without trepidation. Surely the masthead or at the least the fragile wind indicator would be smashed! It seemed there was no way we could make it as we slowed to a crawl, first looking at the bridge, then at our towering masthead. A fisherman we had met noted the 2½-knot current, stating perfunctorily that there is little chance on an ebb tide to change your mind once caught in the swirling waters around the bridge towers. If in doubt, he concluded, it's best to accept the extra miles of going around Great Wass Island.

At thirty yards I put the engine in neutral, and as we were swept along I threw the gear into reverse, for there is no way of gauging from the deck whether you will clear. The boat lost steerage, and Andra ducked below (just in case). But realizing that it was graceless to go through sideways, not to mention dangerous, I threw the transmission back into forward and damned the torpedoes. By what proverbial hair we cleared, we will never know— perhaps even the foot-and-a-half I had calculated, but we will be hard to convince it wasn't a shave.

The anchorage at Jonesport is shallow and the holding ground poor; beyond quick provisioning there is little reason to linger there. Like a pot of gold, Roque Island beckons at the eastern end of the reach, so we pressed on, entering the craterlike enclave late in the afternoon. Ten boats were anchored off the mile-long white-sand crescent beach; this indeed was the cruising man's Mecca Down East.

Under the canopy of needles and leaves the moist forest floor was covered with spongy moss and duff, and from the limbs hung drab species of choking vines and runners, creating the foreboding sense of trespassing on a taboo burial ground—I wouldn't have been surprised to see human heads stuck on sticks, or feel the air whistle near my ear as an arrow flew by, for it was also eerily dark in the forest, lit only by the occasional shaft of sunlight piercing the dense overhead.

All too soon it was time to sail on to Bucks Harbor, where Andra had a childhood friend to meet. Jeanette Delvecchio and her common-law husband, Christopher Rudd, saw us approach from their strange castle of a home high on Miller Mountain, overlooking the harbor. Quickly, they drove down to greet us on the dock.

There is little work in Washington County (unless you're good at raking blueberries), and most of the people are poor.

"What do you do, Christopher?"

"Oh, I can do a lot of things."

There were few new materials in their home, but the timbers and windows salvaged from homes and barns Christopher had helped raze were lovely. The economy of rural Maine is in part an under-the-table system of bartering and shared labor; what little money a man earns is often spent on beer. Christopher had an affinity for six-dollar a rack imported Becks.

Electricity had just been added the year before, and running water was expected any day. ("As soon as I can find a guy who knows deep wells.") When we arrived, Andra asked for directions to the bathroom. Jeanette led the way to the back door, which opened onto their forty acres of wilderness. "Pick a tree," she said.

It was difficult to imagine raising two small children in what we perceived as primitive conditions, but two-year-old Elliot and six-month-old Ian were healthy and happy, the younger crawling naively over Christopher's power tools strewn about the unfinished living room and the elder peeling after him on his tricycle, Gordon Johncock stroking the gun lap of the Firecracker 400, trying to run over his little brother's dimpled fingers.

Here were no Gobots, Transformers, skateboards, Sesame Street television, or Monday Night Football. The folks who move here from out of state aren't interested in cellular phones to keep by the patio pool, or the twenty-four-hour convenience store down the street.

Curiously, Christopher had recently developed a passion for golf, though the nearest course was an hour away. During one run into the regional metropolis of Machias (population 3,000), we stopped at a small park with a monument to the patriots of Fort O'Brien, who engaged the British in the first naval skirmish of the Revolutionary War. While I read the tablets, Christopher lifted his irons out of the truck and began chipping shots at the old bunkers, which he pretended were greens. Soon he had me doing a Gerald Ford imitation, hacking balls over the heads of passersby and into the tangled undergrowth on the park perimeter.

"I bang a few balls here on my way into town," Christopher said. "Must have a dozen or more lost in the bush. Used to pay a neighborhood kid to look for 'em, but even he got tired of it."

While Christopher played the nines, Jeanette tended the children and her prodigious garden. Each morning she headed for the plot on the rocky crest above the house, armed with a baseball bat to beat off a vicious pet goose and a pair of scissors to snip the slugs that ravaged her lettuce.

Jeanette and Christopher left their dogs, chickens, rabbits, and geese long enough to sail with us the eight miles to Cutler. Friends of theirs would pick them up later and drive them home. Before nightfall we picked mussels for appetizers, and Andra made a delicious crabmeat fettucine dinner. The surroundings were quaint and quiet despite the thousand-foot submarine-tracking radio towers of the U.S. naval installation a few miles away. In a coincidence of superb timing, at the very moment Andra served the fettucine, Christopher and Jeanette's friends hailed us from the dock, and the lobsterman whose mooring we had commandeered returned and asked us to leave. Adding insult to injury, Andra had, on the recommendation of a cookbook, boiled the pasta in seawater. Perhaps we had erred, but suffice it to say the dish tasted awful, like licking a salt block.

Josh and Terry rented Christopher's Larrabee camp—a cheap alternative to trailer living without electricity or water, just a running stream nearby for drinking and washing. Escaped inmates from the new state prison (converted from the nearby and now defunct air force base) had broken in a few months before Joshua and Terry had moved in, Christopher said, even though the door had been open. Yes, I thought to myself, those are the kind of guys I knew in the clink.

Terry was a free-lance weaver for the New York garment industry, sufficiently talented to work in a backwoods so remote that, to the locals, L.L. Bean has the same snobbish, upscale image as Ralph Lauren does to the rest of us. Josh was a Food and Drug Administration inspector, exiled to the Maine woods for a winter of blueberry inspecting. Washington County alone produces forty million pounds a year. He was boiling countless samples looking for maggots; more than four per pound, and he would get rough with the growers. It takes a trained eye to distinguish the bugs

47

from the stalks and skins melting in the pan, he said; he had trained his eyes as a professional photographer before his scientific career.

The dinner conversation turned to the implications of being native.

"If you weren't born here, you'll never be from here," Jeanette said. "We've been here twelve years, and they still treat us different. We'll never be from here, and neither will our kids."

"The fishermen don't care about the environment," asserted Christopher. "They eat the small lobsters instead of throwing them back, and they pump diesel fuel overboard. The diggers have numbed the flats, and the draggers have numbed the banks. Now they're deep-sea dredging for quahogs and they're all driving new pickups. Give 'em another season and they'll numb those, too."

As summer waned, we made the final push along the desolate stretch of coast that extends between Cutler and Lubec. The only harbors are exposed, and one is well advised to choose good weather for the trip.

With Grand Manan closing from the east, we motored farther into the Bay of Fundy. The air was still. Dolphins kept us company for a time, the only life in sight. Then we rounded West Quoddy Head and entered the Lubec Narrows, where currents run up to 8½ knots; it is impossible to make it through with a foul tide, so timing is of the essence.

The Franklin D. Roosevelt Memorial Bridge to Campobello Island, New Brunswick, has a vertical clearance of forty-seven feet at high water, so we didn't worry about losing the rig this time. We found an open anchorage near the town landing and an abandoned canning plant, in forty-five feet of water. Setting two anchors 180 degrees apart to deal with the current, we went ashore as close as possible to slack water after once nearly failing to make it back to the boat . . . and this with a six-horsepower motor on the dinghy!

Lubec seemed a strange place. The streets were nearly deserted, and almost half the homes were for sale. ("Oh, you went to the Empty Homes Festival," quipped an acquaintance in Blue Hill later.) A few canning companies still package sardines and smoked kippers, but it is an ailing industry. A downtown sign, courtesy of Uncle Kippy's Game Room, reads: "Welcome to L.A.—Lubec, America."

Viewed from the water, the town's skyline resembles a children's storybook illustration, with swaybacked buildings teetering over the water, smoke billowing from every crevice, and the dark sky filled with screaming sea gulls incited by the thick aroma of fish.

It is a pleasant walk across the bridge to the international park that preserves FDR's summer cottage on Campobello. The gardens are colorful and meticulous, and several nature and documentary films make for a good introduction to the Passamaquoddy Bay region. Here, in the 1930s, Roosevelt entertained the wild notion of harnessing the power of the tides to generate electricity. The huge project was eventually scrapped, but more recent studies in the U.S. indicate that tides may yet provide a natural source of energy.

Lubec and Eastport, a few miles up the bay, share honors as the easternmost cities in the United States. The people are proud to point out that the sun rises here first, and this fact provided us with another subtitle to our cruise—from the easternmost to the southernmost point in the U.S.

At Eastport, where FDR was transported by boat when first stricken with polio, we paid for our first dockage—at the Cannery Restaurant. Our arrival at dead low tide prevented us from entering the town wharf, sheltered by a massive breakwater where ships of the Georgia-Pacific timber company sometimes dock.

We passed a pleasant afternoon doing laundry, filling the boat's tanks, and browsing in the *Quoddy Tides* reading room, elevated above the harbor and equipped with easy chairs and binoculars. Here we watched the fog roll in, keeping us another day and postponing for a short time the sadness and exhilaration of having reached one end of the long road before us.

There was also a good grocery, where we made a major foray to replenish the canned and other foods consumed or chucked during the past few weeks.

In the canned-goods aisle I found fruit cocktail and asked Andra if she wanted any. I needn't describe the look she returned. I put it back on the shelf and followed humbly, smiling to myself, to inspect natural fiber cereals and fresh produce.

The galley, I deduced, was no longer my domain.

Several hours later we returned to the Cannery and were met by a dour-faced customs agent, who obviously had been called from town and had been waiting longer than we cared to inquire. The restaurant-marina manager drew up behind us, convinced, I'm sure, that she had helped bag a boatload of illegal aliens, drug smugglers, or spies from the Russian fishing fleet.

The customs agent swaggered up to us. "Yer boat?"

"Yes," I answered.

"Where ya come from?"

"Lubec," I said, pointing down the bay.

"Before that?"

"We haven't been to Canada, if that's what you mean," I replied forthrightly.

Suddenly his face broke into a grin. "That's what we like to hear!" He pointed to the rigging. "But tell me, what's that flag you're flying?"

Only then did I realize the source of his consternation. "Texas!" I exclaimed. "Obviously you've never owned a pair of Tony Lama snakeskin boots or cried at the gates of the Alamo."

"Oh," he said, almost disappointed. "We've never seen that one here; we thought maybe you was from Monrovia."

The next morning we left on an ebb tide, motoring back through the Lubec Narrows, under the International Bridge, and following the buoys to West Quoddy Head where the bay meets the Atlantic. A wall of fog fell on us, obscuring the coast. We had no choice but to retreat to Lubec with the fog following, a low-lying thermocline of white billowing over the fir-crested point. Above was a compressed bank of dense gray clouds.

Against our wishes we spent another night in this medieval monument of stacks and steam, and there was little to do after dark but chase Andra around the dinette. It was a race with a fateful consequence and a foregone conclusion — amazing how one's life turns on the act of love.

5
Bumming

Andy was sitting in a corner of the cockpit reading a trash novel, one of a dozen she had bought for a nickel apiece at the Jonesport town library's annual sale.

"Oh, Pook!" she exclaimed. "They're falling in love!"

"Who?"

"Arnie and Raven."

I was thinking more of this new nickname—Pook—the most recent in a string of silly and, I presumed, affectionate appellations. Sweetie had evolved to Wheat (to confuse parents), Pongo was an unabashed ripoff from the Walt Disney movie *101 Dalmatians,* and Snookie, which she used only when I yawned, was later appropriated by Peter. When it had been his turn to wash dishes, he had pushed back from the dinner table and whispered sleepily, "Dad, Snookie's got me pinned." Snookie came to life as a separate persona. In her drawing tablet, Adria had depicted him as an elf with a big nose and a nightcap.

So, who was this Pook character? No answer ever came. It is just me.

I drove on, aiming southwest back along the coast, watching my wife slyly as the boat punched through the small waves, giving no quarter. It was an easy day, a day for reading, a day for dreaming at the wheel.

An hour later, Andy dropped the book in her lap. Her eyes were moist. "They're having a baby!"

Thirty minutes elapsed. "Arnold died. I could just sob."

After another ten minutes, she threw the book into the cabin. "The baby died, too."

Many people, when they think of Maine, think of lobsters. This is logical since the best lobsters in the world live in the cold waters of the continental shelf off Maine's vast and intricate coast. And catching them is a major industry, despite the fact that there are no employees punching time clocks and no Gyro Gearloose machinery—belts, rams, or robotic hammers—to crack shells and extract meat. From harvest to table, it is all handwork.

The lobsterman is a unique, taciturn individual, as indigenous to Maine as the quahogger is to Rhode Island and the oyster drudger to the Chesapeake Bay. Mike Brown, a lobsterman who wrote a book called *The Great Lobster Chase,* had this to say of his ilk: "The lobsterman and the creature he pursues are remarkably alike in their different worlds. There is an uncanny compatibility in their coexistence. Just as the lobster has survived the æons by his solitary habits and independent senses, so has the lobsterman. They were made for each other."

You cannot travel the coast of Maine without becoming keenly aware of this peculiar symbiosis. Ashore there are scores of restaurants advertising the crustacean entree with neon cartoons of *Homarus americanus* in all manner of silly poses, sometimes ready to dine himself, with knife and fork clenched in his claws and a plastic bib to catch the drippings of melted butter. You can buy them live, boiled, broiled, or steamed, and whole or shelled. They are sold at restaurants, co-ops, smelly fish markets, and from galvanized washtubs behind the lobsterman's garage.

On the water the lobsterman and his boat are everywhere, striking out before dawn, the lobsterman gunning the Buick engine in the belly of his low-slung boat from buoy to buoy. A warp, or rope, connects the buoy to the trap on the bottom, and with a gaff he leans over and hooks it on the move, throwing the transmission into neutral at the last second so as not to overrun the mark. He hands the line over a pulley driven by a takeoff from the engine.

In moments the first trap rips from the sea and is swung aboard. With elbow-length gloves the lobsterman extracts his catch, perhaps a few lobsters, crabs, sometimes a fish, often sea urchins. Not all the lobsters are "keepers." Any that are questionable must be measured, and the "shorts" thrown back in the ocean along with the egg-bearing females, to be caught another day. Keepers, crabs, and urchins are disposed of in their respective places aboard the boat or over the side (some lobstermen keep crabs, few if any keep urchins), the trap rebaited and dumped on the run like a depth charge. The work cycle of a lobsterman with two hundred traps is not unlike a bridge painter; when he gets to the end of the run, he simply starts over.

It is a poor, deprived soul who doesn't like to eat lobsters, for the meat is as sweet and rich as any food on Earth. When we were of the mind, Andra and I bought direct from the lobstermen, usually at half the local market price. Larceny had had its day with me, and never were we tempted by the easy pickings on the ocean floor. Weep for the fool who pilfers a lobsterman's traps; retribution is exacted by means of a frontier justice that could cost him his boat (mysteriously sunk) or, if some stories are to be believed, his manhood.

At the Southwest Harbor Oceanarium and Cutler Marine Hatchery, we made a brief study and learned some facts about the odd submarine life of a lobster.

He is a decapod, having ten legs, and lives on the ocean bottom in depths ranging from mean low water to two thousand feet. He is a careless scavenger, feeding mostly at night on crabs, clams, algae, echinoderms (starfish and sea urchins), and hydroids. He also has a cannibalistic taste for other lobsters.

Lobsters molt or shed their shells to facilitate growth. As if embarrassed to be seen in their birthday suits, they hide in holes, and in preparation for the event, very sensibly, they stop eating. Their joints grow rubbery, and with the control of a contortionist they pull their heads back and their tails up, exiting through a joint between the two.

In order to maintain his equilibrium each lobster keeps one

grain of sand in a special hole in the top of his head. Every time he grows a new shell, he kicks sand over his head until one single grain settles in the receptacle. Then the shell grows over it, encapsulating the grain; it is, in effect, a primitive gyro.

The female must mate within forty-eight hours of growing her new shell. To attract males, she gives off a scent called a pheromone. (Humans manufacture pheromones too, but only mystics and anthropologists claim to sense them.) After mating, the female carries the sperm around in a belly pocket for eight or nine months while she makes eggs. When she's ready, she lies on her back and secretes the eggs from holes in her legs. The sperm fertilizes them, and a glue she manufactures enables them to stick to the underside of her tail. It is a reproductive cycle that lasts nearly two years and results in the release of 15,000 to 100,000 eggs. Nobody knows the mortality rate, but it is high. Some estimates say that only one-tenth of one percent survive.

At first, the baby lobster looks like a pale blue mosquito, eating other plankton. After two weeks of drifting willy-nilly with the surface currents, the young lobster drops to the ocean floor.

The regenerative powers of the lobster are considerable. Growing a new antenna is simple. His sense of smell, centered in the hairs on his legs, is about one million times more acute than a human's, but his eyesight is worse than Mr. Magoo's. So it is not uncommon for a lobster who has lost an eye in a scrap to grow a leg from the vacant socket.

I have said that Andra and I bought lobsters direct from the men who harvest them, and this is true. But lest I give the wrong impression, it was a rare treat. We were adjusting to a one-hundred-dollar a week budget, more inclined toward poultry and beans. Andra's sister Gay was in charge of our small nest egg, but in Maine we frequently couldn't find pay phones to plead for advances. In Winter Harbor we were down to our last dollars and change. We bought a bottle of wine, a newspaper, and a pack of smokes. We might starve to death, but at least we'd die happy and informed. We'd know how much money Fawn Hall or Donna Rice or Jessica Hahn had made in the last week, or how much our paltry stock in The New York Times Company had dropped in the hysterical plunge of October 19, 1987, or what the temperature was in Key West.

With more than two thousand miles to go, at an average speed of five knots, it seemed we would never make Florida. Nor, like Sam McGee, did it seem we'd ever again wear shorts and T-shirts until our cremation.

On the good days we chuckled at our fortune, hardly believing we had escaped the drone of office machinery and traffic gridlock or skipped out on the sailing-industry advertisers' parties where you had to be seen to be counted.

On the bad days we felt like bums. It was cold in Maine. In Lubec, in late August, we had built our first fire in the Tiny Tot wood and coal fireplace. And when it was cold we grew lethargic, often wearing the same clothes for days because we had only ourselves to confront. The hot-water shower was a tease, a beguiling mistress who threw you from her warm, soapy bosom to the frosty wolves at her doors. We couldn't get dressed fast enough, and the chill clung to our bones like an infection.

When we weren't sailing there were always things to be fixed. *Adriana,* though stout and worthy, was twenty years old. A boat is not like a house, which endures its cancers and ruptures in silence, like a stone marking the passage of æons without a whimper. A boat is nothing like that. She is dynamic, full of friction, an intricate system of parts all trying to separate from one another under the loads and stresses of the sea. And inevitably, from time to time, something strays. A pump fails, an instrument short-circuits, a rock is hit, a beer spills, and you want to cry from frustration. Why, I sometimes asked myself, had I not availed myself of the prison vocational rehabilitation programs and learned something useful like refrigeration maintenance, small-engine repair, or how to weld steel in the army-cot factory?

Still, I had enough tools on board to open a garage. They were heavy, all my hammers, drills, vises, and clamps, cunningly distributed about the boat to keep her in trim. I packed them according to frequency of use: under bunks, in binocular cases screwed to the cabin sides, in canvas duffel bags, and squirreled away in plastic wraps under the cockpit seats. Despite my best precautions, they rusted and jammed, falling prey to insidious corrosive processes.

Andra called me "The Tinkerer," as if I were a codified mole for the CIA, a convict with tunnel vision, or the village idiot in a Hawthorne novel, always at risk of having his neck and wrists slapped in the stocks. For it was my vow to repair at least one item of gear every day, even if only to whip the end of a line that had frayed.

The repair of a mare's tail, as sailors sometimes call it, is simple: First dig into the tape drawer for an elastic tape; cut a length and wrap it around the rope just above the loose threads. With a sharp knife and cutting board (look under the stove), cut off the offending tail. Now locate the sailmaker's twine and needle (behind the toilet in the medicine cabinet?). Open the book on marlinespike seamanship and reread for the hundredth time the various methods of properly whipping rope ends. Choose the easiest.

Your thumbs are too big and sore to handle the fine threads, which only people like Penelope can knot. After all, you are Ulysses, weary from years of wandering terrible seas and unfriendly lands; you wield swords and tillers, not needles and threads. But you do it. Fancy knotting is also the craft of the Queequegs and Billy Budds who climbed the rigging of tall ships, their muscular bodies flung like peas from the whipping spars into the frothing waters of Cape Horn. Yes, you effect the repair and it has taken you only six tools and an hour fifteen minutes. But you have the satisfaction of knowing that learned men will admire your attention to detail, your consummate seamanship. Then one day you wake and realize they are all retired naval officers. You will never let them near your boat again, and the mares' tails sweep the deck and be damned!

On those bad days—when the skies threatened, mildew ate our clothing, and the milk curdled—we did feel like bums. Five bucks for a flop sounded like a night at the Ritz. Know any friends in the next thirty miles? Good, bring a holiday turkey and invite ourselves for the weekend. Who cares if it's only August. Perhaps they'll at least let us do our laundry, those few torn and smelly garments we call clothes. Oh, for a bag to claim from a bus-station locker!

On days like these, Andra would turn to me and say, "You gave up a good job for *this*?"

In early September, just before Labor Day, we returned to Southwest Harbor. What a difference a fortnight made! The boats were gone, and we had our pick of the empty moorings. We ate aboard and later watched the waxing moon cover with haze, rising in a lavender light over the town. The sun fell the other way into an orange stripe beyond Mount St. Sauveur, her half of the sky painted with black, smoky clouds. The pogies were silent and so too the voracious blues that in August sent them skittering across the water like a ruffling breeze.

Standing in the cockpit, watching the night fall around me, I suddenly felt alone. For the first time I realized summer was gone. We were too far north and had been caught with our pants down.

It was autumn in Maine, a season that would be our companion for the rest of the year. Speed south as we could, we only made five knots. About six miles per hour. A snail's pace by any human standard. But one doesn't take up sailing unless he's comfortable with his own company, and we enjoyed the brisk air, scent of pine, and the comparative emptiness of the coastal waters. Monday through Friday the only boats we saw were those of commercial fishermen, which gave us a sense of belonging.

We stopped in Blue Hill, as pretty a harbor as we were to see anywhere. The entrance is a tricky set of doglegs between rocks visible only at low tide, opening into a tranquil anchorage banked by pretty wooden homes and substantial piers. The community is well heeled, and the children play with model yachts and learn to sail on Dyer dinghies with varnished gunwales.

The reason for our visit was an advertisement on the radio that ballyhooed the state fair, and in particular, the world's largest pig. We hiked two miles up an interminable grade, forsaking the thumb on the ill advice of a girl who said, "It's just over the hill."

The Blue Hill Fair belongs in the Midwest, or at least the Midwest I knew growing up in Michigan. What do New Englanders know of good posture in a goat? Fullness in the mammaries of a Hereford? Perhaps Maine doesn't deserve being summarily grouped with her smaller sister states to the south—Connecticut and Rhode Island. Country and Western music is popular, tractor pulls and 4-H clubs. And of course the pig, which weighed 2,660 pounds, transported in a painted trailer that said: "Warning: Giant Pig Inside!" For fifty cents we were admitted inside to file around the beast's cage and to shuffle our deck shoes behind the cowboy boots, and mumble such hesitations of disappointment as, "Sho is a big mother, ain't he?"

Perhaps we had expected too much, or were simply naive. He was most believably the world's largest pig, and most assuredly a total bore. Either he was too fat to stand, happily sleeping out his days having cheated the butcher's knife, or as most observers asserted, drugged into Nirvana. Pigs, by nature, are an excitable species. Later we telephoned Peter and Adria. World's Largest Pig. It was such a good opening line.

First light told me this was a special day. We were anchored again in the Isles of Shoals. Andra was still asleep when I saw the sky and climbed out of bed. I made a pot of coffee and sat in the cockpit. Across the harbor a father and son on a motorsailer putt-putted out of the harbor, capturing the proverbial jump on the day.

The sky was the color of rose water, and the gulls were awake, screaming at the new day. They were hungry, as they always seem to be. The colony was in flight, circling—the young and old and near-dead. It was a desperate, eerie ritual, as if they were calling for our blood, to pick us apart if we faltered, leaving our bones to lie with our fallen brethren, our bones as whitewashed as those pale rocks, the fabric of our clothes rotting in the salt, torn away by beaks and wind and time.

These were not sad thoughts; as I have said, the Isles of Shoals are strange. Peter had felt uncomfortable there. It is an unnatural place, inhabited only by gulls and Unitarians.

Later that day we were sailing freely toward the Annisquam Canal, happy to bear true south, when suddenly a dozen dolphins ripped past our bow. We stood and watched, gape-mouthed. They moved like lightning, throwing themselves out of the water in a rainbow of spray, leapfrogging each other's backs, spinning, diving. For a moment they careened toward us, and we whistled. Abruptly they changed direction, heading off toward the openness and the Gulf Stream beyond Cape Ann. And just when we thought we had seen the last of them, they were back, crossing our stern. Try as we might to flatter ourselves with their attention, they had no mind of us, and I am sure they were just kids playing, like twelve-year-old boys tumbling about a vacant field on a fine summer Saturday while their parents are indoors washing clothes and balancing accounts.

Our luck ran out in Salem, Massachusetts. We stopped to visit Andra's Great Aunt Stel in nearby Swampscott, picking up a mooring on an ugly day beneath the brown brick stacks of an electric plant. The wind built and blew for four days until we could stand it no more. We took the bus back to Stel's and threw ourselves on her mercy. She fixed us up in the reading room, me with my portable computer and Andra with a stack of magazines and paperbacks. She brought lunch on a tray, and we watched a little television for the first time in months. Outside, the rain pelted the windows and the wind continued to blow.

Once I hiked down the street to an overlook where I could see the finger of land called Nahant. A few boats were moored along shore. I was looking for a break in the clouds, a sign of abatement, a promise we could leave the next day, but there was no forgiveness to be read in the skies. I dragged my wet feet back up the steps of Aunt Stel's porch and dialed in another football game, doing, I surmised miserably, just what I would be doing had I never decided to cruise.

Back aboard, we felt nauseous and depressed. The season was escaping us. Long ago I had vowed that when I sailed south I would leave Newport by early September—no late-fall departures for me. I'd be on the Intracoastal Waterway digging Carolina clams before the first frost in Newport. Now it was late September, and we were stuck in Salem, too lethargic to investigate the witches' house or the candy stores in Marblehead.

By the end of the fourth day we had exhausted every topic of conversation. I could barely raise my head in the bucking cabin to make a Scrabble move. Andra tried valiantly to be a sport.

She pondered her next move. J-O-K-E-R. Thirty-eight points and an insurmountable lead. "Pook," she said, "I'm pregnant."

6

The Book of Whys

Ugly, growling waves rolled into Massachusetts Bay as we pushed *Adriana* past Boston and on toward the Cape Cod Canal. The "graybeards" were a mirror image of the clouds overhead—ponderous and slow. Without the wind that created them, the waves lumbered over the banks, forcing us to motorsail. The sails slatted in the troughs, and the ten-foot seas rocked us with a rough hand. Forty miles of bad road lay between us and Plymouth.

Now, knowing as only a woman knows that she was expecting, Andra realized she should also be experiencing the dread morning sickness. And there were moments when she was severely tested. But she has a stronger stomach than most people, and not even the wallowing, nauseating rollers could force her chin to the rail. If she were to be cheated of some fundamental part of the child-bearing experience, this was one facet she didn't mind missing.

In fact, Andra's maternal instincts had always turned at low idle, more intellectual than biological. It had been our understanding that we would, in all likelihood, spare this crowded planet additional progeny. So there was some hard thinking to do, and to me at least, every alternative was painful. On the one hand, abortion seemed repugnant, yet on the other, changing diapers was not the way I had planned to spend my middle years. Life was supposed to begin at forty, not tick away in a moonless nursery.

My solitary recollection of Plymouth is staring dumbly at the famous rock upon whose dull surfaces America's favored ancestors supposedly stepped forth in the year 1620. Done with their miserable passage from England, the Pilgrims were eager to colonize, propagate, and plant corn with an Indian named Squanto. Unfortunately for these seekers of religious freedom — Brewster, Smith, Standish, and the chaste Priscilla Mullins — the ship missed its Virginia destination by a wide margin. The *Mayflower*, like all square-rigged ships of her time, was a downwind tub, incapable of pointing into the wind. The Polynesians had already solved the mystery of sailing upwind with fore-and-aft sails, and China, with its junks and fully battened sails, had also figured it out, but Europe was hundreds of years behind.

The Pilgrims first landed on Cape Cod, near Wellfleet on the north shore. The barren, windswept dunes, scraggly trees, and brambles were less than hospitable. This was not the Promised Land. In the ship's pinnace, the men explored westward, sounding their way among the sandbars into the shallows of Plymouth Bay. There were trees and brooks and materials to make shelter. The men erected a stockade, built crude, thatched-roof houses, and read the Bible to savages. That the Indians never listened should have come as no surprise, dressed as the Pilgrims were in black pantaloons and white bibs.

We transited the canal on September 22 and found a cozy anchorage in Hospital Cove, near Pocasset on the southwest coast of the Cape. On the perimeter were green-lawned country estates, not quite old enough for ivy, and along the sandspit to the west we saw middle-aged men jogging in shorts with Irish setters, and women strutting briskly, swinging their arms with exaggerated enthusiasm.

63

The following morning, which opened pink and moist, we set the sails and headed down Buzzards Bay for Cuttyhunk. The wind was a wish, and in less than an hour I was forced to start the diesel.

We took a mooring in the nearly deserted harbor and rowed ashore in the dinghy. This had been the first anchorage of the cruise, the haven we had found through the fog and rain after leaving all our friends behind. I remembered Adria's fantasy dream about the old fisherman and his macabre bait, and on leaving, Pete offering me the best and only thing he could—his company. The memories made me sad in a curious way, and I wanted to move on.

A paved path leads to the island's highest point, protected on the steep side by a stone wall. Below, the ragged brush is too thick for man, though we saw several deer frozen in the seemingly impenetrable brambles and rose hips. Standing there, one could easily imagine Bartholomew Gosnold, who discovered the island in the seventeenth century, enthralled by the same vista. We could see Martha's Vineyard to the east, the red cliffs of Gay Head vaguely discernible through the mist. To the west lay the Massachusetts mainland and the port of New Bedford, from whence the world's greatest whalers once set to sea.

On a clear day one might see all the way to Rhode Island and the Sakonnet lighthouse marking the entrance to East Passage. Standing on the grassy, windswept knoll, contemplating our brief stopover in Newport to reprovision, I had strange misgivings. After all, we'd already had our bon voyage party, and you can only say hello, good-bye so many times. The temptation was strong to set out on the morrow across Rhode Island Sound, straight for Block Island and Long Island Sound beyond, skipping Newport altogether. It felt like bad luck to show our faces again so soon. Recalling the feeling a few days later, I wished I had sailed on into oblivion, never knowing the news that awaited us.

The steering wheel felt cold on my hands the next morning as I gave it the customary tug left and right. It was a crude system check. Sometimes the wire cables that connect the wheel to the rudderpost stretched, and when the transmission engaged, the whole boat shuddered as though it were a great, shivering animal lifting itself from a winter's sleep.

Andra stood on the foredeck waiting for me to tell her it was okay to bring up the anchor. I stood aft in the cockpit, looking for my gloves. Sometimes cruising couples work out elaborate hand signals to communicate during anchoring maneuvers—port, starboard, forward, stop. For some reason I can't explain, we just yell. By nature I am not a loud person, but sign language seems to overcomplicate the procedure. When we first started sailing together, Andra thought I was angry when I raised my voice; now she understands that I just want to be heard over the clattering of the cold diesel.

Respect, people seem to think, means talking in low volume. It takes awhile to get over that.

That morning ours was the only boat left in the salt-pond harbor at Cuttyhunk. The other two sailboats in the anchorage had gotten the jump on us, filing out of the dredged cut when first light was just visible in the eastern sky. Hearing their engines kick over and the water from their exhaust pipes splash like a mountain freshet on the surface of the still pond, I had stuck my head out of the forward hatch, only to withdraw at the feel of frost on the deck. Better, I thought, to wait for the sun. Besides, we were in no particular hurry to reach Newport. The run to Rhode Island is twenty-two miles, and with any luck we would cover it in four to five hours. And though Newport was home, we weren't expected today. Yesterday's misgivings had evaporated with the night, and we were both excited at the prospect of tying to our own mooring and surprising friends. Perhaps that was why I had gone back to bed when the other boats had left—by postponing the pleasure I might savor it a little longer.

"Ready!" I yelled.

Andra turned her back to me and stepped on the small black foot pad sunk in the foredeck, activating the sturdy, bronze capstan of the electric windlass, which began to turn slowly, raising the galvanized chain and anchor from the bottom of the pond. It's a good thing we have this windlass, I thought. Raising the anchor by hand requires considerable strength, and Andra is smaller than she looks all bundled in loose-fitting sweatpants and blue jeans, double sweaters, and a sailing jacket.

A faint breeze ruffled the waters of Cuttyhunk Pond, gently pushing *Adriana* sideways.

"Up?" I yelled. It's important to know when the anchor breaks free of the bottom.

Andra was still staring down at the water, so I killed time by looking around. The Coast Guard station showed no sign of activity; possibly it was shut down for the season. The white painted sides and red roof looked freshly scrubbed in the bright light of the early morning sun. The yellow beach beyond was pristine. The Gosnold town dock was empty, and there was no sign of the wharfinger who last night had motored out in his skiff to collect the ten-dollar mooring fee. If I'd known he still charged after Labor Day, I would have anchored instead. Three boats in a harbor with room for a hundred! We were cruising on a tight budget, and I was a little peeved at myself. Better to have saved the money for the movies, which we hadn't seen in months, or at the least Jamaican coffees at Cafe Zelda where a lot of our friends met.

"Okay!" Andra called back.

She bent over to lift the thirty-five-pound plow anchor up over the bow roller. I wondered if I should dash forward to help. The pond was small, and with no one at the helm there was a risk of being blown into shallow water. But she was a month pregnant.

"Need help?" I asked.

She turned and shook her head.

Standing on my tiptoes I looked over the cabintop to see that she'd already set the anchor in place. After lashing it she returned to the cockpit, gave me a hard grin, and stepped below for another cup of coffee while the water was still smooth. Soon we'd be hoisting the sails in Buzzards Bay, a body of water known for a stiff chop in the prevailing southwesterlies. The wind hadn't come up yet, but it would. We'd made this trip many times, and there was always wind. Always smack on the nose.

Once outside Cuttyhunk Harbor I turned southwest and raised the mainsail, though it was still calm. I wanted to be ready when the wind came. To our right was Penikese Island. Once it was a leper colony, but their mark on this rock has long since been erased by the scouring of sleet, spume, and salt. Now the State of Massachusetts preserves Penikese as a bird refuge, and the summer caretaker is a school for troubled boys. In winter, the island takes care of itself.

As we came out of the lee of Cuttyhunk the waves began to build, and the mainsail filled lightly. For a time Andra and I said nothing. After two months of twenty-four-hour days together we didn't need to articulate every thought in order to communicate. On the boat our concerns were elementary. We'd developed a series of subtle facial expressions that no one else would understand. We read messages in our eyes and in the creases of our cheeks. One told me Andra was cold, another that she wished we were already at our destination. Mine said there was nothing I could do about either one.

I thought about the troubled boys of Penikese and wondered how successful are these programs, in which inner-city kids are removed to some wilderness where psychosocial problems are supposed to evaporate in the raw air and new values emerge from the pitting of wits against Nature. The island is so small, the biggest challenge would be how to swim to the mainland. You could build a rep on that feat.

As we passed the Hen and Chickens Reef, the waves began to build. When they got too steep, the tops tumbled forward in whitecaps. It was the wind that drove them, and now it buffeted my face. The bow rose to each wave, rearing like a spooked horse, then slammed down into the trough on the other side. Before the boat had a chance to recover, another wave would wash over us. Spray flew back in white sheets. Andra huddled under the canvas dodger that protected the companionway hatch and the forward end of the cockpit seats. I had to duck, and for a moment was forced to steer by feel. But I had been sailing this boat for so many years that the feedback came to me through my feet and hands and stomach — I believed I could steer her true even if I were blind.

The wind, as usual, was dead on the bow. *Adriana* heeled hard over, and water began to shoot up through the sink drain, pouring into the cabinets behind, ultimately draining into and filling the bilge. The cabin sole was awash with an oily film. The dinette cushions and pillows slid into it. Andra retreated to the cabin and, convinced that we were sinking, was ready to deploy the liferaft. I shouted below, telling her to close the seacock to stop the ingress of water through the sink. She opened the cupboard door and was hit by a torrent of water. She didn't have to say it—I knew her thoughts: "Get me off this boat!"

I started the engine to ease our motion, but it too was fed up and quit with a chug. The deck lashings on the dinghy oars came undone, and the oars nearly washed overboard. Andra still had her wits about her and saved them.

We limped up the Sakonnet River and anchored at Third Beach on the west side of Aquidneck Island. Newport lay over the hill, beyond the Gothic spire of St. George's prep school. In the lee of Sachuest Point, we licked our wounds. But our streak of bad luck wasn't over yet. My favorite pipe fell in the water, and I leaped into the dinghy to retrieve it, forgetting the oars. I paddled back with my hands, cursing my stupidity. Later, after ruining a chicken casserole with a can of rancid cream of celery soup, we ate a dinner of boiled canned vegetables. Showers seemed the perfect antidote. Wouldn't you know, the drain was plugged, sending water into the bilge, which overflowed with a scum of bilge oil onto the cabin sole.

"Too bad the wind was on the nose," I said philosophically.

Andra scowled. "You mean, 'up the nose'?"

We decided to cut our losses and go to bed.

Lying there, I was glad at least that Peter hadn't been with us. Though he loved sailing, he was frightened when I yelled and jumped. "Dad," he'd whisper after a fire drill like this, "why don't you just buy a motorboat?" I would try to explain that motorboats cost more money to operate and aren't as safe offshore. Maybe that was his point—why go offshore in the first place? I missed him and Adriana terribly.

They didn't know Andra was pregnant; perhaps they never would. It seemed we had just gotten underway and now were forced to make critical decisions, not only about the cruise but about our relationship as well. Her first child was growing in her womb, and I could tell she was changing. I didn't know what to think. With Pete and Adria nearly grown, I had begun mapping a plan for adventure with Andra as my partner, trying to make up for the experiences I thought I'd missed and the places I'd never seen. I felt derailed, my course plotted with disappearing ink. We conferred endlessly, but the best we could do was to keep heading south and see what would happen.

Our layover in Newport was hectic. There were groceries to be bought, propane tanks to fill, friends to see, and slides to caption for coming *Cruising World* articles. One afternoon I visited the office. My desk had been dumped in the basement, and I felt homeless yet happy that I had at last broken free.

We visited our friends Buck and Lady L in South Kingston. Their saltbox sat at the edge of the Great Swamp, at the end of a country lane that led past the junky camps of migrant workers. The sandy earth was red and the pines scraggly. At night, drinking beers on the back stoop, we slapped mosquitoes and hummed "Georgia on My Mind."

Buck and L had a new baby, Jasmine, which L said looked like a monkey. I couldn't disagree with her. I avoided her eyes, staring out the window. Andy bit her tongue. Neither of us wanted to betray our secret.

Later, Buck led me into the bog surrounding two sides of their house. The Great Swamp is four hundred acres of overflow, black muck, and dense undergrowth. We hopped from hummock to hummock, swinging on swamp cedars and maples, in search of Buck's Lost Rhododendron Patch. In my imagination we were looking for the Natchez Trace, and we were minor characters in Eudora Welty's story about James Audubon shooting birds on horseback. I waited for the sharp report of his rifle, the shrill cry, and brilliantly colored feathers floating to the ground. But here, lost in the Great Swamp, nothing disturbed the perfect silence.

Buck pulled up a quarter mile into the jungle. He had been picking his way as cannily as a Potawatomi, reading the trees and moss for directions. His tall, lanky form reminded me of the hillbilly in the movie *Deliverance*, or the bearded bush guide in *Papil-*

lion. He grew quiet when he had had his herb, cosmic when he spoke.

He stopped to listen for sounds that could lead us to the Lost Rhododendron Patch. After a long silence he whispered, "Sshh. We're near the place I've been before."

Friday night we ate dinner across the bridge in Jamestown with Herb McCormick, his girlfriend Kelsey, and *Cruising World's* advertising design director, Jeff Schipritt. When we finished we stepped outside into the tumultuous night. A storm was forecast, and in my ears I could feel the barometric pressure drop. All day the clouds had hurried by, sometimes obscuring the sun, at other times breaking through just long enough to make one think it was a "nice day."

We drove south to the end of the island and the Beavertail lighthouse. It was cold, the autumn air dry and sharp. We climbed down onto the rocks and watched the surf crash. A full moon came and went behind the clouds, and with it a few stars that gave the illusion of streaking.

Suddenly the entire sky was covered with low-lying clouds, and it seemed it might rain. Then a hole opened over the bay, perhaps a mile distant, and a concentrated shaft of moonlight hit the water. So narrow and focused was this beam, it might have been a spotlight from a hovering spaceship. As we stood shivering, it began to play toward us, picking up speed. And then it was over us, bathing us in light. Just as suddenly as it had appeared, it was gone.

We fell silent. Finally, Herb said, "How about that light? Some kind of Spielberg special effects, huh?"

"Felt like the mothership was about to beam us up," added Jeff.

I cannot say how it affected me, only that it did. That night and the next. I am not a believer in the supernatural, but if ever there was an omen to be read in the strange and multifarious ways of Nature, this was it. Perhaps all was not well in the world.

It was eight o'clock, and we were preparing to fix dinner. Danny Greene rowed over for a visit. In the morning he would depart on his annual exodus to Bermuda and the Caribbean, and we to the safer, coastal route south—Long Island Sound and the Chesapeake Bay, following the Intracoastal Waterway to sun-kissed Florida and the subtropical Bahamas. The kerosene lamps radiated warmth, and it was a happy, nostalgic air that filled our tiny cabin. The boat was provisioned and the tanks full. After years of longingly watching Danny set sail, we felt that for once he would not leave us behind.

Suddenly I heard my name. A shout. I peeked out the hatch, thinking it was Danny Keirns ready to clamor aboard, a paycheck in one hand and a return ticket from Miami in the other.

A white fishing boat, its outboard chattering at fast idle, edged into the dim light. Herb stood on the bow, obscuring the other men standing behind the steering console.

"What's up?" I asked.

"I'm taking you ashore," he said grimly.

Oh no, I thought. He's not going to let us out of town without another round of drinks. We'd worked next to one another on the editorial floor of *Cruising World* for seven years, and it was he, when I was the new editor with the Midwestern nasal twang, who first broke the ice, inviting me out with several of his friends.

Then he was aboard and the fishing boat vanished in the night. "You gotta call Michigan," he said. "Something has happened to Pete. I don't know what, but I think it's bad."

"Herb," I said, looking him in the eye, "do you really not know, or are you just trying to protect yourself?"

"Sorry, buddy," he answered, "but I really don't know anything more."

Silently Andra, Herb, and I rowed ashore. The stars had disappeared, and the harbor chop was cold. George Day waited on the docks. Without a word we trudged up the street and filed into the *Cruising World* offices.

Nervously, I dialed the numbers. Who would answer? Margaret? Adria? Pete? And what could be so terrible? Another fall from his bike? Another operation to straighten his skinny, bent legs?

A recorded voice said, "Sorry, all lines are busy, please hang up and try your call later." I tried again. And again. Finally, I got through, but the line was busy. Meanwhile the office filled. Co-

71

workers Joy Scott and Glennie Ormiston were downstairs with Andra. George fidgeted in his office. Danny Greene stared into space, and Herb sat on the stairs, head in hands. They knew something I didn't. I couldn't ask, and they wouldn't tell.

Operator, I said, give me an emergency interrupt. An old friend, Mary Gibson, answered. "Peter's dead," she said. Say again, I didn't hear you right. "Dan, Peter is dead."

He was hit by a train, knocked off a trestle onto the banks of the Huron River. Seven miles west of Ann Arbor, across the drive from his country home. Two other boys were with him, and I imagine them throwing stones, as I often did, playing on those same tracks when I was a kid. Or heaving sticks into the current, then racing to the other side of the trestle to watch their makeshift boats fly past, bound for Lake Erie.

The train rounded the curve. There wasn't much time, but there was enough. As the locomotive swung around, it first seemed to be on the outer tracks, and the boys jumped to the inside set. The red Amtrak stripes straightened, and now it was obvious it ran on the inside. The other two boys jumped back, one even making it off the trestle to the embankment. Peter didn't. He tripped and fell, his legs impossibly tangled, unable to bounce up like any regular kid. The engineer saw him and blew the whistle. Air brakes were applied, but the distance was short. Pete waved him off. I can see his arm, the elbow twisted inward, his fingers splayed, playing back and forth in a frantic, spastic motion.

The other boys saw him. One instant he was there, the next he wasn't. It was quick, save for those interminable minutes waiting for the train to stop.

When it had passed, finally stopped half a mile down, the boys looked. Pete lay in a cluster of saplings, half in the water, half out. I would like to say like Moses, saved by a basket of reeds and borne to safety on the stream.

My Pete, my Tiny Tim. So many times when his legs gave out, I hoisted him onto my shoulders and carried him.

Our friends comforted us. Danny Keirns said Pete was having an adventure with the boys. Kenn Miller called from Los Angeles to say Tom Sawyer and Huck Finn would have wanted him along. Herb said it sucked.

I knew one of the boys who had been with Pete. During a visit to Michigan the previous fall, I'd taken him and Pete to see *Stand by Me*, based on a Stephen King story called "The Body." Four kids, about Pete's age, set out along the railroad tracks to find the body of another boy who is rumored to have been hit by a train. Crossing a trestle, a train comes. One boy — the fat kid — falls. He is afraid to stand, so crawls frantically toward the other side. The camera switches to the spinning steel wheels of the train. The engineer blows the whistle long and hard. I remember Pete and his friend tightening in their seats. At the last instant, one of the other boys returns, grabs the fat kid, and together they leap to safety.

I remember Pete squealing, then heaving back as the tension passed. I had saved Pete so many times. Why, I asked myself, couldn't I save him now?

A priest could not be found to officiate services. The pope had recently passed through the Detroit suburb of Hamtramck and the bishop had summoned all parish priests in the diocese to a retreat to discuss issues.

At the eleventh hour a priest by the name of Joe Rinaldi was contacted at a Chelsea home for retarded children. He never knew Pete, but he *knew* him, if you know what I mean.

He was a caricature of Father Guido Sarducci. No, he didn't wear a cape or hat; his face was pockmarked, and there was no suavity in his movements. But he had the same hipness, thick Italian accent, and the common man's humor. When we first met, he said to the family in the front row of the country church, "Excuse me. I don't really know what I am doing, but I will do my best."

He told the congregation: "When someone dies, they come to me and say, Father, why? I say to them, nobody knows why. You don't know why, I don't know why. You go to the library, but there is no Book of Whys. Only God knows why. I might like a nice Londoner accent, but I sound like an Italian. I might like a nice head of hair, but I'm half bald. I don't know why, you don't know why. There is no Book of Whys. I didn't know this Peter. I don't know if he was blond or black or red. But I do know he must have been a very special boy, because I been to this church before and I never seen so many people!"

Then it was my turn. That morning I had composed a few thoughts at Robert and Mary Gibson's breakfast table, writing while they and Andra still slept. At that moment, what I wanted more than anything else was the last word for my son.

Adria stood by me at the lectern, in case I couldn't finish. I looked at the mourners, more than four hundred. Standing room only. Faces I had never seen.

Since most of you are Peter's Michigan friends, I want to tell you a little about his summers in Rhode Island.

A lot of our time was spent on our thirty-three-foot sailboat. Some years we lived on it all summer, and on weekends we would take cruises to Block Island or Martha's Vineyard. Peter and Adria have their own bunks in the back of the boat. Pete had a net hammock for his clothes and a bookshelf for his toys. He liked to keep his things organized—he was a good seaman.

This summer was special, because I had left my job to sail the East Coast and write a book. Pete was very excited to help get ready. The biggest job was to build a dinghy. Every day Pete and I went to the shop and worked on it. I called him my helper, because he fetched tools, cleaned up, painted, and generally told me what to do. He thought he knew a lot about boats, and he did.

Pete was never strong enough to row his own dinghy, but when we reached my cousin Sophie's house in Maine, he learned how to paddle a small kayak. It was fitting that her husband, Peter, taught him, because in part we named Pete for Peter.

For the first time Pete could handle his own boat, and he spent hours paddling around the backwaters of Horseshoe Cove. When we had to drag him out for dinner, he was wet, tired, and all smiles.

I believe that Pete was meant to spend his time on Earth as a child, not an adult.

He came to us in the summer and left us in the fall. He never knew the cold of winter.

We're going to keep sailing. We're going to find you, Pete. And we know we will see you in every port, on every ship, in every sky.

Welcome aboard, Mate.

Afterward I drove Margaret from the church to a luncheon for friends at a neighbor's house. On the way she said the strangest thing had happened last Friday, the day before Pete died. She was in the yard. The weather had been "funny" all day and she didn't know if there was time to turn the garden soil. Dark, rolling clouds blotted the sun, and she thought it would rain. As she watched, the sun shone down through a crack in the clouds. More like a beam, she said, so specific and thin was the cone of light. It fell first across the road, on the railroad tracks, then moved up the hill toward her until it fell on the house and was eclipsed. Then the rain came and she went inside.

"Now I understand," she said to me, "that it was a sign, a sign that Pete was about to be taken from us."

I looked at her and said, my heart leaping, "You won't believe this. . . ."

The weather that week in Michigan was splendid, brisk and bright, and the colors in the turning trees full of orange and red. And the season changed. I dreaded leaving almost as much as I dreaded staying—all the grieving relatives in my old house, the delicate, conciliatory greetings of Andra and Margaret, the dark half-moons under Adria's pink eyes. As hard as it was to separate myself from the touchstones of Peter's world, I grew anxious to lead Margaret and Adria through the final steps.

On a fine afternoon I gathered a selection of flowers from the bouquet Lennie Zazzarino had sent and led the way to the tracks. We walked out on the trestle and laid down some blossoms. Below, on the bank, we could see the broken saplings where Pete had spent his last moments alive. There we carefully laid the rest of the flowers, sat in the mud, and cried.

Lastly there was the business of Peter's ashes. Margaret and Adria had already decided he would not lie underground. No fancy casket. We would spread him in the places he loved — on the fertile earth, on flower beds, and on the waters where he had sailed.

He was given back to us in a plastic bag inside a simple cardboard box, the sort that comes with a nice coffee mug. Strangely, Margaret and I were both comforted to have this box, to know we had what was left of our son.

In the car we opened the bag and sifted the ashes through our fingers. They were not fine like tinders from a fireplace, but coarse. Mostly there were pieces of bone and calcium, like broken shells and fossils found on a beach.

We bought a bottle of champagne, and Margaret got a little tipsy. Then we took him home. Adria and Andra were out. Numbly I read the newspaper and when I looked again, Margaret was gone. I called her name, but there was no answer. I looked outside and asked the dog. But Lucy didn't know. Upstairs I found Margaret in her bed, under a comforter, her arm around the cardboard box, a mother who at long last had brought her poor son home.

Back in Newport, Andra and I held a small service for Pete's friends at the Seaman's Institute. In another day our affairs were in order, and we took our leave from the condo docks across from the *Cruising World* office. There was nothing else to do. Many of our friends were there on the dock. After the obligatory hugs and promises to write, George Day pushed us off into the sunshine with the command, "Commence cruising!"

It seemed an auspicious way to resume the cruise, but at the harbor entrance I remembered the company car keys in my pocket. I started to turn the boat around and lost the steering.

Fortunately, we were able to grab a nearby mooring. The steering cable was soon repaired, the keys returned, and an hour later we were again underway. As we broke into Narragansett Bay I gave the helm to Andra and ducked below for my share of Pete's ashes. They were stored in a cookie tin painted with bears. I stood with my knees against the lifelines and sprinkled a portion onto the waters as if I were sowing seeds.

I recited folk singer Joe Hill's last letter, sent to Wobbly president Big Bill Haywood.

> *My will is easy to decide.*
> *For I have nothing to divide.*
> *My kin don't need to fuss and moan,*
> *Moss don't cling to a rolling stone.*
>
> *My body? — Oh! — if I could choose,*
> *I would to ashes it reduce,*
> *And let the merry breezes blow,*
> *My dust to where some flowers grow.*
>
> *Perhaps some dying flower then*
> *Will come to life and bloom again.*
> *This is my last and final will.*
> *Good luck to all of you,*
>
> *Joe Hill*

We sailed on in silence for Stonington, Connecticut, and that night I wrote this in my journal:

> *The light is thin, the land a ribbon of brown and green, with a little red on the trees. It is as if we are wrapped in gauze, everything hazy, as if we too have passed on into another world. We too are in transition. And so the cycle of life goes on, the Earth adding where it has lost, spinning through space on its unknown mission. The lights of the living blink its at once sad and joyful message.*
> *I am changed. I am not the person I was at 5:39, October 3,*

1987. It is difficult to say precisely what is different. Before I was in my thirties, with all hope before me; now in my forties, with a past I cannot bear and a future that seems dimmer, shorter.

And I think of all the old men in the world who have lost sons — in Vietnam, Afghanistan, Nicaragua — to war, car accidents, drugs, and AIDS. We brought them into the world and sent them out, always believing they would bury us.

7
Cons, Ghosts, and Highwaymen

Long Island Sound opened to us at the Race, the imaginary line between Point Judith, Rhode Island, and Montauk, New York. At full flood the water pumps through the constricted opening at speeds of up to five knots.

We carried the current with us on our diagonal course from Stonington, Connecticut, to Port Jefferson, New York. Here, on the autumn coast of off-season Long Island, we could see the lights of Stamford and New Haven, Connecticut, across the sound. It was as close as we wanted to get to the ghetto-burbs of New York City, the tangled freeways, littered corners, and the inevitable street tension that occurs wherever the rich and poor rub shoulders.

Even at midweek, we passed several day-charter fishing boats, large steel vessels like the *Poconic Star II* and *Super Squirrel.* Fifteen bucks for half a day. The rails were lined with the unemployed, blacks and whites with hands stuffed in pockets and sweatshirt hoods pulled over their heads. As in a breadline, you wait long enough, you get your dinner.

The *Poconic Star* came upon us in a calm, stirring up the sound with her diesels as the captain aimed for some secret hot spot.

I know a good fisherman can divine the presence of fish, and I know there are instruments such as echo fishfinders to help, but I do not understand how fish are found. Magazine editor Jim Gilbert, once a commercial fisherman, advised me to think like a fish. Familiarize yourself with its habits, he urged, its likes and dislikes, mating practices, feeding routines, eccentricities. Try as I might, however, I could not put myself in its position, imagining myself swimming through a bed of wavering grass, dodging crabs, smelling the water for the scent of food, then stumbling onto a dangling worm and thinking, "Mmm, looks good!"

I have always supposed that beyond the choice of bait or lure, catching fish is just dumb luck. No doubt this explains my singular failure with the rod and reel. You have to know how a particular species reacts to water temperature, current, and underwater formations, what the expert deep-sea fisherman calls "structure." For me, structure is what you're trying to get away from when you go fishing.

We crabbed along the sound, avoiding the cities and wishing for the Chesapeake. There were long periods of silence aboard *Adriana* as we tried to understand Pete's death. Once or twice a day, often over dinner, we opened up to one another and dissected the experience. This sort of grieving was new to both of us. For me, Pete's death had catalyzed a quantum change in the way I viewed my life and how I wished to live out the second half of it.

It didn't take days or weeks for reality to kick in; I had come face to face with it the moment Mary Gibson answered the telephone. Perhaps I had feared Pete's vulnerability for years, ever since the pediatric neurologist diagnosed his cerebral palsy.

The sadness is something else. Like being rejected by your lover, you wonder what you did wrong, you lose sleep, and when you accept the fact there is nothing more to be done, you still wince at the irretrievable loss of something precious. And you cry. Time, friends say, is the only healer, and in time we learned this truth.

We did not talk a great deal about the baby, not yet. It was too soon. Andra understood that. The night Pete died, we had rowed back to the boat, after sitting up half the night, to pack and rest before flying to Michigan. We climbed into our bunk and held each other, and I told her how my heart had changed. For Adria's sake, for hers, and maybe even a little for mine. Mostly, I told her, for Pete's sake. To me, this baby was a gift from my son.

I began to wonder about the matter of souls, where they go, and when newborns are infused with their unique *spiritus*. In prison I had worked a short time for the Catholic chaplain, and he had taught me Church dogma. I let myself consider the bizarre and mystical possibilities of metempsychosis. Obviously, I thought, a baby doesn't get its "soul" on the first day of conception, for even if a soul is non-matter, there just isn't room inside two cells, and there is nothing—no intellect or personality—for it to act on. By the same reasoning, the instant before delivery is too late; after all, premature babies have souls, right? So the soul must arrive somewhere between Day 1 and Day 266. At one month, the fetus already has fingernails, hair, a brain—seems as likely a time as any, I reasoned. Maybe, just maybe Peter's soul was transferred to this baby, for at the time of his death the baby was one month underway on its fantastic journey.

We spent the last of three nights in the sound at the Sand Hole, a cleverly conceived anchorage near the entrance to Oyster Bay. The approach is an S-curve between sandbars, opening into a pool the size of a football field. There were several dozen boats anchored there, power and sail. Trespass warnings were issued on the mainland side, so we rowed ashore to the spit to pick shells on the sandy beach. There we watched powerboats ripping up and down the sound, tugs towing huge, flat barges, and tramp freighters sneaking through New York's backdoor.

As we stood there with the orange orb of the sun squatting on the horizon like a scoop of melting sherbert, driftwood underfoot, I pointed to the raftup of five boats downwind of us.

"If the wind shifts," I said, "they'll surely drag down on us."

At four that morning I awoke to a bumping, grinding noise. Poking my sleepy head through the hatch, I saw that all five boats had settled around us like a flock of tethered sheep. Our stainless steel bow pulpit had locked horns with the outriggers of a small fishing boat. I dressed and climbed on deck. About the same time the skipper of another boat emerged to survey the situation. He lit a cigarette in his cupped hands and blew the smoke into the chilly night air. "Well," he said, "what's a party that don't get busted?"

One by one the other men awoke and broke off from the raft. I heard the wives whining in their beds—"What's going on Harold? For chrissakes, come back to bed." Few of the men answered. They started their engines and moved off into the night, tossing their seldom-used anchors into the phosphorescent water.

The currents run strong through the East River. The *Nautical Almanac* lists the ebb and flow at Hell Gate, midway between Long Island Sound and Manhattan. During the Revolutionary War the British frigate *Hussar* was turned about in the whirlpools, struck Mill Rock, and sank with paychests for King George's army. Our timing, however, was as impeccable as Phileas Phogg's, the punctual hero of *Around the World in Eighty Days*. We were swept along the famous river safely, past LaGuardia airport, Riker's Island, and the mouth of the Harlem River. The tenements, warehouses, and dirty laundry inched by, eventually giving way to the skyscrapers of Manhattan. How different it must have looked to Henry Hudson when he first explored the river's undulations in the seventeenth century. Then the oaks, elms, and maples flourished; today the Earth lies in the perpetual shadow of concrete canopies, miles of macadam, and bricked-over I-beams.

Andra had been afraid of passing through New York City for fear of seeing "bodies." Ridiculous, I retorted, though I remembered a story in the *Berkeley Monthly*. Submitted under the headline, "My Most Unusual Trip," the story told of a long-distance swim race around Manhattan the writer had entered. On the Harlem River, he found himself alone, the other competitors having either moved ahead or astern. At last he saw another person in the water and maneuvered alongside to ask directions. The rude fellow wouldn't answer! It took several minutes for him to realize he was addressing a dead body.

I did not repeat this story to Andra, nor did I tell her that near midtown I saw a bloated dachshund float by, belly gases swelling the flesh around its bright red collar.

We did not stop in the City. Accommodations are slim; it is not the sort of place one visits in a small boat. Better to spend the night in a five-star Fifth Avenue hotel on company business and a fat expense account.

Instead we pushed on under the Verrazano Bridge and across the brown waters of Raritan Bay. There were so many boats zipping around, there was no pattern to the waves, just an ugly chop slapping us from all directions.

On the other side we tucked into the marina complex at Sandy Hook, New Jersey, under the hill called the Atlantic Highlands. The launch driver for a local yacht club gladly pointed us to an empty mooring, gratis. We called Lennie and Joanne Zazzarino, who drove down from their Rahway home to treat us to dinner at the Chuckling Oyster, and finally, for the first time, we announced the baby. I felt a little guilty not telling Adria first, but both Andra and I needed to share our secret before it consumed us. Especially for her, a public acknowledgment was a necessary milestone. Spending her entire nine-month pregnancy on a boat would be difficult enough without having to try concealing the obvious. Amid toasts, Lennie said he would like to sail with us for a few days, help us on our first overnight of the cruise.

The coast of New Jersey presents a problem for boats drawing more than a few feet. The Army Corps of Engineers has fashioned a waterway route behind the barrier beach, but it is extremely shallow in places and twists so that the 125-mile length of coast between Sandy Hook and Cape May is increased by a third. To make matters worse, access into and out of the waterway is by means of narrow inlets that are subject to shoaling and rough seas in an onshore wind. There are only a handful of inlets—Manasquan, Shark River, and Barnegat—for the first eighty miles. Best to kick up your heels and do an overnighter; give NJ the big miss, our advisors said.

In all fairness to the Garden State, its Atlantic coastline should not be gauged by impressions formed driving on I-95 while speeding past the industrial centers of Jersey City and Bayonne. There are no ports, cranes, or big ships offloading containers. It is a lowlying shore, quick to disappear if you head too far out to sea, a straight line of sand and deciduous trees, less like Connecticut, Delaware, and Maryland than the mid-Atlantic Coast low country of Virginia and the Carolinas. For better or worse, we saw it from only five miles out and can offer no report on the backwaters and winding channels.

Lennie hopped aboard with a compact duffel. He was eager, and that is the great thing about him—always game, never lame.

He'd put his experience taking mug shots in the prison's receiving center to good use. In the following years he held a number of staff and management jobs with portrait studios, mostly the type that visits J.C. Penney stores at Christmas and Easter. Buck ninety-nine for a family portrait, lots more if the photographer can talk you into buying the portfolio. It is essentially a sales job, and he excels at it. But he is also a good portrait photographer. Economical with film, he knows when a situation is worth shooting. He ciphers the light, shadows, subject, and framing. There are few fancy lenses in his bag. Like Jim Gilbert's ability to "see" fish, Lennie sees stupendous snapshots where most people find nothing extraordinary at all.

We left Sandy Hook at nine on a Monday morning, motoring across a glassy sea. Later a breeze appeared, and we set the sails, paralleling the coast. Andra fixed dinner, and after dark she fell asleep. We awoke her for one watch, otherwise letting the little mother rest. It was the first occasion Lennie and I had had to talk in some years, and alone at sea was the perfect place to catch up.

Like soldiers who can only talk to other veterans about the pits of war, ex-cons also share uncommon ground. It is not generally the blood and guts of the wounded, the terror and horror of disembowelment in the field, though there is some of that. Mostly we talked of space and time, ideas that are abstract on the outside but palpable in prison.

There are parallels between prison and cruising. Take space, for instance—a precious commodity in prison. There's never enough of it. Among the general population you share small spaces with a lot of other men. Two men to a cell the size of a closet. One hundred twenty to a cell block. Breakfast with six hundred. For most, penance is not exacted by forced isolation; rather, it is wrought by forced living cheek to jowl with others.

Each animal has its own peculiar sphere into which others are unwelcome. A dog doesn't like other hounds in its yard. Penguins and caribou get nervous if there aren't a hundred others waddling or plodding nearby. And if a man can smell the person he's talking to, he backs off.

Man was not meant to live in barracks or cell blocks. Military and penal institutions organize their subjects in an unnatural living pattern to break down independence and individuality. It is a dehumanizing tactic, justified in the name of teaching discipline. Drill instructors and football coaches are good at it. The tactic works, to a point—you don't squawk, punch the "hacks," or incite riot. Incarceration may be a defensible punishment, but as a treatment plan it creates anger and bitterness. And even if you resist lashing out because America Joe (so nicknamed because of the large flag tattooed on his chest) gave you an ugly haircut, or the mashed potatoes were cold, or the parole judge "continued" your case for another twenty months, you do not like it, and you do not forget.

There was a young man serving five years for sawing off a shotgun and holding the patrons of a bar at bay while his buddies beat the piss out of the man who'd crossed him. Interestingly, the charge had been for failing to pay the manufacturer's tax on a firearm. He told me he wasn't sure he'd ever be released, that there was a crazy streak in him. He subscribed to the *Shooter's Bible.* Ken Kesey's *One Flew over the Cuckoo's Nest* and Anthony Burgess's *Clockwork Orange* upset him. He feared being lobotomized or "reprogrammed," so he memorized the names and addresses of everyone he thought had ever done him wrong. Even if he were released as a guileless, pacified amnesiac, he said, the list would exist in his subconscious. It did not bother him that he might not remember why he had been wronged; the only imperative was getting even. His list, he said, was the size of the New York City phone book.

✳

A cruising sailboat has about as much space as a prison cell. And if you've been shanghaied by a wanderlust husband, you are for all practical purposes a prisoner of the high seas. When we first started sailing together, Andra wasn't even able to row the dinghy ashore. Her wardrobe was reduced to a net hammock, one bin, and half a closet that was all of fourteen inches wide. There was space on her bookshelf for a few quick reads, and in the head a shelf for shampoo and lotion. But no makeup artist would find room for blushes, facials, lipsticks, and cream rinses. Two or three pairs of shoes max, one cold-weather coat, and a suit of raingear. As in prison, the crew on a small sailboat has its possessions reduced to the essentials.

I enjoyed paring my belongings to simple, everyday needs. After owning a country home, two cars, two TVs, pets, and appliances, moving aboard *Adriana* was an ascetic exercise. As the Buddhist monk retreats to his mountain cave to ponder the meaning of life, the sailor also forsakes materialism. Perhaps his philosophy is less coherent, but just as surely his purpose is spiritual. The boat, the chart, and the pipe comprise his personal pleasure dome, and there is no telephone or mailman to disturb his meditations.

Time is the other punishment. Inmates understand it better than Einstein. It is not the fourth dimension, it is a thing with mass, a rock that settles on your chest, making breathing difficult. With Sisyphean futility, it can be pushed, pulled, kicked, and sat on, but never vanquished. "I don't know about you, brother, but I like to do my time *eeeeasy*."

An inmate takes pride in his personal approach to "doing time." Each stalks the treadmill with his own gait, his own tricks to keep putting one foot in front of the other. It is not easy. You do not find yourself saying, my how time flies. It is counted in minutes and quarter hours, on the backs of your hands.

When I was in quarantine at the federal correctional institution in Ashland, Kentucky, for "observation," I spent weeks without seeing another inmate. Just the guards who brought me my meals. After a time, I took up conversation with the man in the cell to my right. One day my faceless friend shoved a copy of George Santayana's *Dialogues in Limbo* around the corner wall and through the bars into my cell. It was a book of philosophy, a fictional continuation of Plato's famous dialogues in the afterworld, with Socrates as the main man, still discoursing after swallowing the fatal hemlock. These were the first written words I had read in months, and I devoured them. It was possible to lose myself for a full half hour before realizing I was still incarcerated.

Severe protraction of time makes life miserable. Never before had I reckoned what an inscrutable bastard Time is. He stuck his screwdriver into the machine and slowed my life to a sputtering idle. Hard time. And when I was eventually released, I felt I had not only licked the Establishment, the System, and Kesey's Combine, I had licked Time. Beaten him at his own game. But even if you've outwaited your adversaries, the hollow in your eyes tells of the toll taken.

Adriana passaged the New Jersey coast in twenty-two hours, and yet it seemed like days. Lennie and I hardly slept. It was cold, though not unbearable. We wrapped ourselves in blankets. The autopilot did our work. When we weren't talking we stared at the stars and watched the giant neon signs of Atlantic City through binoculars. It seemed to take all night to pass the Showboy casino. Time crept on its tail.

Only twice did we sit up, alert, and find thirty minutes lost. The first occasion was when we suddenly found ourselves engulfed in a floodlight. Lennie jumped to the rail. Some druggies looking for a carrier? The Coast Guard preparing to board a suspected smuggler? Then we heard the drone of a big diesel, and against the shore lights we saw the silhouette of a small barge carrying a Volkswagen Beetle, and the tug pushing its load northward. Its running lights were not working, and there was only the sporadic use of its spotlight to warn off other boats.

The second instance occurred just off Atlantic City. Again we were flashed by a high-powered beam. This time it was the Coast Guard, half a dozen young men dressed in rubber suits and life jackets, crouched low in an inflatable craft. They hailed us.

"Where'd you come from?"

"Sandy Hook!" Lennie yelled.

"Have you seen a disabled boat out here? We got a radio report but can't find it."

Lennie answered because he felt there was less chance of trouble with a New Jersey accent. Hell, I thought, these guardsmen are probably Colorado boys, and Lennie's voice is a perfect match with the profile of a runner!

The Coast Guard sped off in search of its phantom vessel, and even though we listened to the VHF radio, we never heard more of its fate.

When at last the sky turned an ashen gray, and the silhouette of the land demarcated itself from the clouds, Time was a passenger, sitting on the seat next to us. We had joked with him, told stories, jabbed him with friendly insults. Of course, he was impervious to our needling. You don't fool with Mother Nature and you don't fuck with Father Time. He is a rap partner in prison and a lazy mate on small boats.

Lennie had been tight with the Hispanics. "Remember Ralphie? Gonzalez? Those were some good cats. You could ask them for *aaannything*. I heard Ralphie died, but I don't know when or where or why."

Ex-cons go like that. "Remember Robertson?" I said. "You know he got out a week after me. He was a gambling fool, even wagered on our release dates. It was the only time I won."

Robertson called me 'Ort,' a contraction of my middle name, meaning a bread crumb or table scrap, and in prison that's what you are, he said.

Robbie got a job running a printing press in Ann Arbor and lived in a small cottage at Whitmore Lake. It was the size of a dollhouse, and the yard was always mud because the lake level was so high that spring. He came over a few times and we got stoned together. Then I heard he got drunk one night, borrowed a shotgun, and sat down in a bowling-alley parking lot. He began drinking and shooting. The cops found him sitting on a concrete parking divider.

"What you doin' son?"

"Jus' tryin' to blow a hole in that there wall."

"How come?"

"So I can rob it."

They gave Robbie two more years in Jackson State Prison. He made some nice things for Adria in the wood shop—salt-and-pepper shakers and a penny barrel that said, "The New Messiah."

I'd given him twenty bucks to get started in Jackson; he was such a good poker player, he soon had all the cigarettes, cookies, and Crest toothpaste he wanted. The day he was paroled he called from the bus station to tell me that someone would come by our place to drop off five hundred dollars for him. He had to go to Grand Rapids first, where the prison placement officer had found him a job making prosthetic limbs.

Robbie said he'd call from Grand Rapids, planning to come down on another bus that weekend for the money. He never called, and no one sent five hundred dollars. Months passed. One day I received a letter from the Memphis city jail. "Dear Ort," it began, beseeching me like Wimpy begging for hamburgers in a Popeye cartoon. "Circumstances prevent me from expounding on my present situation. However, a small grubstake of fifteen or twenty dollars would surely help me land on my feet."

I sent the money and never heard from him again. Perhaps he is dead, or worse, rotting in some dank prison cell. Swallowed whole. He admired horned toads because they can survive decades without food or appreciable water. They've been found in corner stones, he said, fit as the day the mortar was laid. His one regret was that he'd die before a complete inventory of artificial biomechanical organs had been developed. Especially, he waited for a brain. Before you died, the doctors would wire you with electrodes and download everything you knew onto tape. Your new artificial brain would be programmed with the tape, then inserted in your synthetic brain. It was as if he knew there was no hope for him in this lifetime. Even with the hindsight and wisdom of 150 years, Robertson would always be a criminal. For him, there was nothing like easy money, and it's that way with a lot of guys.

Then there was Ned, the fifty-year-old motel proprietor who served every day of a five-year sentence. They put him on work release a few months before his sentence expired, and on the day before his release he forced the trusty driver to stop on the freeway where he'd hidden a fifth of whiskey. Ned got drunk, stole a car, bought a gun, and went on a drunken binge in downtown Detroit, shooting (only to scare) at women and little children. To paraphrase Bo Diddley, they put him so far back this time, they had to pump air into him.

Hubbard, a Jehovah's Witness and the other inmate working with Robertson and me in the parole office, was released to his home in upper Michigan. He lived with his father, who hated the JWs. The one time I visited, we walked up a grassy hill over Torch Lake. One of the seven most beautiful in the world, he said proudly. Hubbard was in love with a black girl, and he had great plans. "Interracial marriage is God's will," he said. I asked how so. He looked at me sheepishly. "God made it easy for blacks and whites to get together," he said. "That's why He gave white men small penises and black girls tight pussies. He arranged the same convenience for white women and black men, only on a different scale, if you know what I mean."

When we tired of talking about old acquaintances, we talked about our families. Lennie's father was a prizefighter. "Young Zazz" they called him. Fought for the world lightweight title at nineteen, in Madison Square Garden. Lennie didn't say he lost, but I gathered that he had. Still he was quite famous. He bought six buildings in Jersey City after he married Lennie's mother, Assunta. She put the kibosh on his boxing. He died of an athlete's heart when he was thirty-nine. Lennie, the youngest of three children, never knew him.

He visits his mother often, and when she makes her famous pasta fagiolo, she tells him about his father.

"When I think of what she went through, whew! It blows me away!

"I went to visit her after Pete died. I wanted to see what she thought. And you know what she told me, Danny? She said, 'That boy had tough times ahead, what with girls and all that.' "

People, it seemed, were always trying to justify Pete's death, but I would rather have had him crippled and alive than dead and "free."

*

90

We motored into Cape May at dawn, guided by tall radio towers that grew like shoots from the low, grassy land. Inside the anchorage we saw half a dozen boats we were to see again and again, for this was the first gathering point for cruisers headed south.

After breakfast at a fisherman's hangout, Lennie was anxious to get home. Bus tickets were available at the local video store, but it wasn't open yet. Lennie began asking truck drivers if they were going to Atlantic City, where he could catch a bus for Rahway.

"You goin' to AC?" he yelled across the parking lot.

The bread man shrugged.

A dotty old man in front of the laundromat heard Lennie. He called me over. "You a fisherman?" he asked. "I fished for fifty years, but there ain't no fish left, and I had enough."

I nodded.

"Look!" he exclaimed, pointing to the pavement a few feet away. "There's a pencil."

I picked it up and offered it to him. He stared at me incredulously.

"I don't want it!" he said vehemently.

I excused myself, the crazy man watching with mouth agape as I grabbed Andra. Lennie was on the highway, holding a sign for Atlantic City he'd fashioned from a piece of trash cardboard. If he didn't get a ride, he was ready to walk.

An old blue Ford stopped, and he hopped in. As the driver gunned away, Lennie turned and waved through the back window. Blew us a kiss. He was gone as fast as Pete, and there were still some things I wanted to ask him. Topics uncovered by the long night, like, Lennie, what was it like selling marijuana in New York City? What if Ralphie showed up on your doorstep tomorrow? Do you believe in life after death?

8

Into the Grand Susquehanna

Cape May is a tactical launching pad for boats headed south. It is the southernmost point of New Jersey, and sits at the mouth of Delaware Bay, as vile a body of water as exists on the East Coast. It is brown, shallow, and contrary, characteristics that may be esteemed in cheerleaders but not in a body of water.

The townies promote an architectural patina of Victorianism in the tourist literature—an enormous white clapboard beach hotel that looks like kindling waiting for an arsonist, and some old homes with gingerbread trim. There is a mall of small shops on a street where auto traffic has been eliminated in favor of brick walkways and benches. A rich bronze plaque in its center eulogizes the inspired man who created it, a former president of the downtown businessmen's association.

Most of the sailors we met in Cape May were waiting for a south wind to kick them in the pants—up the bay and into the Chesapeake & Delaware Canal. Despite his occasional need to show face, in his heart of hearts, the cruising sailor welcomes the excuse to stay put. He can fiddle with gear and engage in other avoidance tactics until the cows come home. But sooner or later he must reckon with the passage ahead, in this case the Delaware. The bay is seldom more than twenty feet deep, with an evil chop, and its color has a diarrheic tinge. Much of the surrounding land is marsh, and the first landmark on which the helmsman can focus is the nuclear reactor on Artificial Island. This specter, looming in the dirty haze, is his reward for thirty-five miles of often tough, wet sailing.

Andra and I spent four days in Cape May waiting for a flood tide and south wind to align. On the third day we thumbed our noses at the guidebooks and gave it a try. The tide was with us, but the wind was not. We lurched out of the Cape May breakwater and were spanked on the nose. The wind was vicious and the waves square, forcing us to slink back to the mooring area, tails between our legs.

There are many turn-of-the-century resorts on the East Coast — Boothbay, Marblehead, Newport, Hilton Head, St. Augustine, Coconut Grove — and there is an appalling sameness about them. It is the curse of the "pretty places."

Beaches are usually the drawing card, but it is no secret that most people come to shop. If there were Laura Ashley and Papagallo outlets in Loyalhanna and Wanamassa, perhaps the people who live in movie sets such as Cape May would be spared the dread American tourist family.

It is no wonder that the only locals who talk to tourists are shopkeepers, and then only to sell them sea shells and brass lanterns. Of course the proprietors aren't really locals, since they close shop and spend the winter in Florida. It is this treasure-seeking mentality that has time-shared and condominiumized the choicest sections of our coast. By the end of the century, ninety-five percent of the Atlantic Coast will be privately held, and those public parks that remain will have corrals for waiting cars, like the waiting gates for rides at Disneyland, and the parking fee will be a day's pay.

When at last the wind turned there was an exodus out of Cape May. More than two dozen boats — power and sail — charged into Delaware Bay as if it were the start of a LeMans race. Most of these were French Canadians, and like that of their famous geese, their flyway south was raucous with the honking and flapping of wings.

The wind was brisk and right for reaching. Cargo ships bound for Philadelphia worked the deeper, marked channel that runs up the bay like a spine. The smaller boats kept just outside the buoys. The tide turned as we entered the canal, and the last miles were tedious and slow.

The C & D Canal bisects the Delmarva Peninsula with the straightline cuts of a strip mine. The embankments are as fine and true as an arrow, and the "project depth" is monotonously uniform, so that not even the depthsounder offers diversion. At the western end it curves into Back Creek, and thence the Elk River. After Turkey Point all of the Chesapeake lies ahead in the inverted shape of a fir tree, its arterial branches fanning into the soft land.

We led the charge of Canucks into the basin at Chesapeake City, about two-thirds of the way through the fifteen-mile canal. The chart showed eleven-foot depths and we ambled in confidently. Without warning we ran aground on a four-foot shoal. I turned to wave off the others, at the same time instinctively throwing the transmission into reverse. We were stuck. I eased off the throttle and took stock of the situation. Where was the dinghy? Andra pointed over the side and down. Sure enough, there it was, three feet under the surface, barely visible. But why? Then it dawned on me. The dinghy painter had wrapped around the propeller, yanking the dinghy completely underwater. Again the gas can and rowing seat floated away, and we were fortunate to snag them with the boathook.

The next morning, with the help of the tide, another boat maneuvered us next to the wall bordering the canal museum, where we hung fenders and tied up to a steel bulkhead. I tied a line to the main halyard, to heel us slightly inward, and led it to the foundation of a fuel tank near the museum maintenance shop. As the tide ebbed later that day, the water receded, and by dusk we could see the keel settle into the mud. I worked on the tangled line from the dinghy. In a jiffy the line freed, then I saw the propeller. The dinghy's bronze towing eye had smacked it squarely and with awesome force, bending one blade into the shape of a tulip leaf.

We were marooned in Chesapeake City, a hamlet of about two hundred inhabitants, none of whom could help us. The town was divided by the canal, yet connected by an enormous bridge on

Route 9. There wasn't much on the north shore except Schaefer's Canal House restaurant and marina; it, like the rest of the town, sat in the shadow of the bridge, dead quiet now, though the large parking lot suggested gayer times. The marine store sold liquor and duck decoys, but no propellers. The southern half of town seemed to hold greater promise, so we rowed to the Dockside Yacht Club and paid the one-dollar "membership" fee for the privilege of drinking in their lounge.

While Andra chatted up the bartender, I checked the Yellow Pages and soon had Bob Greene on the phone. He owned a yard twenty miles to the north. It was late Saturday afternoon. "Bring it in Monday morning," he said. "We'll drop everything." It was the best we could do.

The bartender was sympathetic and talkative. Up and down the coast, we invariably found that when you need to scope a place fast, consult the purveyors of alcohol. They are trained in the business of advice, be it directions or matters of the heart.

"This used to be a tough town five years ago," she said. "There was a bar called the Hole in the Wall where there were gunfights and stabbings. I had to go in once just to say I'd been there. Now it's a family restaurant. Mrs. Du Pont bought it."

In fact Mrs. Du Pont had bought most of the town. The main street was a short string of restored homes, many of which were now stores selling scented soaps and Christmas-tree ornaments. Under the bridge at the old Bayard House restaurant the bar patrons agreed the town had needed some improvement, it was just too bad the locals didn't need anything the new gift shops sold.

Seated at one end of the bar was a tall, distinguished gentleman whom everyone called the Major. He had a gray crewcut, handlebar mustache, and wore a suitcoat and tie that loosened a notch with each successive shot of whiskey.

Suddenly one of the waitresses ran in from the dining room, gasping that a person had just jumped off the bridge. A Volkswagen was found blocking an inside lane. The police, she said, were searching the waters with helicopters and boats.

The Major leaped to his feet and pushed outdoors.

"Look at the Major!" mocked the maître d', "He's gonna look for the body!"

The bar emptied. Above us the bridge was lit with the flashing lights of police cars, and in the cold night air before us we heard the thrumming rotors of the helicopter, its spotlight playing across the fast-flowing waters of the canal.

"The car has Pennsylvania plates," said one bar patron standing near us.

Another remarked: "Remember the guy who jumped off the bridge and landed in Schaefer's parking lot?"

As in Newport, bridge suicides in Chesapeake City are the subject of much speculation as to identities and motives. The Major was the last to return, and when he came in from the brisk night there was a sad, faraway look in his old eyes, as if he were remembering old battles. Perhaps it was the helicopters. I felt a little sorry for him and wished we had talked, for he seemed on the threshold of something important.

Adriana leaned and straightened with the tide. Sometime during the night the tide changed, gently rolling Andra on top of me, and I awoke with a sore shoulder.

Sunday afternoon we hitchhiked into Elkton and bought a wheel puller. On the return trip, we were picked up by a woman wearing blue jeans and work boots. She was driving a Jeep, and as the back was crammed with wire traps, assorted gloves, and cardboard boxes, Andra and I squeezed into the single passenger seat. She was from Raleigh, North Carolina, three months out of college. Her conversation was pleasant. Holding up a molasses jar kept on the front seat, she showed us the crab bait she used to catch raccoons. "You can smell it if you want."

It was no joke; she was a professional trapper for the state.

"Rabies has reached almost epidemic proportions in the coon population," she explained. "After I catch them, I turn the animals into one of our stations where they're vaccinated and released."

Andra asked if special training was required.

"Shoot, no," she answered. "I majored in fisheries, and I'm the best trapper they've got! Caught eighteen last week. My boyfriend's a trapper, too, but he doesn't have my luck."

A friend from Annapolis, Wayne Carpenter, offered to drive to

Chesapeake City on Monday and take us to the boatyard. Wayne has earned justified notoriety in the cruising community for having sailed several years on a twenty-seven-footer with his wife, two daughters, and mother-in-law.

"Don't you have to work?" I protested.

"I work at home," he said, "and today looks pretty slack."

Playing on the computer and checking real-estate ads seemed to agree with him.

Bob Greene met us in the showroom. He was a short man in his fifties. A stroke had closed an eye and one side of his mouth. When he saw the prop, he shook his head. Without a word he led us across the parking lot to a yardhand hanging upside down in the engine compartment of a small power cruiser.

"Can you fix this?" Bob asked.

The man craned his head and took it in his hand. He turned it over as though it were a fragment of meteor and said, "I dunno."

Now I don't know how most people think bent propellers are straightened, but I have always believed that they are "reconditioned" by sophisticated machines, the complex curves exactly reestablished, the fine bronze edges burnished sharp, and the whole sculpture measured by a micrometer and balanced by a scale with very small weights.

That is not the way it is done. Our strapping yardman heated the bent blade with an acetylene torch, then slipped it over a spindle on a massive workbench. Under the prop was an iron casting with approximately the same shape as our good blade. Shape, the manuals explain, is measured by "pitch," which is the number of inches it would move forward in one revolution if turned in some viscous substance such as cold Jell-O.

What followed I can only liken to a scene from Dante's *Inferno*; it is work for the sinners and the condemned who have no hope now or after the Earth has vanished in cinders. Using various-size sledges, raised high above his head, the man bashed the blade as if he were John Henry driving railroad spikes. The noise was crazy, sharp and ringing. Andra and Wayne had to leave the room before their ears split. The methodology was crude, but when the man finished the blade had essentially the same shape as its mate.

"There's a little hollow here," he pointed out, "but you don't get any drive on the inside anyway. All your power's out here at the tips."

By now we could tell when the shaft was out of water because the toilet would no longer flush and the dinner plates required shimming to hold a side of baked beans and the shifting gravy. At the next low tide we refit the propeller and were on our way. It worked so well that for weeks I had a basic distrust of the repair. In bad weather I was convinced it would fly off the shaft and rip through the hull, severing major arteries as I stood wide-legged at the helm.

The Chesapeake Bay is actually a flooded river valley. Before the last ice age, the water level was much lower, and the western shore of present-day Maryland was 70 miles farther east. The antediluvian river, which geologists named the Susquehanna, was the watershed for thousands of square miles of plains. Then the ice melted and the water rose. The Susquehanna flooded and formed the Chesapeake Bay—85 miles long, 3 to 22 miles wide. The 5,000-mile coastline encompasses more than 3,000 square miles of fertile shellfish beds, fed by nineteen rivers and four hundred streams. It is the world's largest estuary, a natural resource of inestimable value.

Between Maine and the Carolinas there is no finer cruising ground, especially in autumn. Gone is the oppressive heat that drives Congress out of nearby Washington on European junkets and to North Woods fishing camps, as well as the swarms of Annapolis racing yachts choking the narrow channels (the ultimate Heimlich maneuver is to follow a freighter through, but that is risky).

In the fall the winds freshen, and the blooms of jellyfish, known as nettles, wither in the brown water. These gelatinous drifters are the bane of swimmers and have given rise to an unusual cottage industry. The patented Nettle Knot Net, as an example, is a clever device deployed over the side of a boat for swimming. It is a large net bag kept afloat by a Styrofoam collar and tethered to a stern cleat. In a current it has a tendency to collapse, so that you end up dogpaddling in a pen nine feet long and two feet wide.

I tried the Nettle Knot Net some years ago. At first I shrank from the absurdity of throwing myself into a contraption that looks to belong in a fish hatchery or ostrich ranch. But the heat and humidity drove me to it. I leaped, suspended above the narrow orifice, just as the lookout shrieked, "Jellyfish!"

Andra and I sailed *Adriana* out of the canal and into a back creek on a drizzly, gray day. Baltimore lay twenty-five miles ahead, but we needed time to lick our wounds. It was not that we hadn't had ample time to rest in Chesapeake City, but there had been unforeseen expenditures and the anxiety of spending money, losing time, and suffering damage to the boat. We needed to sit somewhere and collect ourselves, stationary as a lily pad.

Andra was experiencing the usual schizophrenia of a new mother-to-be. Her clothes didn't fit, and she thought she was ugly. She fell on the words of men who said they disliked flat tummies. It was often too cold to shower, and she felt seedy. Our plan to lead the autumn season south had failed; it was increasingly clear that we were destined to chase its trailing edge, trapped in a band of faded foliage, crisp nights, and blustery days.

Andra, to her credit, was patient. She even betrayed signs of liking some aspects of cruising, but of course she wouldn't admit it to me. According to her code, it isn't cool to get too gung ho about sports like skiing, tennis, and sailing. But she is by nature an agreeable person, and on her gravestone they will surely scribe: Andra Lee Spurr—A Good Sport.

In the 1970s Baltimore needed a serious facelift. Always a comfortable residential city and major shipping port, there was little that appealed to visitors. Many of the famous rowhouses were gutted, civic pride was nonexistent, and the harbor, well, you'd have had more fun in Newark or Cleveland. Starting with the Charles Center, Mayor William Schaeffer set about a mammoth refurbishing of the downtown. Rowhouses were sold for one dollar with the stipulation that owners live on the premises for at least three years. The city was on its way out of the ashes. Then, when the glitzy Harborplace markets opened in 1980, Baltimore's Inner Harbor was reborn.

Andra and I heard many good things about the harbor as we planned our East Coast cruise. And since I had attended Johns Hopkins University in the mid-seventies, moving my family out when Adria was just two, we figured it was a good place to balance the burgs and backwaters we normally prefer.

We arrived in Baltimore from just such a place — Worton Creek on the Eastern Shore. It was a slow reach across the bay to the mouth of the Patapsco River, and the commercial traffic was heavy. Dredgers, tugs, barges, container ships, and car carriers plied the narrow channel. There were boats sailing on the Patapsco (the marinas in Stony, Rock, and Back creeks are crowded), tacking in harm's way, but as the river shallows in peculiar places and we were anxious to put down for the night, we motorsailed the ten miles from North Point to the Inner Harbor.

It is not a pretty cruise upriver. The eastern shore is lined with heavy industry, cranes that move awkwardly against the sky like dinosaurs in low-budget Japanese horror movies, and shabby warehouses through whose portals pass all the fixtures of our lives, from baseballs to baby dolls, Toyotas to time clocks, iron, salt, chemicals, and industrial gases. The smell from Bethlehem Steel is enough to numb your nose, and the strobes on the electric plant on the western shore are not the sort of thing you want to look at if you've been up all night marching to Bolivia.

We perked up at about mile eight, where the Patapsco divides, for there, squatting on a green hummock, is the shrine of Fort McHenry. The American flag flutters in the breeze, and sentinel cannons are strategically stationed on the stair-stepped lawn. For non-Americans or the unfortunate products of progressive education who do not know its significance, Fort McHenry was the site of a major battle during the War of 1812, when the British attacked the port, in part to destroy shipyards building the famed Baltimore Clippers. A prisoner aboard a British frigate, Francis Scott Key, wrote a poem entitled the "Star Spangled Banner," which later was set to music and became the country's national anthem.

The West Channel jogs another mile or two past more warehouses, a few marinas, and the bohemian Fells Point neighborhood, which has more bloodlines than a junkyard dog. Shortly after, it terminates in the cul-de-sac of the Inner Harbor. It is like finding yourself in a dream; suddenly you are surrounded by modern skyscrapers dressed with one-way amber-tinted windows that look like giant Vuarnet lenses, bronze and blue steel facings extruded on a cold star, and blue supergraphic neon waves wrapping the angular rooflines of the National Aquarium. At the foot of the city, aligned with Pratt and Light streets, are the two pavilions of Harborplace. Modeled, at least in concept, after Boston's Quincy Market, each houses dozens of informal food stalls, produce, apparel, and gift gadgetry.

As novelist John Barth pointed out to me later in our visit, the Inner Harbor is used by common people and so has an authenticity and vibrancy that might be missing if its only patrons were brokers and investment bankers. "When was the last time you saw a black in Quincy Market?" Barth asked.

When arriving by boat, your choices are threefold: Rent slip space from either the privately owned Inner Harbor Marina or the city docks, or anchor in the northeast corner. We chose the latter, finding the depth about twenty feet and the bottom an accumulation of two hundred years of sludge.

East of us was the aquarium, busy all week with tours and school kids as well as a maritime museum featuring the mothballed U.S.S. *Torsk* (the last U.S. sub to sink a Japanese ship in World War II) and the lightship *Chesapeake*. To the north was the World Trade Center and its twenty-seventh-floor observation deck somewhat pretentiously called "Top of the World." West, in the corner of the Harborplace malls was a ship built in 1855 to replace the original *Constellation* (constructed in 1797 and torn apart in 1854), the first commissioned warship of the country's new navy and the oldest warship continuously afloat. All this, framed by brick walkways, landscaped shrubbery, and heraldic flags, made a good setting for a party.

So we called some friends who had moved here from Rhode

Island. After weeks of marsh living, it is a distinct pleasure to seat yourself at a good "bar bar." Now there is nothing more honest than a Budweiser, but it cannot compare with the sixty-five-year-old McGilvey Scotch that Pat Kerins ordered for us at Birds of a Feather.

We are not shopping freaks, so we gave the Pratt Street Gallery, with catalog shops like Carol Reed and Williams-Sonoma, a quick pass, pausing just long enough to imbibe a nonalcoholic daiquiri at the Flying Fruit Fantasy while studying dumbly the four stories of hanging plants, dyed waterfalls, and elevators that run off in every direction in the illusory organization of an M.C. Escher drawing.

Unfortunately we didn't have time to visit the Maryland Science Center at the southwest corner of the harbor; our bartender at Phillips told us the giant-screen IMAX was the best sphincter-tightening show of all time.

Baltimore is a city easy to underestimate. It isn't the biggest or best at anything, but it does have the Orioles professional baseball team, is hoping to regain a pro-football franchise (Robert Irsay, your name is still mud here), Center Stage Theatre, superior medical services at the Johns Hopkins Hospital, and now a harbor that is friendly to cruisers as well as merchant mariners.

In the brick rowhouse neighborhoods, stacked like dominoes on gentle inclines, little old ladies with aprons still scrub their famous white marble steps above the sidewalks, and in the evening the old men — bald Italians, stocky Germans, and rheumy-eyed blacks — haul out easy chairs to read H.L. Mencken's *Baltimore Sun* and watch the sun set over the heather- and thistle-laden hills of western Maryland, which lie beyond their vision, but not their ken.

We powered out of Baltimore's Inner Harbor on the last day of October. As we passed Fort McHenry I spread some of Peter's ashes on the waters. There the channel meets the Patapsco River, which in turn flows into the bay, the Atlantic, and all the oceans of the world. This was the city in which Peter was conceived, and though he never lived here, I needed to observe and honor this landmark of his short life.

Andra cut the engine and we sailed lazily into the stream toward our own unknown destination.

I stood at the rail and said to myself quietly, "You're back where you began, Pete. Hope you enjoyed the trip."

9

Voices from the Eastern Shore

On the last day of October I guided *Adriana* away from the spewing factory stacks lining the Patapsco River, away from the slopes of brown brick rowhouses, the cataleptic shade trees, and black wrought iron fences. It is a heated place, capped with concrete; even in autumn the only breeze is frequently vertical.

Like the clipper ships of the last century, we rode an ebb tide toward the mouth of the Magothy River, halfway between Baltimore and Annapolis. The wind filled in outside the city, and the hull cooled. It was the kind of afternoon to wear T-shirts and thermal leggings, because the sun was warm on the back and the fiberglass seat cold on the butt.

It was also a Saturday, Halloween in fact, and in the distance, in the middle of the bay, a regatta was celebrating Chesapeake Appreciation Days. Just north of the Bay Bridge that joins Annapolis to the Eastern Shore was the *Queen Elizabeth II* presiding over the event, its massive black-and-white structure dead in the water, dwarfing the puny land. It is easier to imagine her in New York Harbor or Southampton, where there are skyscrapers and hangars and great halls built on the same grand scale; here, on the Chesapeake, there was only the Bay Bridge arcing across the muddy water to soften the juxtaposition of scales.

The regatta played out in the distance. By standing up I found I could "dip" the hulls of the racing sloops below the horizon, which is a navigator's trick for determining the distance of an object with a known height. Around the QE II the tiny triangles of white sails tacked for unseen marks, and it looked as though the passenger liner had spawned a swarm of fruit flies playing out their short-lived dance of life.

By the time we approached the Magothy on a dying breeze, we were chased by several dozen other sailboats. It was four o'clock, the regatta finished, and all the boats converged at the green and red buoys marking shoals at the river mouth. With fuel jugs lashed to the shrouds, the dinghy heeling behind, and laundry pinned to the lifelines, we labored like a glue-factory horse among polo ponies. The faces of the racing sailors were slack and drop-jawed as they fled past.

"Sea gypsies," they seemed to be thinking of us, "a quaint but impractical idea for the eighties."

We found Wayne Carpenter at a small marina a mile up the Magothy. Rather he found us, hard aground on a sandbar. I had *Adriana* dead center in the small channel, but as is common throughout much of the East Coast, winds and currents had rearranged the swirling shoals like finger paints. The Coast Guard, it seemed, was late adjusting the buoys, and the water was too brown and colored with silt and leaves to read the depths from on deck.

As I gunned the engine, rocking the mired keel forward and backward, a few motorboats puttered past. "There's not much water there," one said. "You can't go that way," yelled another. "Find something hard?" jabbed a third, a note of ridicule in his voice that made me ram the throttle harder. My predicament was obvious; they might as well have been saying, "Hey, your mast is sticking straight up!"

The prop wash kicked up a cloud of silt as the keel eased off into deeper water. Then I saw Wayne waving from the marina dock. Carefully I worked my way in, again running aground just as we pulled alongside the swaybacked structure.

Wayne had already helped us fix the propeller in Chesapeake City, and now I was counting on him to pilot *Adriana* six miles up the Magothy to a free dock belonging to his friends Tom Taylor and Jackie Karkos. It was tough, but I was learning to accept handouts. I apologized for the inconvenience we were causing. He waved me off. "Hey, so many folks helped us when we were cruising, I figure the only way I can pay them back is by helping others. What goes 'round comes around. And you're the first to come around!" He smiled, and the tips of his blond handlebar mustache jumped. Then he hopped aboard and told me to go back to the main channel and turn north.

"How's the prop working?" he asked.

"I know it's hard to believe," I said, "the way that poor soul laid into the blades, but there's very little vibration." I rapped my knuckles on the wooden cockpit coaming.

After another mile we passed Wayne's home, set back on the other side of the beach road. A shallow canal ran behind it, and there was a small dock for his twenty-two-foot sailboat. Most of the homes were originally constructed as summer cottages, and the mismatched additions were obvious through the naked trees. "I own the beach lot too," he said. "But I don't plan to build on it. Kristina and I are serious boardsailors, and we keep it open for the neighborhood. Built a big deck on it, and on good days, when the wind's blowing, everyone sails until his arms drop."

As dusk settled we entered Dividing Creek at the headwaters of the Magothy. Wayne stood in front of the wheel, telling us that every man should try selling cars once in his life. Without warning we struck another shoal. The bow tripped, and the mast shuddered. Wayne was thrown forward, his back crashing into one of the companionway doors. The Plexiglas window cracked. He had a stunned, "I've been hit!" look on his face.

The channel banks were very steep, which prevented the keel from riding up gracefully into a shallow, untenable position. Wayne shook himself and laughed. "My mouth is always getting me into trouble."

Adriana had stopped dead in her wake, still afloat, a boat length from a small orange-and-white signpost. In hard-to-read letters it said "Danger—Shoal."

Dividing Creek bends into the hardwoods in a gentle curve, then splits like a serpent's tongue. There was red and yellow in the oaks and maples, and the bark was black and dun to remind us we traveled on the trailing edge of the season. Brick and wood homes were built on the banks, and though they seemed exclusive beyond the windrows of fallen leaves, we later saw that from the streetside they looked just like every other 1960s "colonial" in the neighborhood. The same houses are found in Indianapolis and Columbus, where a postage-meter salesman can be fired for wearing a blue button-down shirt.

If you saw from the creek a home you liked, you might try to refind it on land. Drive deep into the all-American suburbs of Severna Park, lose yourself among the guttered streets and manicured lawns, disrupt a gang of boys playing touch football, then round up in a cul-de-sac. One of these homes has access to the world through its backdoor. One has a trail through the woods to a dock and boat on the creek. But all of the homes sit above the street on berms, too close together to see between. There is no evidence of water; after all, this is Beaver Cleaver's neighborhood. You could ask Ward there, raking leaves, which is the house you seek. But what is the point? One of these homes is worth a lot more money than the others, and Mr. Beaumont thinks the boys are too tender to have their utopia rocked by class distinctions. Eddie Haskell, from the other side of the tracks, would tell; for a piece of chocolate cake and a Parliament cigarette he'd show you where he tortures the bullfrogs he finds hibernating in the rich, organic muck.

There is nothing except crab traps in the side yard and life jackets on the clothesline to distinguish the "waterfront home." Such was the two-story colonial belonging to Tom and Jackie.

In the fading light Tom waited for us on his dock, directing our approach with long fore-and-aft sweeps of his arm. I shoved the transmission into neutral and glided toward him. There was no wind in the creek, and the water was stained with tannic acid. The color of tea it was. *Adriana* stopped about ten feet from the dock. Aground again.

"Farther to your right," Tom called. I backed up and tried again. No luck.

"It's soft," Tom said. "Goose it."

This time we got close enough to throw a line, and between

the engine's pushing and Tom's pulling we drew alongside the dock. It was only after the lines were made fast and the diesel silenced that I noticed the moon. It was a harvest moon, shining through the black, silhouetted lace of limbs and branches, magnified by layers of atmospheric gases, seemingly larger than at its zenith. The Magothy had played some good tricks on us, and it was easy to blame our groundings on the moon. Not only does its diurnal orbit influence the tides, it opens the cages of goblins and the graves of ghosts. I know it was a harvest moon, a full Halloween moon, because I recognized it from my childhood when Jim Dunlap and I scampered through the Cleavers' backyard, plotting revenge against the cranky old geezer who lived on the lane above our street. Bags of candy swung from our belts like ammo pouches, and bags of dogshit and fistsful of cherry bombs were clenched in our fiendish little hands.

Tom and Jackie, perfect strangers, were extraordinarily gracious in opening their home to us. After introductions, Wayne left and we sat down to dinner with our hosts. Anyone who can serve leftovers to new acquaintances must be either well adjusted, very poor, or simply not give a hoot for decorum. Assuming the latter, we liked them immediately. Andra and I spent three pleasant days in Beaver's neighborhood, showering on a whim, reading mail collected for us by Wayne, and running errands in his Toyota pickup.

Wayne was busy killing off a small publishing company. The family was in flux. Kristina had just quit her job with a Washington defense contractor and said she wanted to sail around the world. Wayne yearned to go too but needed cash. An old friend had offered him the presidency of a small California company that builds motorcycle trailers. Wayne liked sailboards better but was giving it serious consideration. As far as I could tell, the cruising community, active and on shore leave, was still a drain on the taxpaying public. I wanted Wayne to show me how, but I suspect he would have advised real estate, and if I asked from what crumbs of money does one whisk together a down payment, he would advise selling cars.

*

The story of Pete's death preceded us everywhere, and people treated us tenderly. Usually, Andra was broached first, to see how I *really* felt. Later, perhaps, when one was alone with me in a car or at a kitchen counter, he or she might say, "Sorry about your son," and I would say, "Yes, thank you," and the subject would change before I burst into tears. I could always tell who had suffered some terrible loss, because they were the ones who gave me the chance to talk about mine.

All this talk about Peter overlooked Andra. She listened to me tell others about my son, and how if it weren't for his death, we wouldn't be gestating another child now. She indulged my sorrow and bore her own. Sometimes I found her with tears in her eyes and Pete on her lips. But more and more this thing in her stomach grew, and she withdrew from irrelevant conversations. She had never anticipated pregnancy, and her thoughts were filled with wonderment.

"You know what I can't believe?" she said one day, "I'm going to be somebody's mother!" And she laughed, as if the idea was too square for words. She—once a rebellious, back-talking teenager, the girl who rode a van west to Los Angeles rather than suffer another humiliation in speech class—a mother?

It was difficult for me to understand how we had slipped so easily from our mutual agreement not to have children, but I knew that Andra had changed her mind incrementally: first by observing me with my children—her first real exposure to parenting; next with marriage, which naturally raised the possibility of having her own children; then the ultimate persuader—finding *herself* pregnant. In her first month of pregnancy we had been at growing odds, and only Pete's death had had the power to change my mind. That I might not have relented out of respect and love for her was a righteous cause for resentment. When I told her that night that a life was too precious to be arbitrarily snuffed, I think she expected I would come aboard full of enthusiasm. But it wasn't that easy.

My views about myself and my life were a concretion of plans made hard and unassailable in the years since my divorce. Pete's departure blasted that rock, and I had no idea how the fragments would reassemble themselves.

Andra, in her wisdom, said little—afraid no doubt of tipping me the wrong way. But clearly she wanted to have a child. This should have been a joyful time for her, a time to share with her friends and family, to be pampered and fussed over. But she was stuck with me on a small boat, biting her lips, confronted with a husband who at times must have seemed as cold as the fiberglass hull that cradled us. What got her through, I think, was the knowledge that above all I loved her deeply.

Dim cabin lights and a slurring stereo clued us to a bad battery, necessitating a brief stop in Annapolis. Then we moved southeast across the bay to the Eastern Shore. I was beginning to research a book on the history of fiberglass boats, and there was a man in Oxford I wanted to meet.

The quickest route to Oxford and the Choptank River is through Knapps Narrows, a small cut separating Tilghman Island from the thin, curved peninsula of mainland that enfolds the fashionable hamlet of St. Michaels. A small drawbridge spans the channel, and the current runs fast, ebbing and flowing as the bay breathes, nourishing its rich beds of shellfish. The sheltered banks of the Narrows are lined with drudgers and tongers, and when a pleasure boat passes through, the fishermen stare with tired, reproachful eyes.

The people who live around the Chesapeake Bay possess an abiding love for it; she is, in their estimation, the most sublime body of water in the world, large as an ocean, refreshing as a spring-fed lake, ancient as the Dead Sea. And their devotion to her is as fierce as that which Melville felt for Nantucket, or Faulkner for his humid, incestuous Yoknapatawpha County, or Steinbeck his breezy Monterey. In the 1970s, when James Michener was living in St. Michaels and writing his book *Chesapeake,* the newspapers doted on sightings of the famed author. That the natives loved his book is no surprise to me, for they are all minor historians easily fascinated by the most minute details of the bay's past. The bookstores are full of dull pamphlets written by the wives of country squires. These endless genealogies of community life bear titles such as *A Life on the Eastern Shore* or *Oxford: A Brief History.*

What these histories don't tell you about is the inbreeding common on the bay islands—the Appalachia of the East Coast. Several years ago, I took Andra and the kids on a bay cruise, and we spent a night tied up to a derelict skipjack in Knapps Narrows. The next morning Peter told me a man had been watching the boat. Stepping into the cockpit I was surprised to see a skinny, middle-aged fellow standing on the dock, studying us across the buckled decks of the skipjack. He was dressed in a gray worksuit and baseball cap, leaning against a piling.

"Good morning," I said.

He gave me a queer, toothless smile and mumbled something I couldn't make out.

"Excuse me?"

He repeated himself, and still I was unsure of his meaning. Then he climbed onto the skipjack and shuffled closer. We talked for an hour, he and Peter oddly sensing one another the way a wolf and a husky might.

"My brother's a drudger," he told me. "I used to go out with him, but not no more. Me, I like the shop best. One time we almost sunk. We was in the middle of the bay when the wind come up. The waves were gettin' bigger and I tol' my brother the boat don't feel right. I say to him I know we're goin' down.

"He asks how come and I say I just know. I can feel it, that's all.

"There was a nigger on the crew and my brother says to him, 'Go check the hold.'

"The nigger stuck his head under the deck and come back to the helm.

" 'Wha' did you see?' my brother asks.

" 'Nuffin,' the nigger answers.

" 'Look again,' my brother says, 'and this time climb down the ladder.'

"The nigger looks again and come back. 'Nuffin,' he says again.

" 'Did you go down in the hold to look?' my brother asks.

" 'Yassir,' the nigger said.

"My brother looks at me and says, 'You still think we goin' down?'

"I say, 'Yes,' so he gives me the wheel and goes to look for himself. He comes back wet to his knees and grabs the nigger.

" 'How come you lied to me?' he yells.

"The nigger say he don't lie.

" 'Then how come my legs all wet?' says my brother.

"The nigger shrugged and say he don't know why.

" ' 'Cause you never went down and looked, that's why,' says my brother. 'How come you lied?'

"The nigger say he did go down in the hold and there wasn't no water.

"Finally my brother give up and says, 'Can you swim?'

"The nigger says no.

"My brother says, 'Well, you're in deep shit, cause we only got two life jackets on this boat—one's for me and one's for my brother.' "

"Umm," I nodded, "but tell me, did the boat make it in?"

The man twitched and looked over his shoulder, as if he were worried he might be missed at the shop, caught telling stories again.

"Oh yea," he said. "We got the pumps workin'. But I ain't been out since. Neither has that nigger."

The man I wanted to see in Oxford runs a small boatyard there, Cutts & Case, Inc. We lashed *Adriana* abreast of some pilings in front of the big shed on Town Creek, just off the Tred Avon River. Ed Cutts is a talented boatbuilder of the old school, having cut his teeth at the old Nevins yard in City Island, New York, when he was a lad. Great wooden yachts like *Bolero* were built there, back when an adze and a spokeshave were common tools. Cutts says he knew Nathanael Herreshoff, the grandfather of American yacht building, and his son L. Francis Herreshoff, designer of *Ticonderoga,* perhaps the most beautiful boat ever built.

The Nevins yard was a replica of Herreshoff's Bristol, Rhode Island yard, and in the 1950s there wasn't a better place to learn the trade. Cutts still builds in wood, developing a method of winding Kevlar fibers through hollows routed in the planks. But what I wanted to know most was his early experience with fiberglass, and why he had ultimately rejected it.

Cutts was sleeping when we knocked at the door of his office, in the walled-in porch of his long, single-story home. His wife called their son, Ed Junior, and bade him show us the boats abuilding in the sheds. When we returned a few hours later, it was dusk, and the old man received us in his living room. There were ship models on the end tables and prints of square-rigged fighting ships on the papered walls.

Mr. Cutts stood a hand over six feet. His hair was cut short, and he had the thick, calloused fingers of a man who has bruised his knuckles all his life. His wife and son and all the workers regarded him with mild reverence, as though they were the pupils of a Zen master. Then again they might just have known who signed their paychecks. They looked after his small wants, telling him when to eat and when to sleep and when to talk to strangers, leaving him free to think and work with an exceptional singlemindedness.

"I usually sleep in the afternoon," he said. "That way I can work at night when there's no one around to bother me. The neighbors used to complain about the noise coming from the sheds, but now—I'm sixty-two—I spend most of my time at the drafting table. Did they show you my designs?"

Yes, I said. I had seen the blueprints for several custom motor-yachts, long and lean, throwbacks to the "old days," before the world wars, when there was less emphasis on palatial accommodations and more on easily driven hulls with economical power plants. Plumb bows, fantail sterns, flat coachroofs, and vertical pilothouse faces with brass bells and ornate steering wheels.

Andra and I settled into an old sofa; Mr. Cutts sat opposite us, in front of a window that, because there were no lights in the room, made it difficult to focus on his face. His features disappeared in the shadows, as if he were a bigtime drug dealer being interviewed on "60 Minutes." Still you could see his mustache and the curl of his lip, and I thought that if I were some Mafia kingpin and this dude had crossed me, I'd know him if he so much as farted in the same county.

"Tell me about those decks you laid up with fiberglass back in the fifties," I started.

He was eager to talk, but not about fiberglass. Instead he rambled about his youth and how an apprentice ought to be handled, about tools and caring for them, the problem with modern hull designs, and the inherent goodness of wood. When I attempted to bring him back to the subject, he'd say, "Well I do run on a tangent, don't I," then launch off in another direction without remorse. When I could barely make out his face in the growing darkness and could smell dinner cooking in the kitchen, I was abrupt. "Listen," I said, "we really must be going. Andra is pregnant, and we must get her to the ice cream parlor before closing time. But you still haven't told me how you laid up the fiberglass decks of those Nevins 40s."

"Well, we built a lot of S boats—you know the Herreshoff design—six, eight, even ten of them. Nevins had a spar loft that was exactly like Herreshoff's. Everything was exactly like Herreshoff's, because Murray, the guy who was in charge of all the woodwork at Herreshoff's . . . well, when the Herreshoff company went on the bricks, he left. He left because Nevins sent someone up to see if he wanted to come down there. Murray had enormous knowledge by osmosis; he had worked there for so long . . . at Herreshoff's. The Herreshoffs never talked. I knew them quite well. L. Francis taught me yacht design for the twenty-five, twenty-eight years I knew him. Over there is the last drawing he ever made in his life."

On a corner table was an old sheaf of drawings.

"Lay 'em down on the floor," Cutts said.

I did, and I saw the lines of the sketch trail off, as if the author were shot while writing for help.

"It's a powerboat," Cutts continued. "Look where his pen stops . . . it says, 'I can't do this work anymore. . . .' "

It was a poignant story, but I was growing increasingly uncomfortable interviewing this man about fiberglass, a material he regarded as crass as fast food, electronic music, and computer art. His hands were still folded on his lap.

"Ah yes, well Owens-Corning had this resin, and they thought you could build boats with it. I think they wanted Nevins to run with it. They sent me out there to do these decks. We hadn't gotten molds yet. We were just putting this stuff on top. The first job didn't work. It turned out just like molasses. Later, after we'd done one, they wanted more. Ed Cutts, they said, we want you to do it. Sort of carry this group along. You know how it's done.

"Now, in a fiberglass boat, if you've got it screwed up, you add microballoons until you get it; but in a wooden boat, you got to hit it right the first time. I said, 'I can't stay. I can't mix a boat in a pot.'"

Mrs. Cutts leaned through the door, and I realized this was all I was going to learn from his cluttered memory. Still, he was immensely likeable. We stood and showed ourselves to the door. He followed us into the office.

"You guys accept articles on boatbuilding methods?"

Andra and I wandered down the main street of Oxford. There was a pleasant park on the west side facing the Tred Avon River. We walked past Doc's Quik Shop Market and Brigman's Tred Avon Confectionery expecting to find more shops, but there were none. We backtracked and went inside the variety store looking for Doc. But Doc, it seemed, had passed on down the river. The shop was run by an old woman—perhaps his widow—and her fat son, whom I judged to be in his mid-forties. He looked like a cross between Steve Allen and Roy Orbison. He wore black horn-rimmed glasses and sat on a stool behind the tall wood-and-glass countertop like a circus bear. Andra bought an ice cream. I browsed and found a sign advertising steaks. Andra hadn't eaten red meat in ten years, so we ate a lot of fish and poultry. But I needed a fix and asked to see them.

The son pulled himself out of his chair and opened the freezer door. He selected a frosty prepackaged hunk of colorless meat and laid it kindly on the glass in front of me. He pointed at the edges. "The fat and gristle tend to disintegrate on the grill," he said. "Sometimes I get a box of these frozen steaks that's unreliable; first one'll melt in your mouth, the next one you couldn't cut with an ax. Then I found this outfit in Vermont. I've sold 'em all summer, and ever' last one is good."

"How much?" I asked.

"Four bucks," he said, "and worth ever' penny."

I must have hesitated, because his mother jumped up and wagged her finger at me.

"I don't like steak!" she yelled. "But my son Bill here said one night, 'C'mon mamma, let's take us some of these frozen Delmonicos and a baked potato and make ourselves dinner.' I'll tell you, I ate the whole thing, fat and all!"

Double-teamed as I was, I coughed up the four dollars and left.

"Let me know," Bill called after us, "if you ain't one-hundred-percent satisfied!"

The loss of Pete was completing a change in me that had begun years earlier in prison: No longer did I feel vulnerable to the vagaries of justice, afraid of my own death, or anxious about being dealt a handful of jokers. The healing left scar tissue, and that numbness told me I could never again be hurt so badly. War veterans, I'm sure, must feel the same way.

For the inmate, the cauterizing begins in jail. My first night in the Wayne County Jail in downtown Detroit was a scene from *Apocalypse Now:* two inmates, one fat and sweaty, the other old and mean, slashing at each other's throats with single-edged razors melted into the ends of toothbrushes. Red ribbons wept from the fat man's dewlap. The old man fell, cracking his head on the steel track on which the cell bars rode. The furor of twenty screaming men subsided as one shook the old man and got no response. They yelled for the guards, who did not come. And why should they? The noise and the slamming was the usual background. We waited in a circle, and when at last a guard sauntered down the hall to investigate, the old man's life had bled away before our eyes.

By comparison, prison was a relief. The food was better, there were books to read, and work—however menial and mind-numbing—to pass the time. You were still in charge of your own survival. Leaving quarantine for my assigned cell block, I was stopped by two brothers (the accepted term for blacks) on the stairway.

"You a girl?" one asked.

"What?" I replied, thinking I hadn't heard them correctly.

"You a girl?"

After several repetitions, I realized they were hitting on me. There are, naturally, some true homosexuals in prison, but there are various grades of others who engage in homosexual sex out of pure deprivation and need. A "girl" was someone who submitted and liked it. A "punk" was some weak-willed kid, often too small and timid to defend himself, who gave in to survive. A "daddy" was a strong man who protected his girls and punks from attack by others.

The two brothers were trying to find out if this new kid was a possible target. Regardless of how you might handle such a situation on the outside, there is only one way to respond in prison, assuming you've already made the decision to resist.

Dropping my issue of clothes and bedding, I slammed both hands into one brother's chest, drove him into the wall, and yelled in his face, something to the effect that he'd have to break my back before I'd bend over for him or anyone else.

Though he was much stronger than I, he backed off. "Okay, okay," he said, straightening his shirt indignantly. "Back off mo'fucker."

This cell block was a single huge room with four rows of about thirty steel cots each. All eyes were on me as I checked the painted numbers for mine. To one side was a brother named Jackson, playing chess with a friend. After a time I offered to play the winner. At first they ignored me. Oddly, no whites played chess in prison, only the brothers. Several days passed before Jackson turned to me and said, "You wanna play?"

Jackson fancied himself one of the better players, and after I had beaten him, I became a challenge. We played often and in due course became solid friends. My father mailed annotated games of the masters, which we played through until the lights went out. And some nights we lay on our bunks playing "blindfold" chess in our minds, alternately calling out moves:

"Pawn to queen's bishop three."

"Knight to king's rook five."

"You can't move there, you got a pawn on that square!"

"The pawn's on rook four."

117

"No it ain't."

We weren't Capablanca or Morphy, Alekine or Nimzovitch, but we got pretty good. And no brother ever tested me again. But some nights when walking past the latrine you could hear the grunting of men raping a new kid, and you might think to do something before the lookout waved you on. There's two things you don't want to be in prison: A punk or a snitch. So you walk on, guarding your own butt and your own honor.

And years later, when you're walking down some dark street in a strange town, and a shadowy figure hangs in the doorway ahead, you may play it smart and cross over. But in your heart you're ready and you're not afraid, because you know they can't hurt you. Not really.

That night I awoke and heard the Canada geese honking across Town Creek. I opened my eyes and listened. The night air was filled with their cacophonous din. I might have heard in their calls the shrieking of men fighting, the jeers and taunts, the demand for blood, but those memories were fading. I liked the idea of being surrounded by geese, and all I wished for was a good night's sleep on the flyway.

1 0
Dead in the Water

Roughly midway down the bay, just above the surly mouth of the Potomac River, the Chesapeake bends slightly westward in the shape of a Mexican pepper. To minimize distances on our cruise down, we switched back to the western shore and stopped at Solomons Island on the Patuxent River.

Before the white man arrived, the Patuxent Indians lived along the river's shores, fishing and hunting for subsistence. The forty-one-acre island was settled in 1662 by Edward Eltonhead, whose grant required that he bring in fifty settlers. Despite a time extension, he failed and the land escheated to Lord Baltimore. Isaac Solomon bought the island in 1865 and built an oyster cannery that is preserved to this day. The fishing and oystering business grew, and by 1880 there were more than five hundred vessels operating from the harbor.

Soon after, a local blacksmith invented the "patent tongs" that are still used to harvest shellfish in shallow water. In fair weather and foul the tonger is there, sensing the bottom through the long poles. It is hard work, like digging a post hole with twenty-foot handles, and his shirt is wrung through with sweat. And when at last he muscles the tongs aboard, his gloved fingers tear at the thick mud for the hard, black shells of the oysters. At dusk there is a gathering in the dirty bilge that represents his day's pay.

In the pubs and restaurants along the bay and farther afield, a good man can scarf them as fast as the shucker shucks. Priced at better than a buck apiece, everyone profits, including the scarfer, who it is said fortifies his virility. The fisherman's bumper sticker reads: "Eat Fish, Live Longer, Eat Clams, Last Longer, Eat Oysters, Love Longer."

We anchored in Mill Creek, a mile or two beyond the town. Nearby was a nineteen-foot Lightning-class daysailer moored with a stern anchor in deep water and a bowline tied to a convenient tree. On the soft, low banks the man had pitched his tent, and around it was the sailor's mess — evidence of a fire, some cookery, a sleeping bag. Chesapeake Bay had not been kind that day, and I pictured the man huddled in his red nylon world, stripping off the wet jeans, his flesh blue, his mind dreading the night.

"Crazy fool," Andra muttered as we passed up the creek.

Already we had formed impressions of this man, though we had yet to lay eyes on him.

As the sun set I decided to try my hand at crabbing, having bought a pack of frozen chicken necks for the purpose. It is surprisingly simple: Tie a length of string around the neck (the smellier the better), lower it to the bottom, and wait. When you grow curious, haul in the string. The blue crab will hang on until it breaks the surface, at which point it releases its grip and falls back. If your net is not at the ready, you will see it drift away, its arms frozen in a semicircle, falling like a plate until the murk closes around and *Callinectes sapidus* is vanished.

After an hour I had five in a plastic bucket. Each time I tossed in another there was a furious clatter of shells as they fought. This lasted perhaps thirty seconds, and when I looked again they were locked in one another's spiny grasp, ten pincers fixed in tension like the tubes of a pup tent.

Andra dropped the bucket while transferring them to the pot. The crabs scattered. One hid behind the toilet, set back on its haunches clacking at her. I rounded them up with tongs, care, and a frying pan.

You must cook them with Old Bay seafood seasoning as no other method is deemed suitable in the State of Maryland. The spices include celery salt, mustard, pepper, laurel leaves, cloves, pimento, ginger, mace, cardamom, cassia, and paprika. And crabs fried or baked with Old Bay are delicious, though you tend to burn off more calories cracking shells than you gain from the small shreds of meat. Soon you appreciate the high price of crabcakes and canned whole meat.

Motoring down Mill Creek the next morning I got the jump on the camper. He was knee-deep in the cold creek water, fussing with his boat.

"Better him than me," Andra mused.

The boat's name was *Sundog,* which meant he was a visitor here, a traveler from some place far north of Maryland. I'd never seen this Arctic phenomenon of the sundog, a small round halo on the parhelic circle, but I wanted to. I supposed this man had, and I wanted him to explain it to me, for it seems to possess a mystical significance in folklore.

My thoughts ran back over the years to my first boat—a fifteen-foot open Snipe. At one time it was the most popular boat in the world. Red-hulled *Culculine* was all I could afford, but I loved her. On long weekends I trailered her to northern Michigan. Often I grabbed an old friend who didn't know enough to avoid me when I had that wild, fool look in my eye.

Jim Dunlap and I launched the light hull at Leland on the Leelanau Peninsula, and we sailed ten miles "offshore" to the Manitou islands. Ballast was the tent, sleeping bags, and cookware. If a reef was indicated we dropped the mainsail. Jim turned green and slipped into a funereal silence until the bow sliced into the sandy bottom and we stepped into the clear, cold waters of Lake Michigan. We pitched our tent and built a campfire. Cooked a steak on the flimsy grill, pretending we were Lewis and Clark feasting on buffalo hump. And when the fire died and only the embers lit our tired faces, I lay on my back and saw Ursa Major and Ursa Minor spiraling over the dunes.

The Potawatomi Indians believed that the Sleeping Bear dunes were made by a mother bear who had swum the lake with her cubs. The little fellows struggled to make it the eighty miles from Green Bay to Michigan, and she lay down to wait. They never made shore. The wind blew sand over her, and she was covered in sorrow, abiding her loss in eternal sleep. The drowned cubs turned into North and South Manitou islands.

Sleeping there on the smooth-pebbled beach of North Manitou, chilled by the thin air of the North Woods, the white pine whispering in the breeze, the myths seemed real. Real until some thug pulled up in a jeep, rifle slung across his lap, and told us to scram. Private herd of deer, he said, property of the Angel Foundation. Arthur Hailey had nothing good to say of the mysterious outfit in his book *Wheels*. I wanted to recon the island, and the next year we tried again to slip across the strait. Then a plane dropped out of the sky and threatened to shorten our sails before we bore off for South Manitou. I never did learn the identity or purpose of the Angel Foundation, though years later the U.S. Government appropriated the island as part of a lakeshore national park.

The wind gushed down out of the northeast, pushing the needle on the anemometer to thirty knots in gusts. I dropped the mainsail and we barreled along with just the genoa pulling us south. My plan was to again cross the bay to the Eastern Shore, putting in at Tangier Island for the night. On the horizon a freighter was making its way up the bay, and I decided to stay west until it passed.

For a time we plugged on, and I did not at first notice how slowly the distance between *Adriana* and the freighter closed. Beginning sailors are cautioned about a freighter's deceptive speed: A ship making twenty knots covers five nautical miles in fifteen minutes. I checked the clock and noted that almost an hour had transpired since the first sighting. Strange, I thought, she's dead in the water. Had I recalled the warnings in the coast pilots and cruising guides, I would have understood.

The freighter was about eight miles east of Point Lookout, marking the northern lip of the Potomac River. By now I had maneuvered well inside her, and as we approached I trained our powerful Swarovski binoculars on the bridge. "Of course!" I exclaimed. "It's one of the navy's target vessels."

And so it was, the S.S. *American Mariner,* intentionally run aground on a reef twenty years ago as a target for navy pilots. Though punctured like Swiss cheese and wrapped in a blanket of rust, she has been kept more or less intact with inert ordnance. Fated to this ignominious end, the S.S. *American Mariner* is one of the last Liberty ships mass-produced by industrialist Henry Kaiser to supply Europe during World War II.

The mouth of the Potomac River is reputedly rough, especially in a norther. As the skeletal remains of the *American Mariner* faded astern, we drew abreast of the famed river, and the waves rolled down from Washington like concussions from a great explosion. The dinghy began to take on water, and I chastised myself for not having stowed it on deck. The thought of losing her was scary, reminding me of the letter Danny Greene had left on *Adriana* while we were in Michigan. "One of my fondest memories of Pete," he had written, "was watching you two build a dinghy to one of my designs." It had been Pete's pride and joy, and I was desperate to save her.

Fortunately, she was tethered by two painters, and I managed to winch her bow nearly to the transom, one line to each quarter cleat, so it did not careen past us, digging in its nose like a pig roguing for truffles. Had it completely filled, we would have had no choice but to cut it loose. Trying to bail a foundering twelve-foot boat in eight-foot seas and twenty-five-knot winds would have been dangerous and certainly futile.

When at last we had passed the Potomac, we licked our wounds on the Wicomico River, Virginia. Several miles upstream was tiny Horn Harbor, and no more beautiful anchorage have we found anywhere. At the entrance, a narrow dogleg between two sandspits, one can literally jump off the boat on either side and land on firm, tawny beach. Inside is a tranquil pond surrounded by wooded hills and one house, rather hidden. The night sky was unusually clear, and I found myself standing in the cockpit remembering my childhood fascination with the quivering mysteries of the heavens—endless time and infinite space. The temperature plummeted. We built our second fire of the cruise in the Tiny Tot and turned in early.

Fog greeted us the next morning and followed us down the coast to Mobjack Bay. The wind had blown itself out, and for hours we were forced to motor in a cool haze.

Andra went below and lay down.

"Are you taking a nap?" I asked.

She reappeared at the companionway. "No. Why? Do you want to be alone? You can tell me these things."

I smiled. "Being with you is like being alone," I said. "Even with you right here I can drift off in my own thoughts whenever I wish."

"I know," Andra replied, feigning peevishness, "whether I'm talking or not!"

A few days later we were steaming for Norfolk, Virginia, when I spotted a dead whale floating in the quilted water. Three sea gulls sat on its side, looking at one another as if to say, "What now, Mac?"

I trained binoculars on the big, dead, majestic beast, fascinated by the sharp demarcation between black and white where its belly met its sides, and its tail, which seemed to wave in the gentle undulations of the bay. Suddenly he was there—Zelig in the Lightning—on the other side of the whale, motoring for Hampton Roads. "Hey!" I wanted to yell, "Check out the whale!"

But he was too far away and too low in the water to notice this great, lifeless thing. We passed on, but somehow I knew we would meet again.

Norfolk crouches on a neck of flatland a few miles west of Chesapeake Bay. It is the last stop coming down the bay before the serpentine bridge-tunnel combination that rises and drops into the waters, shuttling auto traffic between Cape Charles to the north and Cape Henry to the south. Beyond is the broad Atlantic, Bermuda, the Azores, then Africa and Europe. The port is deep and strategically located. No surprise that Norfolk, Newport

News, and Portsmouth comprise the largest shipbuilding and repair complex in the United States.

Hampton Roads is the impressive-sounding name given to the meeting place of the James, Elizabeth, and Nansemond rivers. It is a dizzying cauldron of giant freighters, cloud-gray missile cruisers, shrimpers, tugs and barges, and hundreds of small craft, all competing for space in the narrow entrance channel. Apprehensively I turned *Adriana* into the swirling currents and aimed toward Fort Wool at the entrance. We slowed to a snail's pace, and it was only after careful, anxious calculations that I cut in front of a freighter to hug the south shore.

Wakes rocked us, and the mast whipped across the dazzling sky as we inched forward. At the Hampton Roads bridge it seemed we would be swept backward, reeling out of control, then driven asunder by one of the big three-story ocean-going tugs pulling barges as big as a football field.

Eventually we labored into the reach and out of harm's way. To starboard was the big-ship anchorage, large enough to accommodate an 80,000-ton aircraft carrier, and the U.S. Navy base at Sewells Point. Farther along to port was the S.S. *United States,* built in 1952 at Newport News. Mothballed here since 1969, she long held the Atlantic Blue Riband for the fastest ocean crossing. She lies stately there, a patina of rust belying her undeniable majesty. The two stacks are raked aft as if shaped by her tremendous speed, and it is impossible to pass by without lamenting her unkind fate.

Everywhere about her are the navy's warships — frigates and destroyers, their thin plates dented between the frames, guided missile cruisers with square launching blocks angled skyward, flat-topped aircraft carriers, small mine sweepers, orca-shaped submarines, and gunless supply ships, sometimes rafted three-deep along the piers. All in various stages of fitting out, they are ready for combat. After a cruise along this row it is easy to see why the nation's defense budget runs to the hundreds of billions.

We spent the night anchored up the Lafayette River in a pretty cove bordered by the Hampton Boulevard Bridge and some navy offices. Opposite was the Norfolk Yacht Club, which refused our request to land a dinghy. After five days without going ashore, we were resolved to stretch our legs on solid ground. Looking about, we decided to head upstream under a road bridge and tie the dinghy to some shrubs overhanging the bank.

The larder was thinning, the milk and meat gone. We flagged down a city bus and rode it several miles to a supermarket. The place was filthy and the prices noticeably higher than any we had seen. "Of all people to stick it to," Andra said, "they pick the poorest."

Now also was a rare opportunity to make phone calls. It was November 8 — thirty-six days since Pete's death — and we hadn't yet told Adria that Andra was pregnant. Tell her too soon, I worried, and she might be offended. Tell her too late, and she might feel left out. Peter's death hung heavily on her conscience, for she felt some sense of responsibility for watching him that day, and I was afraid she might resent Andra's pregnancy. Most days when I thought I had it figured out, I couldn't call anyway.

Luckily she was home, and after filling her in on events since our last conversation, I broke the news. "Really?!" She said it was great, but I could tell she was a little stunned. Who could blame her? Andra talked with her awhile, answering the usual questions about a due date and morning sickness. I got back on to say goodbye, and then we began the trek back to the boat.

"How did she sound to you?" I asked.

"I don't think she knows what to think," Andra answered.

Neither did I. But I hoped fervently the news hadn't driven a wedge between us. I wished I could have held her as I told her. It would be rough enough on Margaret, if only because I was getting another chance.

"You better call her again, soon," Andra said.

I nodded, working my hand through the handles of four plastic grocery bags. "There's a taxi," I said.

The driver, an old man with silver hair, helped load our bags in the trunk of his dilapidated Plymouth. Only after we were seated, running down the road, did I realize this wasn't a cab at all, just an enterprising man's effort at making a few bucks. As with the underground postal system in Thomas Pynchon's *Crying of Lot Forty-Nine,* in Norfolk you can save fare with jitneys in jalopies. The only problem is, you can't find them; they find you.

∗

The next morning we pressed down the Elizabeth River to the city docks.

Waterside is yet another James Rouse creation, modeled after the marina/shopping gallery developments in Boston and Baltimore. It lacked the vibrancy of Faneuil Hall and Harborplace, but the docks were well maintained and the staff friendly.

I noticed a handsome powerboat a few slips down, and later the owner, a middle-aged fellow named Roger Miller, came by to borrow a hose. "Stop for a drink," he offered.

It was past eleven that night when we finished our dinner in one of the arcade restaurants and shuffled home arm in arm like young lovers. Suddenly a voice yelled: "Hey, step aboard!"

It was Roger, seated in a canvas captain's chair on the afterdeck of his lobster-type trawler yacht. "It's late," I demurred, "but sure." Moments later I had a scotch in hand and was seated next to him. Andra lounged on the padded engine cover.

Roger was high spirited, having just quit his job, and on impulse was heading south to Key West.

"Why?" I asked.

"Well," he said, "some mornings you wake up and you just know today's the day. I had a good job repping for a small company that makes the tiles for NASA. You know, the ones that are always falling off. Not our fault though. It's a good product. Blame it on the damned adhesive!" He laughed and poured another scotch.

"I used to own a sailboat," he went on. "Took my wife and kids across the Atlantic on a thirty-five-footer. There was a mutiny, and that was the beginning of the end of that. I live with a woman and her seventeen-year-old daughter now. Or I did until yesterday. Nobody can believe it. Some of my friends from work were just here, kind of checking me out. They wanted to know what was wrong, and all I could tell them was, 'Hey, you guys got it mixed up—everything is *right!*'"

As the night wore on we talked of many things, the cruising life, the marine industry, boats, his daughters, Peter and Adria, and ultimately our unborn.

"You don't look pregnant," he said.

Andra looked at her stomach. "The rabbit died," she quipped.

"Bah! Let's give you the cookie test!" Roger jumped up and went below to rummage in his compact galley. A moment later he handed Andra a pack of chocolate marshmallow cookies. "If you're really pregnant," he said, "you'll scarf down this whole pack!"

The next morning I was just awakening when I heard his engine spring to life. I poked my head through the forward hatch just in time to catch his eye. He throttled up and left Waterside with his building wake jumping up the pilings.

"Key West! January sixth!" he yelled, and was gone.

11

The Boat Wore Blinders

Andra and I rubbed the condensation from *Adriana's* windows and peered out at the sleet and snow that blew horizontally across the docks. We were waiting for our Michigan friends Robert and Mary Gibson to join us for a few days. And we were anxious to begin the Intracoastal Waterway, for we were practiced at the art of self-deception and saw it as a symbol of dramatic and sudden movement south. Surely the Tropics lay just beyond the Virginia border!

Through the gloom I saw them lugging duffels along the seawall. Dressed in hooded parkas and animal-skin boots, they looked like Inuit Indians ready to hunt walrus. They were prepared for the savagery outside. Andra and I were not. It was mid-November, and we hadn't been warm in months. The picture I had painted her of slipping lazily down the Carolina streams, a pair of old reptiles sunning ourselves in the cockpit, was an honest though gross miscalculation.

The Gibsons clamored below, slamming the hatch behind. They had three days to cruise, but the weather was miserable enough to postpone the Iditarod. The four of us debated. Finally Robert said, "If you want to smell roses, you're gonna be pricked by thorns."

He was right. For every beam reach and sunny day, there is a dark and sometimes ugly flipside—knockdowns, pooped cock-pits, oatmeal in the bilge. The veterans are revisionists who learn to amend and forget. So we cast off our lines and steamed down the Elizabeth River toward the first of seven bridges standing between us and the Great Dismal Swamp Canal cutoff.

Just when we thought it couldn't get any worse, the channel was enveloped in seasmoke, and the ghosts of mothballed navy ships advanced and retreated in the low-lying fog like mannequins in a house of horrors.

We pressed on, huddled in the cockpit, feeling as morose as the last members of Scott's ill-fated expedition to Antarctica, poised to lop off our frostbitten toes for a macabre game of poker. The last bridge, a fixed concrete structure supporting Interstate 64, appeared in the frozen swirls, and beyond it we knew was our right-hand turn into the canal. But how far? Ten yards? A hundred? A quarter mile? The chart was an inadequate guide.

And then the bridge was gone. Whiteout. The snow fell and the ledge of fog swept across our bow. I felt like a coach driver on a Transylvania movie set, dashing up the snow-whipped mountainside to Vlad's castle.

I drew in my horses and drifted under the sixty-five-foot span. The arch appeared briefly, and when it vanished astern there was nothing else. Just white all around. The numbers on the digital depthsounder dropped with insidious precision—18, 13, 8. Hastily I ordered the ground tackle made ready. Soon there would be no recourse but to anchor in water too shallow for the tugs and barges that moments earlier had choked the river. Then wait, till when? Dusk? Dawn?

Suddenly a sign appeared before us. It read "Great Dismal Swamp Canal," and an arrow pointed thataway. I eased the reins and probed the white vapors grudgingly. Minutes later I saw tree-tops appear above the fog, and a faint opening in the boughs. We were creeping, eyes keenly fixed for a break in the seasmoke. And then the dull forest took shape to either side, and we realized we had crossed the threshold of the canal.

"See that sign?" I chuckled. "Lucky us, eh?"

"Yeah, I read it," Andra snorted. "That was a 'Surrender Dorothy' sign if I ever saw one."

We anchored in a small pondlike appendage to the canal, and that night the snow fell wet and thick on the decks. An accumulation of several inches. It was cold, and we built a fire, made popcorn, and played Christmas carols on the stereo.

To Andra and me, it seemed the farther south we moved, the colder it got. "Hey," Robert countered, "it's warmer than Michigan, and for us, this is an adventure."

And so it was, the beginning of a 1,100-mile odyssey through Virginia, North and South Carolina, Georgia, and Florida—virtually all in the protective shield of the Intracoastal Waterway. And what a strange initiation it was, motoring on the straight-and-narrow Great Dismal Swamp Canal, overhung with red maples, tupelo, and bald cypress, brightly banded by yesterday's snow.

George Washington was an early proponent of the canal, for young America was keenly aware of its need to move men, food, ammunition, and supplies on an inside waterway impervious to blockade. The Great Dismal Swamp Canal, utilizing five locks to move shallow-draft barges between the Elizabeth River and the Pasquotank River, opened in 1805. Later a hotel was built on Lake Drummond and named the Halfway House. It was there that Edgar Allan Poe wrote "The Raven." At the South Mill lock Robert chatted up the aged keeper; when he returned to the boat he reported, "This place is so far out of the way that the last memo on the wall is from the Army Corps of Engineers, dated 1939!"

The Gibsons would leave us in Elizabeth City, North Carolina, at the free city docks where a Canadian cruiser had shown passersby how to make snowmen. Front-page news. A couple of retirees greeted us in a golf cart. Fred Fearing, the ringleader, handed long-stem roses to the ladies and chamber of commerce brochures to the men.

"This wasn't my idea," he said almost apologetically. "The Rose Buddies were started by Joe Kramer. He loved this town and wanted to give something back to it. I'm just carrying on for a friend. We buried old Joe last week. His son moved the rose bushes down here for us."

Fred pointed to the season's last flowers, wilting by the small brick building that was the centerpiece of the dock area. Local businesses had donated the docks, and their names were painted on the wall behind the roses. Fred told us the canal was their life-blood. When it was closed during droughts, the waterfront businesses died. Willard Scott, weatherman on the "Today" show, once did a broadcast from the piers, dubbing the gang the "Rose Buddies." Their pride was manifest, and you would have thought they had been decorated by the president.

Everyone we met had a sales pitch for Elizabeth City. An energetic old woman at the chamber of commerce begged us to attend the Mistletoe Festival and practically insisted we take a walking tour of Queen Anne homes, "Gothic revival–style" churches, the "utilitarian Greek revival design" Cobb Building, and various other structures with "Tiffany-style windows" and "full Doric porticoes." However, its charm was hidden to me, and I could not help feeling that Elizabeth City was a dusty, nondescript shadow of history struggling against extinction.

A recent ordinance permitting liquor by the glass, presumably to spark a nightlife, was controversial. Robert hired a cab to take us to dinner, and I asked the driver's opinion. He was a big, heavy, black fellow, about sixty, with a frosting of white in his hair. There was a gentle way about him.

"Don't smoke or drink myself," he said amiably, "but you get the guy who maybe don't want to buy a whole pint. Maybe he jus' tired after work and want to stop for a shot or two. I think people gonna drink a lot less than the others think."

He noticed my pipe through the rearview mirror and continued: "When I was a boy, I went behind the barn to smoke myself a cigarette I made of corn silk. Holy Jesus! It was coming out of my nose and eyes, ears, everywheres! My daddy didn't say nuthin' at dinner, but I know he seen me. At three o'clock in the mornin' the covers was pulled back, and when he was done with me, I didn't want no more cigarettes. My smoking career was short," he chuckled. "It ended and started that one day!"

Robert and Mary bade us adieu the next day. Despite the promise of free-flowing wine from a local vineyard, we decided to pass on the second free night at the docks, and the hello/good-bye party sponsored by the Rose Buddies.

A lazy breeze bore us slowly into the Pasquotank, and though I regretted leaving such good friends, I was heartened by the message Adria had confided to them. "This baby," she had said to Mary in Ann Arbor, "is the best thing that could happen to me."

Ten miles downriver I looked into the rigging for a sign of stronger wind and was startled to see a large spider drop onto the dodger. My eyes focused, as if waking from a dream, and I saw yards of cobwebs streaming like telltales from the stays and halyards. The delicate crosshatching connected the three shrouds on each side of the mast, forming a faintly colored tepee.

Andra rolled her eyes. "Yeah," she said, "that's what happens when you stay too long in Elizabeth City."

The course took us south across Albemarle Sound to the mouth of the Alligator River on the other side. Enjoying the calm weather between two violent fronts, we sailed a little. Sitting behind the wheel, chin in hand, with nothing to do but follow a distant mark on shore, is a posture conducive to the sort of melancholy reflections that follow when you leave old friends. By now Robert and Mary would have returned to their car in Norfolk and begun the long trek home. Home to the place I had left so quickly, with so much anxiety, eight long years before. A piece of me traveled with them, for I knew the road well—the beltway skirting Baltimore, the dark and mountainous turnpike snaking across Pennsylvania, finally coming down onto the big sky and rolling expanse of Ohio—and I knew the destination like the beat of my own heart. Ann Arbor, breezy as Walter Van Tilburg Clark's Reno, it too a city of trembling leaves.

The Little Alligator River, a shallow sidestream that bent behind a point of leafless sticks, presented a secluded anchorage. Nearby was the rusting shell of a steel shrimper, run aground and forgotten. The sun set in a lavender wash, and the shore was a swamp from whose sphagnum softness rose the ghostly silhouettes of gnarled, dead limbs. The wreck turned like a chameleon from a weak yellow through shades of darkening brown and ultimately, when Venus rose, to an indissoluble black.

A twenty-one-mile landcut brought us to the Pungo River and then the town of Belhaven on a Sunday night. There are several good marinas in the area, but true to our pecuniary code, we anchored inside the town breakwater. However, the nightly buffet served at the River Forest Manor was so highly recommended we took the dinghy ashore and splurged. The Southern-style cooking—chicken, roast beef, turnip greens, black-eyed peas, and oyster fritters—was superbly arranged on hot trays.

At the table next to us were two middle-aged men, and before long we were sharing waterway tales. Their boat was a Bayliner Express Cruiser named *Another Bad Czech.*

"How much fuel do you burn?" I asked. I was trying to sound knowledgeable about the concerns of powerboaters, failing to realize how soon I too was to become obsessed with the equations of consumption.

"Gallon a mile," the Baltimore lawyer said. He pulled out his wallet and flipped credit-card receipts on the table. "Hundred seventy-five, hundred sixty-six. . . ."

I couldn't tell whether he was proud or irritated. "When do you expect to reach West Palm Beach?" I asked.

"Saturday," he answered perfunctorily.

I left the restaurant shaking my head. "How much can he possibly see?" I said to Andra. "It's like driving cross-country on freeways, when all the sights and smells are on the backroads. This is a classic case of the tortoise and the hare; he'll have breakdowns and we'll arrive at the same time. And, of course, we'll have seen so much more."

The next morning we crept out of Belhaven into Pamlico Sound. The guidebooks warn of dangerous storm conditions in all the shallow, inland waters, and for a time we joked smugly. This was the last open body of water we would see until Biscayne Bay, Florida. I hoisted the mainsail and #2 genoa, and we rounded Maw Point into the Neuse River. Then the skies darkened with squalls, and the wind pounced on us like a trained Doberman. While we thrashed about with the mainsail and engine, several trawlers tooled by. The shrimpers steamed purposefully toward the ocean inlets, and the sportfishermen with their great deep-vee hulls made fools of us all, handling the seas with agility and grace. Slowly it dawned on me that sailboats do not belong on the waterway. They are craft out of their element, with no business plodding down the winding alleys. A thousand miles of motoring lay ahead, more than enough time to examine Nature in excruciatingly microscopic detail.

A series of squalls screamed overhead, and anxiously we watched the depthsounder as we aimed for the windward shore. The tree line disappeared, and we wallowed into Oriental, a gale on our tail. With just inches beneath our keel, we anchored in the calm water of Greens Creek, surrounded by manicured lawns and pleasant homes.

Katy Burke and Taz Waller invited us for dinner that night at their deep-water bungalow. Author Herb Payson and his wife, Nancy, were there, having just commissioned a Pacific Seacraft 34. Taz and Katy had bought one too, and much of the evening was spent praising this feature and diagnosing that idiosyncrasy. Of course, they loved their boats.

We talked a bit about Peter and Andra, now 2½ months pregnant. One of my children had left this world at the same time another was arriving, and I frequently drifted into reveries, trying to understand this cycle. My idea of it was pure naturalism: Our bodies, like rainwater, dry up, condense, and rise into the heavens, then fall to nurture the ground and give life.

Andra was starting to feel outright fat, waiting anxiously for that "radiant beauty" ascribed to happy, peach-faced mothers-to-be. All her pregnant friends at home had it. "And I'd have it, too," she said cynically, "if I could shower three times a day."

"Just wait," I consoled. "Soon we'll be in weather so hot you'll spend every day lolling on an air mattress, trailing your toes in the tepid, aquamarine bays of the Bahamas."

There was probably a time, before she was pregnant, when the promise of a summer idyll on some palm-lined desert beach sounded exciting to her. Now, not surprisingly, all her thoughts focused on her belly. The prospect of childbirth was frightening. And traveling through the backwaters of coastal America, way beyond the range of telephone booths, doctors' offices, and ambulances, did little to reassure her. Her first obstetric examination in Florida was still more than a month away.

Some days she'd look up from her book and say, "Let's think of names."

"We don't know what it is," I'd say.

"You're supposed to pick one boy's and one girl's," she'd say.
Then a long silence would follow.

"At least you could pretend to be interested," she'd sigh at last.

"I am," I'd say weakly. And I'd again fall into silence, staring at
the markers ahead as if these totems held the answer. We would
not get much beyond Florida and the Bahamas, and the realization
was difficult to accept. All the years of planning, saving, and boat
work seemed for naught. Worse, a picture of our lives after this
aborted cruise was slowly materializing: house, cars, pets, jobs,
quibbling about money and who's pulling or not pulling his or her
weight—the "full catastrophe," Zorba the Greek called it. The
image was depressing. Andra's sister Linnea wrote and said she
thought we could raise the kid on the boat, that we were well
suited to such an alternative lifestyle. But I knew it wouldn't
work. This cruise was my idea, not Andra's. Given her choice,
she'd be hiking in the Rockies. The thought that perhaps we were
not such a good match after all was sickening.

But Peter's death made these gripes seem trivial. Every time I
turned from the immediate question of where our lives were leading, I was slammed by the impenetrable, unscalable wall of truth:
He was dead, and I would never see him again. Hadn't seen him
since that day in Portland when we watched him walking up the
ramp to the airplane. There would never be a chance to say the
things I wanted to. It was a small consolation that my last words
had been, "I love you."

It is an easy run down Adams Creek from Oriental to Beaufort,
the latter lying just inside the barrier islands of the Atlantic coast.
Many Caribbean-bound captains who have come "inside" to avoid
ill-tempered Cape Hatteras take their leave of the waterway at
Beaufort. Here, the miles of sailing close-hauled to the trade
winds are less than farther down the coast, which bends steadily
westward, away from the Caribbean islands.

The anchorage at Beaufort runs the length of the waterfront,
but it is narrow, and one must use two anchors in a Bahamian
moor to swing with the strong currents. And Beaufort is a decent

provisioning port. The shopping center is a few miles away, but the North Carolina Maritime Museum has loaner bikes and a car for cruisers. Naively we tried walking to the nearest propane fill station. Like dullards who can only be enlightened by cattle prods, we were beginning to realize that the distance estimates of well-meaning locals are always wrong. "Oh, it's 'bout two blocks up the road and just round the corner apiece." This means at least two miles, and you cannot carry four bags of groceries and a propane tank with the equanimity of a packhorse. Eventually, we learned to double all distance estimates, take city buses, or simply wait for the next town to shop.

Fortunately, our friend Mark Balogh drove down from Cedar Island to help us with our chores. He is a sailmaker in a strange, anachronistic community where the neighbors still speak a form of Elizabethan English salted with hillbilly. As in Maine, Mark said he could spend his entire life on Cedar Island and never be wholly accepted by these descendants of British seamen who jumped ship centuries ago. He seemed eager for companionship and chirped like a mynah bird as he chauffeured us from mall to mall.

Somewhere around Camp Lejeune, where marine gunners lob artillery shells over the waterway, the weather turned nasty. Temperatures dropped into the low forties during the day and below freezing at night. The wind was relentless and sharp. Rigging beat at the mast, and the canvas dodger tugged at its seams. After eight hours at the helm, which was the best we could do in those short, winter days, I eased my stiff legs below, feeling as though I'd spent the day inside a tambourine, rattled in the wind and banged on the knee of a musician possessed with superhuman stamina.

Each morning we got out of bed at sunrise, put on a pot of coffee, and began dressing. Two pairs of socks, two pants, four shirts, sweater, and two jackets. We wrapped longsleeve T-shirts around our heads and pulled wool watchcaps over the top. I made a muffler from a dish towel. Andra wore socks under her gloves, and when that wasn't enough she stuck her hands in Peter's fuzzy duck and seal puppets. In the mirror we looked worse than the poor bums who sleep on sidewalk steam vents. Unfortunately, we discovered no practical way to double up the shoes.

Sailboats on the waterway tend to travel in packs. It is a herding instinct, and the common denominator is the vulnerability caused by slowness. We are wagon trains ready to circle up at the slightest threat of danger. Powerboats run alone mostly, because their speeds vary so greatly. The awesome sportfishermen are the mavericks, I think, fast and purposeful. But the sailboats all run within a knot or two of each other and spend the night in the same anchorages. Eight hours at five or five at eight still gets you forty miles of bad road.

Adriana was the slowest boat in our pack. For a time we tried to beat the others by rising earlier and running later. The fastest boat in our group, a forty-foot British motorsailer, invariably caught us by noon and waited for us at dusk in a cozy sidewater. The skipper of *T'Morn* would amble out of his toasty pilothouse and wave, always looking like cocktail hour. Secretly I was chagrined, until I got hold of myself and realized there was no reason to drive headlong into an unwinnable race. I was becoming crazed by speed, intoxicated with arriving first, and ultimately I would be destroyed by my own obsession never to rock in another's wake.

Our little coterie of plodders bucked along past Wrightsville, Carolina Beach, and on into the Cape Fear River, where the buoys marking the big-ship channels run roughshod over the fragile squares and triangles of the waterway. The river swept us toward the angry Atlantic. At the mouth we had a glimpse of it, white and cold, frothing like a plague at the door before we hung a sharp right into Dutchman Creek. Inside the barrier island the water was serene, the wind muted by the banks and trees.

As it happened, I recognized the man on a slick racer who had just joined the pack. He was alone, as anyone who knew him might suspect. He was a man with few friends. Not that there was anything terribly offensive about him. He was good looking and had a pleasant smile. I guess it was his tendency to be overbearing, always asking for one more favor and never knowing when to go home. What I mean is, I didn't want to spend the next six weeks stupefied by his conversation.

Andra, however, felt sorry for the guy, and each time he passed she wanted to invite him to dinner. "Wait another day," I pleaded, donning one-way sunglasses and looking the other way as if an exotic species of parrot had flown over the boom, or a black bear had just lunged at me from the near bank.

Just as suddenly as he had entered our pack, he left. Or perhaps we did, I'm not sure. You move up, you move back, never really knowing where you are. I felt bad for our singlehanded friend and if we met again, I resolved to buy him dinner. Well, drinks at least.

My recollection of the days that followed are of bone-chilling cold and the slow procession of sailboats that each morning crept from their berths into the frigid air. We were weary as settlers following one another down the Chisholm Trail. Each day members of the chain changed only slightly, adding or dropping a boat that had either sped up or slowed down. Some simply grew disgusted and went offshore.

The wind clocked twenty knots and more for days on end. At the wheel I shifted my feet and wriggled my toes to keep the blood circulating. Despite the beauty of the passing shores, the boredom at times was crushing. My only interest was the position of the boat in front and the boat in back. We had little fear of running up somebody's ass end, but we were ever mindful of being passed, which occurred constantly. And all I could think of was Hannibal crossing the Alps with a procession of elephants, creatures unfit for the task demanded of them. There was something pachydermatous about our file, I thought, and an economy in linking trunks and tails as we lumbered south. But as Will Tuttle had told me months ago at the Jamestown Boat Yard, Hannibal didn't have half-tracks, and we didn't have wings.

You fear falling asleep at the wheel, and so you take the most trivial interest in the boat ahead. You notice how the helmsman reads his chart, whether he pays attention to the magenta line that shows which side of the narrow channel to favor. Yes, he's dodged the shoal at Marker 179. Good work! He is obviously a skipper to be trusted. Then, just as you lighten your concentration, he drifts off below a green marker and slams aground. You pass, leave him for dead, telling yourself there really was nothing you could do. "Don't get into jams you can't get yourself out of," you scold. The cold is so bitter you cannot conceive slowing down, failing to make your destination. After all, the best anyone can do is row an anchor into deep water and kedge off. Sailboats are gutless tugs.

After a time the scenery all looks the same, a high-banked avenue nicknamed "The Ditch." The egrets and herons stalk the shallows, the gulls mew in the wind, and you imagine all the toads and snakes in their warm holes, smartly hibernating until spring.

You become so mesmerized by the drone of the engine and whine of the wind you begin to marvel at how well the boat anticipates turns. It seems you aren't even holding on. Then you look down and are surprised to see one hand clenched to the wheel. Amazing! You'd forgotten about that hand an hour ago, ceased to feel the severed limb that seems to do its work with a mind of its own.

In a fifty-foot-wide trough, you put a cap on your brain, blinders on the boat, and keep heading south.

12

The Salt Marshes

Since about Mile 308, where the waterway meets the Cape Fear River, currents had become an important factor in our daily piloting, and I studied the tide tables assiduously. Because water ebbs toward the ocean inlets from both directions—north and south—running with a fair tide is not always possible. Our hull speed in unperturbed water was about 5½ knots. With a 2½-knot current, we would make 3 or 8 knots depending on its direction. The Loran displayed speed over the bottom, which, at the passing of every ocean inlet, rose and fell. And when we were halfway between two inlets, it was anybody's guess.

My mood swung with the tide—six hours on, six hours off—morose when the nearby trees seemed almost stationary, exuberant when the docks and houses flew past.

Planning was useless. If we waited for a fair tide until, say, noon to begin the day's motoring, there was no way to make up the lost hours. To complicate matters, our ten hours of sunlight were rarely evenly divided by the ebb and flood; some days we enjoyed a push for the majority of hours, other days the situation was reversed.

There are no street lamps on the waterway and no headlights in *Adriana*'s bow. Nighttime trafficking is hazardous. There are sharp turns, hidden shoals, and floating logs big enough to damage a hull or at the least mangle a propeller. With limited daylight, the best we could do was move from sunrise to sunset and take our licks.

Near Prince Creek, *Sundog* darted out of a hidden side channel. The 3½-horsepower outboard buzzed like a dentist's drill. The young man kept her close to the shore, near enough to catch snakes draped in the boughs of sour gum and cypress. It took some time to pass him, and when we were abreast there was a moment to throw a few questions over the din of engines:

"Where you from?"

"Alaska!"

"Where you heading?"

"Florida Bay!"

"You camp every night?"

"When I can!"

"You know, some people think you're crazy, but I used to cruise in a Snipe. I can relate, man. Still, I like my comforts."

He smiled and gave me a short, offhanded wave as we moved ahead.

Suddenly I felt ashamed. Me, acting like some fat cat in my thirty-three-foot "yacht"! Me, poor enough to sell pencils, my hands and feet cold as steel, condescending to this hardy lad.

Many mornings we'd rise early, and just as we rounded a bend in the river, sipping our second cup of coffee, there would be *Sundog,* buzzing along next to shore. Some days we'd spot him several miles ahead, and it would take the rest of the day to catch him. By the time we pulled even, we knew the details of his transom the way a quarterback knows his center's hind end. Like football, the waterway is a game of inches.

Approaching South Carolina we began to see live oaks, green all year, and a sharp contrast to the gray, deciduous woods all around.

Adriana chugged across the border into South Carolina, her diesel humming rhythmically. Sometimes I talked to the iron

142

heart in her, praising its consistency and dreading the sounds of palpitations, real or imagined. The owner's manual for the engine suggested an oil change every fifty miles, but an every-other-day maintenance schedule was impossible. Often I remembered the story of the little engine that could. "I think I can, I think I can. . . ."

Every hundred miles and every state line was a milestone worthy of celebration. We found Calabash on the border of the two Carolinas, nestled among the yellowing marsh grasses of Little River, half a mile from the waterway.

It is a small place, a crook on the wide side of the stream. The inside of the bend is shallow, maybe six inches deep at high tide. At low tide it's a flat of warm, oozing mud.

The main game in town is serving seafood to tourists. There are enough restaurants to feed the U.S. Army, each advertising delicious "Low Country" or "Calabash-style" cooking. Call it homestyle—boiled peas, baked potatoes, and everything else deep-fried. We treated ourselves to dinner at the Dockside, paying extra for *boiled* shrimp and fish. The maître d' allowed us to tie up to the dock free of charge, saying that management wanted to attract more boats. The sharp operator rings them in from land and sea.

The Low Country of South Carolina opened before us in broad expanses of salt marsh. The tall spears of green and yellow sawgrass ran off in every direction for miles, only here and there a clump of trees telling of firm land where roots could put down into real soil. The channel was cut like a swath, and everywhere were sidecuts, as though some giant had run amok with a lawn mower.

Sundog continued to flit among the side channels like a bat flushed from its perch in a many-chambered cave. I almost caught the lithe skimmer on the banks of the North Edisto River one morning. The skipper was just breaking camp on a sandy sliver of spoil island, and I thought I had him, a chance to say, "Hey dude, you got it right!" But the engine's alarm sounded, and we were forced to execute an emergency anchoring. He slipped away as I rolled up my sleeves, broke open the engine compartment, and sighed.

While I worked, Andra watched two winsome river otters frolic on the mudbanks, and it seemed as though I was the only creature on Earth too stupid or compulsive to throw away my tools and my schedule and enjoy the little pleasures of life.

In the Cape Romain Wildlife Refuge we saw duck hunters flying about in camouflaged jonboats. They were usually young men, dressed in mottled brown-and-green fatigues with thatches of grass tied to their hats. Sometimes they were so well concealed along the channel's edge we didn't know they were there until we heard the loud report of their guns.

In the salt marshes days passed during which we never saw a house or town. Steering became a mind-numbing exercise, and my thoughts turned to matters both serious and mundane. Sometimes memories of Pete were triggered, often by the mere glance at his favorite cockpit corner. Andra seldom saw my eyes mist over, or knew that my mind ran back over his life to the instant of his birth, his death on the tracks, and all the milestones in between. How many times I replayed the critical drama, when he crowned too quickly, then dangled between his mother's legs while the doctor leisurely "scrubbed in." The old nurse's aide and I stared at him, and all I could think to do was spot him as she wrestled the two onto a gurney. I chased them down the hall and held my hands under his head as they were transferred to the delivery table and Margaret's feet were lashed into stirrups. And still the doctor didn't come. His passage was quick. The nurse laid him in the bassinet under a heat lamp. His skin had a blue tinge, and I reminded myself that all newborns do. The nurse suctioned him, flipped him over, patting his face and bottom. He peed. Once she had left, I put my hand on him and he quieted. His skin turned pink and the panic ended.

But something *had* gone wrong. Perhaps it was constriction of the umbilical cord or failure to suction his mouth and nose promptly. CP, caused by a lack of oxygen to the brain during pregnancy or birth, is not a degenerative condition or a disease, but the starved cells never come back and only time reveals the toll on nerves, muscles, and the child's ability to think.

Then Andra would bring lunch into the cockpit, and I would snap-to. Homemade soup and grilled cheese perhaps, and I would see that her stomach had grown. I kept having the same thought—that Nature adds where it has lost, sweeping us all down the eternal stream. My eyes would drift away, and I was lost again.

Piloting was a welcome diversion, a thing to focus on. In the narrow channels, charts seemed almost unnecessary, but plotting progress by the totemic markers gave me something to do and occupied a mind alternately hyperactive and comatose. I would reach for the binoculars to pick off the number of an upcoming marker, find it on the chart, and make rough calculations for distance traveled and distance to go to our next anchorage. I did this maybe twenty times a day. Bearings and fixes were irrelevant. I knew precisely where we were at all times, how far we were from where we had started. Like an escaped convict who hears the dogs sniffing his scent, it was never far enough.

Where the channels merge with larger rivers, navigation becomes more complicated. Transferring from one big-ship channel to another is in effect changing freeways without cloverleafs. And when you see the orange-and-white range markers out of line, your eyes whip to the depthsounder, and you wait for the shudder of impact in the keel. How stupid of you to lose track of your position! You see boats aground everywhere, stuck on the flats like helpless turtles.

When you run with the current the scenery seems to fly past, and your heart pumps a little faster. Your eyes study the water's color and the bends along the shore for clues to shoaling. It is as though you were in a real-life arcade game, racing an Indy car through the countryside. The road comes at you, unfolding from a drum. Obstacles pop up—a barrier, another vehicle—and your success depends on reaction time. But it is never fast enough on a sailboat, and sometimes you wish you could just put the hammer down and get the old bitch up on a plane. Take this slalom course at forty knots, slide into the corners with a rainbow of side spray, and put the nose down on the straightaways. *Another Bad Czech.* Palm Beach Saturday night. That's the way to do it.

Herb and Nancy Payson caught up with us in time for Thanksgiving dinner in Charleston, South Carolina. We treated ourselves to a night at Ashley Marina, where we could walk into Old Market and shop. It was our first taste of the antebellum South. The cobblestoned streets were lined with grand old homes and the yards defended by tabby walls, wrought iron gates, and strategically placed palmettos to ward off inquisitive noses. And the Spanish moss hung on the live oaks like tinsel, covering the yards and walkways in a shadowy indolence.

We left Charleston on a rainy, blowy day, and the best we could say about it was we'd made another twenty miles south. The anchorage we'd targeted at Oyster House Creek proved too shoal, and we were forced to anchor in a corner of the main channel, near a flashing red marker. It was an unnerving night, particularly when a big steel crewboat roared past in the dark. Later, when two sailboats stumbled by, repeatedly running aground in their mad dash for open water, we listened to their curses and expletives until our weary heads could take no more.

One day we came across a fellow drifting in a jonboat, his only companion an old, raggedyass, shit-brown and dirty-white spaniel sitting in the bow. Its hair was wet and matted, and there were a lot of old bird stories in its eyes. The man hailed us, and we slowed.

"My engine quit!" he yelled. "Can you give me a tow to the next river?"

We threw a line, which he made fast to his bow cleat, and as it drew taut we talked to him over the transom. Almost unnoticed, the bulbous eyes of an alligator cruised past, scoping us.

"Any luck?" I asked, recovering from my surprise.

This guy, I supposed, was used to reptiles. He lit a cigar and eased back in his muddy boat. "I'm the game warden," he said. "Every time I borrow a boat something breaks." He cursed his luck.

"Big cigar you got there," Andra remarked.

"Gotta carry 'em big when you spend the day out here."

We fell into an uneasy silence, and twenty minutes passed.

146

Then he stood up and said, pointing at the junction ahead, "You can cut me off now. I saw some boys up on the South Edisto earlier this morning. There's a fishing camp a mile up. Maybe I can drift down on 'em and salvage something from this otherwise wasted day."

He wobbled into the bow and threw off the towline. The boat promptly started spinning, doing two three-sixties before the warden straightened it out. The last we saw of him, he was paddling with a single, stubby paddle, shifting sides with every stroke. Then the wind caught him, and he took off up the river, spinning, spinning. . . .

Beaufort (pronounced Bew-fort as opposed to Bo-fort, North Carolina), our last stop in South Carolina, was also one of the loveliest. The town is situated on the shore of the Beaufort River, surrounded on three sides by an S-curve. Stately homes line the drives, and the Spanish moss is cool on the ancient oaks. The streets are clean and the people friendly; reason enough, I thought, to contact real-estate agents.

Walking down the main drag, we suddenly came face-to-face with the mysterious skipper of *Sundog*. Carl Shoch was his name, six-foot-six, slender, with a handsome, boyish face. There was a girl with him, Cecile, a nurse from Ungava Bay, Quebec. Her long hair was knotted up, her face pretty though plain, and her slender body wrapped in suede, fringe, and colorful cottons. I invited them to dinner. Sure, he said, but tonight they were in search of a motel. Either that or pitch camp on the green lawn of city hall, under the canopy of oaks and moss. "We're going first-class now," he said, "at least until Cecile leaves." She seemed uncomfortable, and I gathered that even Ungava Bay looked like a Holiday Inn compared with a night on a spoil island.

That evening I slapped my first mosquito since Robinhood Cove, Maine. The gravid females, the only ones that suck blood, are my personal nemeses. But I was excited to see them, for it meant only one thing — warmer weather!

On the last day of November we passed into Georgia, crossing the Savannah River on a cool and cloudy day. Over the marsh we could see the stacks and tops of downtown Savannah, nine miles to the north. Facilities for boats are poor there, so we berthed on the waterway at Thunderbolt Marina. Free donuts and a newspaper every morning, and as advertised, "The best showers on the waterway."

On a Monday night we took a bus into the city and had dinner on the waterfront, afterwards prowling the sleepy shops as the clerks fixed window displays for the holiday season. The streets were nearly empty, and we ducked into a hotel lounge for a nightcap. Andra, as any good expectant mother would, restricted herself to sparkling waters and near-beer. The place brawled with football fans cheering a televised game. I suspect it is one of the most dependable rites of autumn, and despite all the changes we had witnessed—in topography, climate, and culture—there was no doubt we were still in America.

We took a cab back to the marina. The diver was a middle-aged woman, talkative, rough around the edges. She was short and stout, square-jawed. Christmas was hard times; there was never enough cash. She said she was earning some extra money playing Rudolph the Red-nosed Reindeer at a local mall.

"What are your duties?" I asked.

"Usually nothing. Stand around," she retorted. "But sometimes I have to ask the kids what they want for Christmas."

"Isn't that Santa's job?" I asked.

"Yeah, but he's a real prick, and a lot of the kids are afraid of him."

The weather had moderated, but still it seemed that powerful forces were at work, as though we were visiting an active volcano on its odd day off. This foreboding was partly the product of the fast-moving rivers that cut through the salt marshes, three or four of them—the Rockdedundy, South, and Little Mud—merging roughly into a brackish sound. They are powerful and quick, moving huge volumes of water into the crotched coastline. Frequently they are at odds with the eight-foot tides, which rise and fall like a steam pump. The collision of water mass can only push up, and it does, kicking and pitching so that even the local fishermen can make no sense of it.

There was no sign of civilization, no homes, no docks, no loom of city lights in the night sky. Big shrimp boats worked the rivers, their booms outstretched and the trailing nets faintly visible as they followed side channels beyond the fields of grass. From afar we watched heavy clouds move inland the way thunderstorms come across the wheat fields of Kansas. The storm rolled toward us like an implacable war machine, drenching the coast.

I had last been in Georgia in 1966. Nick Bohr and I had driven my Volkswagen sunroof down I-75 to Atlanta, then swung east to Columbia. Our friend Kenn Miller was jump training at Fort Gordon. We had to see him before he was shipped overseas. The 82nd was bad, and he planned to kick some yellow butt in Vietnam.

I was in training, too. My brief career as a bank embezzler ended abruptly with a startling accusation from the president, and a hollow confession. For a time it appeared the authorities might be appeased by restitution. Of course, all the money had been spent — on cars, furniture, a television. What a way to impress the new wife!

My job at the gas station paid a dollar and a quarter per hour. I needed about six grand, quick. My logic unfolded thusly: If you can't make it as an inside thief, why not try the outside? Fact: Money, that dirty stuff I had counted over the past two years, is kept in *safes*. I remembered licking my thumbs to separate the bills and scrubbing the silver grime ground into my skin after an afternoon packaging quarters. I knew the feel of money, and I knew where to find large quantities. No, not the bank; I wasn't that good. Grab it in the stores before it was deposited. Forget listening to tumblers with a stethoscope! A crowbar and a heavy machinist's hammer can peel the face off a Diebold in thirty minutes. It was crude, but then I didn't have much style either.

I liked the second-story jobs. Entering through darkened panes, above eye level, out of the light. Cat burglar. "To Catch a Thief." There was a couple of hundred dollars under the back seat of the Volkswagen Nick and I drove to Georgia. Too many coins, though, which I put in a cigar box to keep them from rolling around. We slept in cheap motels, but when we found "Caveman" Miller, I bought his buddies all the whiskey they could drink.

In six months he would be creeping through Asian jungles, leading a long-range reconnaissance patrol behind Charlie's lines. Leeches and mines, and punji sticks tipped in human feces. After the war, he'd win acclaim for his novel, *Tiger the Lurp Dog*.

In six months I'd be behind bars, suffocating in the 110-degree heat of the Wayne County Jail. During the summer of 1967 Detroit was on fire, and the cells were overflowing with rioting blacks. I slept on the floor, the third man in a two-man cell. At night the cockroaches came out from behind the crack in the commode, and I woke in the middle of the night picking them out of my nose. Henry, a mug artist, would teach me how to empty the toilet bowl and talk through the pipes to the women's floor. He had a girlfriend there, though he had never seen her. Another guy got connected to an evangelist, who sent him the entire Bible through the pipes. And he read it, one page a day. When the Bible was history, still he awaited trial.

Miller crawled on his belly and dug his fingernails into the earth, hid in thorny bushes, and muffled the sound of shitting his pants when Charlie passed.

I sat in a concrete cell and studied the patterns of water stains on the ceiling.

Yes, we were both in training, and we both got what we deserved.

Two snapshots: a thin, pale young man standing in a brick courtyard, his arm around a pretty girl in a short pink dress. He wears army-surplus fatigues. A cigarette fits easily in his free hand, and there is a nonchalant, fatalistic smirk on his face, like some Mexican revolutionary trying to psyche-down a firing squad.

The second print shows an equally tender-aged man leaning against a bunker of soil-filled burlap bags. An M-16 in one hand, a cheap magazine entitled *SEX* displayed in the other. He has a cigarette, too, stuck in his grinning lips. If looks could kill. . . .

13

The Conquest of Florida

The 137-mile coast of Georgia is deceptively rugged. Its dominant features are the narrow sounds—Ossabaw, St. Catherines, Sapelo, Doboy, Altamaha, and St. Andrew—formed by fast-moving rivers that rumble down to the ocean through the wild marshland. Not since the most remote regions of northeastern Maine had we felt such extreme isolation. The miles of wet grass block the intrusion of man, his bulldozers, highways and girdered high-rises, left begging at the distant banks of firm earth like dogs afraid of the water.

The small cruiser sneaks through the waterway with trepidation (Odysseus in Cyclops' cave), as if afraid to awaken a sleeping giant. The power of the rivers and sounds is somnambulant, waiting to bolt upright, swell, and burst.

About midway down the coast, on a peaceful side channel, lie the grassy remains of Fort Frederica. It is here that the history of Florida is first announced, on St. Simons Island. To its east is the Atlantic Ocean, the Hampton River to the north, and to the west the Frederica River. It is difficult to discern the line between land and water, lost among the grass. From the deck one sees islands of trees—palmettos and oaks—scattered in the wavering, yellow sea.

On a cool and sunny day, the west wind blew us through the rustling grass to a bend in the Frederica River and a narrow anchorage along its banks. Secured by two anchors set 180 degrees apart, the boat came to rest in range of the ancient magazine. Once armed with eighteen-pound cannon, it is all that remains of the once bustling fort. Deeper, among the live oaks, are ruins of the town — the barracks, guardroom, storehouse, and a handful of houses. The preserved battlements are made of coquina, a shell-stone cement, and the houses tabby, hand-laid of burnt oyster shells and concrete. Crude as they seem, these solid walls represented a significant improvement over the primitive thatched palmetto huts in which the pioneers first lived.

Fort Frederica was founded in 1736 by James Oglethorpe, operating under a grant from King George II of England. Forty-four men and seventy-two women and children raised the buildings and gathered the earthworks that were meant to forestall Spain's frequent campaigns to expand its sphere of influence north of St. Augustine, Florida.

When war broke out between Spain and England in 1739, Oglethorpe protected his town with a ten-foot-wide moat, then set out to attack St. Augustine. Nine hundred troops and eleven hundred Creek and Yamacraw Indian allies laid siege to the Castillo de San Marcos. But after several months Oglethorpe was unable to breach its defenses and returned to Fort Frederica.

Two years later Spain took the initiative. The governor of Florida, Manuel de Montiano, led a force to within sight of Fort Frederica, but was repelled. Later that same day Oglethorpe's 42nd Regiment of Foot surprised the retreating Spaniards at Bloody Marsh. The water ran red among the reeds, and by day's end the British had scored a decisive victory.

The years rolled on, and with the coming of peace Fort Frederica was of little use to the Crown. By 1760 the town was abandoned.

Fort Frederica is now a state park, managed by rangers knowledgeable about every detail of its history and fauna . . . except, we regretted to learn, the distance to the nearest convenience store. Seeing that we had arrived by boat, a ranger seduced us into trekking up the road for a fresh supply of milk. "It's 'bout, oh, half a mile; three-quarters at most," the ranger motioned. "I mention it to you 'cause lots of cruisers ask where to buy food." We succumbed. After all, baby's bones require a quart a day, without which, Andra believed, its legs would warp like noodles.

Despite repeated victimization at the hands of well-meaning people who drive and never walk, we had yet to learn our lesson. Just before sunset we set out. The store was more than two miles away, and by the time we returned old Ra was saying goodnight to San Francisco.

As we crept southward, Andra and I endeavored to learn what we could of the towns along the waterway. St. Simons Island is illustrative of the rich history we encountered. Besides the fighting at Fort Frederica, the earnest researcher learns of a visit in the sixteenth century by French explorers Ribault, Laudonnière, and Le Moyne. The accompanying Jesuits and later the Franciscan order of missionaries failed in their pious attempts to convert the heathen Indians to Christianity. With Oglethorpe sailed John and Charles Wesley, who later founded Methodism. The U.S. frigate *Constitution*—Old Ironsides—was planked with St. Simons oak; Aaron Burr found respite on the island following his famous duel with Alexander Hamilton. James Audubon visited, and poet Sidney Lanier wrote of the Marshes of Glynn as stretching "leisurely off, in a pleasant plain, to the eternal blue of the main."

And the people are not beyond manufacturing their own histories, myths, and legends, kept alive by the memories of lesser-known personalities. Consider the slaves unloaded from a ship at Dunbar Creek, who, turning away from shore, marched together into deep water singing, "The water brought us in, the water will take us away." It is said the clanking of chains still can be heard on eerie nights.

Two more days of motoring brought us to the St. Marys River, and suddenly we found ourselves crossing the magical boundary into Florida. Mile 713. Its very name makes you feel ten degrees warmer. We anchored off the town wharf at Fernandina Beach and rowed ashore.

The enormous electrical plant that rears up behind town like

153

Godzilla belied the charm of the stuccoed, Spanish-style buildings. It bore a canny resemblance to any dusty, tumbledown village in Mexico, where the sun beats on the trees and tiles, as if shade were its sworn enemy; the dirt builds in the gutters and catches in the eyes for wont of rain.

The once-famous welcome station that dispensed free orange juice was gone, the first indication that cruisers are not as welcome in the Sunshine State as they once were. Anchoring restrictions and occasional outright prohibitions are on the increase in fashionable Florida communities. Ninety-six-hour anchoring limits are intended to keep out the "dirtbaggers," the motley assortment of vagabonds, deadheads, boozers, free spirits, and ne'er-do-wells who drift down from the north in all manner of derelict craft. Where they run aground they stay, for without money for repairs the shallow sand is all that keeps them from sinking into oblivion. Locals complain that the dirtbaggers land their dinghies on private property, dump garbage in private dumpsters, attract nefarious types who traffic in drugs, play loud music, and generally create a blight on the water. The waterfront owners pay big bucks for waterviews, and they'll be damned if some ratty-haired, rheumy-eyed sailor, bleached as a piece of driftwood, is going to ruin their perfect peace.

In fairness, they all—according to some authorities—may claim a constitutional right to the ocean and its adjacent waterways. Some court cases have ruled in their favor, but most side with municipal interests.

Andra and I were sensitive to local attitudes as we pressed on. Our immediate destination was Boca Raton, where she was to have her first obstetric examination. Boca Raton—where there are no marinas, no anchoring, no jogging without a T-shirt, and no music that can be heard from more than fifty feet away—is an overrated, overpriced enclave of yuppies, millionaire contractors, and retirees where liveaboards are prohibited. Even town residents aren't allowed to sleep on their boats at their own docks!

But the anchoring ordinances didn't bother us, only because we saw no purpose in dallying. Miami and the Keys lay more than three hundred miles distant, and we still weren't warm.

✳

The waterway runs like a knife cut down the coast. The shore turns tropical, with palms shading the modest homes, a runabout at every dock. This is fish country. The men and boys, and sometimes even the wives, sit four-abreast in their Sears aluminum jonboats, rods poised and bobbers bobbing. And when, perchance, a fish is hooked, not the slightest exclamation is heard. A pair of pliers calmly wrenches the hook free of the gaping jaw, the fish is tossed into a bucket, the line rebaited, and the bent posture resumed, as if the fisherman had merely tossed a few coins into a church collection cup. These are the golden years on a platinum budget.

Everywhere comical brown pelicans divebomb jumping mullet, swallowing the catch in their pouches with a jerky, ghastly convulsion. In the shallows herons and snowy egrets patiently stalk minnows, and the shore rustles with the movement of other animals, heard for an instant but never seen.

"I'm finally starting to relax," I said to Andra. "We've finally made it to Florida, and now we know we'll make our doctor's appointment on time."

Andra looked up from her book, paused, and said, "If I get any more relaxed, you'll have to carry me off this boat in one of those canvas bags."

Aside from Eric the Red's voyage to North America about 1000 AD, or perhaps St. Brendan's visit in a leather coracle during the sixth century, America's earliest history leads to the northeastern coast of Florida. In the fifteenth century, the Canaries and Azores were the outposts of European civilization. Men whose names we will never know set out and wandered back, telling of islands that shimmered on the horizon as perfect as clouds. Eventually these stories amalgamated the islands into one—Antilia. A map made by Beccario in 1435 expanded the picture, showing four islands west of Portugal—Antilia, Reylla, Salvagio, and I in Mar. Antilia, meaning "the island opposite," is supposed now to be Cuba; Reylla appears as Jamaica; and I in Mar, perhaps one of the Bahamas. But there is little doubt that Salvagio, the "Isle of Savages," is none other than Florida.

Christopher Columbus landed in the Bahamas in 1492, and perhaps in the following years some Spanish sails were sighted by the Tekesta Indians along the Florida shore. The first reliable account of the coast is credited to John Cabot, who sailed down the East Coast past Florida until, according to biographer Richard Hakluyt, ". . . hee had the Island of Cuba on his left hand, in manner in the same degree of longitude."

But it was Juan Ponce de Leon who earned the distinction of being the first white man to land on the flat and hostile peninsula. (And no, he was not in search of the fabled Fountain of Youth; this was total fabrication on the part of the historian Herrera, who borrowed liberally from the relation of a folktale by Fontaneda, a Spanish lad who had been held captive by Indians.) Bounced from his governorship in Puerto Rico, Ponce de Leon gained a grant from Charles V to explore and settle Salvagio. In 1513 he landed somewhere near Cape Canaveral and named it La Florida—"flowery Easter."

More would come—Navarez, Hernando de Soto, and the castaways of treasure ships wrecked along the cost. Ironically it was the French who established the first colonial settlement in Florida. Jean Ribault sailed across the Atlantic in 1562 and built a camp at Port Royal, just north of St. Augustine. A year later the men were gone, dead, or enslaved by Indians.

Three years later Menéndez de Avilés came on the scene. Like his Spanish forebears, he envisioned a land of great wealth—gold, silver, tobacco, and silk. Florida historian Marjory Stoneman Douglas tells of his conquest: "On August 28, 1565, Menéndez went ashore and took possession and named the place St. Augustine. He had encountered the French fleet under Jean Ribault sailing to the relief of Fort Caroline. He took Fort Caroline, killed or took prisoner all the people of the fort, marched with difficulty by land to St. Augustine, fought Indians, captured a group of French from Ribault's fleet, and had all but about eighteen Catholics among them killed. There was not food enough for both conquerors and prisoners. Menéndez was now master in the north." From that bloody beginning, America traces its first permanent city.

*

On December 5 we raised our anchor from the shallow, sandy depths of the Fort George River and left behind unexplored the old plantation grounds. Late that afternoon we anchored in St. Augustine, off the Castillo de San Marcos. Busloads of tourists and military personnel disgorged on the waterfront. Sightseeing trolleys circled the narrow sector, and the distorted voices of tour guides carried across the water to our mooring. A reenactment of some military maneuver was underway, and the town was gaily prepared.

Rowing ashore we found men and women dressed in period costumes, playing the parts of colonial housewives, bakers, smithies, and soldiers. In the parks and yards conquistadores and redcoats bivouacked, muskets were stacked in tripods, small fires readied for the night, and a score of cannon stood sentinel. The scene was reminiscent of Newport, where history buffs reenact French general Rochambeau's breaking of the British blockade during the Revolutionary War and his triumphant landing at King's Point—right down to the Newport Field Artillery's cannon, popcorn wagons, and fudge factories.

Day by day the weather was more kind to us, and now and then we bared our skin to the sun and sky. In Daytona we stumbled onto a great boatyard for do-it-yourself cruisers. The Seven Seas Marina is a funky community of long-term hangers-on, who are usually found at the small restaurant on the grounds. Our waitress was proud of the food. "Made from scratch," she said. "And there's pinochle Friday nights." It was a comfortable, unpretentious scene we would not often see in South Florida.

But we were still in central Florida, and a good number of days were spent on the 120-mile-long Indian River, an area famous for its citrus crop. The trimly marked channel of the waterway does little to disturb the widening of the river, known as Mosquito Lagoon. It is 3 or so miles wide and very shallow. One night we found ourselves unable to tuck behind one of the spoil islands and were forced to anchor in a hard-to-find six-foot spot a hundred feet off the dredged channel. The wind blew, and clouds covered the stars. No lights marred the perfect blackness, and I slept restlessly until the morning when the sound of a lobsterman retrieving his traps ended my strange dreams of interplanetary travel.

En route to Melbourne, a Florida Marine Patrol airplane buzzed us three times before losing interest. The drug-smuggling hysteria intensifies as one moves closer to the Cuban refugee camp otherwise known as Miami. Random boardings by the patrol boats become frequent, and by the time you reach Biscayne Bay the water is roiled by the wakes of innumerable agencies—Customs and Immigration, Florida Marine Patrol, the Dade County Sheriff's Department, and the Food and Drug Administration— all crisscrossing in flashy Cigarette-type speedboats, chasing suspects, and, on occasion I imagine, chasing themselves. Indeed, we once saw a police video crew in a Cigarette chasing other agents in a Cigarette, apparently, we were told, for the purpose of documenting a possible arrest.

We anchored at Eau Gallie, a pleasant harbor rimmed by neatly manicured homes and several marinas. The trawlers and motor-yachts were festooned with Christmas lights, and along the docks the yachties and cruisers clinked glasses and passed unbreakable plates of hors d'oeuvres.

In the middle of the night the boat suddenly shuddered, and it seemed we had dragged anchor and run aground. I poked my head out the hatch and saw a dark form in the water. It was our first manatee, lumbering dizzily away from our anchor chain, snorting and wheezing in the still, soft air.

At Wabasso Beach, a sign on shore advertised dock space for five dollars. The pier was gray and rickety. It was no marina, and only a few old houses, set back from the water, interrupted the thick vegetation along the water's edge. A narrow dirt road followed the shore, but there were no cars. I pulled in and ran a sliver deep into my palm tying the lines. Soon, a tall old man ambled up with three grapefruits, which he exchanged for our dock fee.

Afterward he presented me with his card—Jones' Pier. Wabasso Beach.

"Lived here sixty-eight years," he said. "Used to have a lot more fish, but where man comes, Nature moves out. Snook, yellowfin, whiting, we had them all. Manatees, too. I remember my Daddy killin' them right off this pier. Good meat, but you won't find many left who've tasted it."

I stood next to him on the dock, arms folded, nodding assent as he waved his arm across the water, beholding the domain of his long life in this humid jungle.

"We have a blue heron that's been here thirteen years," he continued. "I call him the Democrat, 'cause when we have fishermen on the dock, he comes around and begs!" He didn't laugh, just looked at me hard as if to say, "Don't say nuthin' derogatory 'bout Ronnie Reagan!"

Mr. Jones owned a small orchard, and I was surprised when he told me he sold fruit "mostly to the Japs."

Soon we had passed the so-called Space Coast and Treasure Coast and found ourselves on the Gold Coast, the famed stretch of condos and beaches that runs from Palm Beach to Miami. You can't see the beach from the waterway, but you tread in the shadows of pink-and-blue towers where the widows and pensioners buzz like honeybees in their great cinderblock hives.

And on the water there are other telltale signs. Long, evil-looking muscle boats plow deep furrows in the congested waterway as they slash between drinking orgies at places such as Bar Balu, Shooters, and Dirty Nellie's. The drivers are skinny blond guys and dark Latinos with open shirts and gold chains as bright as supernovas. The girls lounging on the rear sunning mattresses wear string suits, and their hair is whipped like Old Glory as they burn by. They are unsmiling, perhaps a little afraid of high speeds, perhaps a little disdainful of sailboats that drag their feet like crossbearers.

We stopped for two weeks to see friends in Boca Raton, 332 miles *into* Florida. Dave Landmann had arranged for us to use a dock at his grandmother's house. Just as we turned off the water-way we hit a submerged log. Thunk! *Adriana* shuddered. I backed off the throttle, inspected the bilges, then returned to the helm and inched into the canal. There was an unmistakable vibration corresponding to engine speed. I cursed our luck, realizing all too clearly that the propeller had been bent again.

With the boat safely berthed, we called Ken and Karyn Green, who hosted our weary carcasses in a spare bedroom. The next day Andra had her obstetric examination. Dr. Daniels pronounced mother and baby healthy, prescribed vitamins, and issued a bill for $780 — the difference between his fee and what our insurance company considered "customary." Malpractice insurance is especially high in Florida, we were told.

With newfound confidence and security, Andra lounged by the Greens' pool and picked tangerines for breakfast. The wind couldn't reach us here behind the citrus trees and coconut palms. And when we stirred, the beads of sweat on our foreheads broke into rivulets and rolled down our cheeks.

Warm at last! Warm at last! Thank God Almighty, warm at last!

14

The Keys Disease

Andra did not find it difficult to leave *Adriana* during our brief stay in Boca Raton. To her great relief, her tummy had at last popped out, declaring to the world it was not a potbelly but the home of a real baby-to-be. But with it came a sudden sense of caution—maintaining an extra margin of distance between it and kitchen counters, taking stairsteps one at a time, and, when sailing, a fear of falling overboard.

She began to lose her sense of balance and crawled whenever she left the cockpit. Where once she had been afraid to steer with other boats around, she now willingly took the helm rather than teeter to the foredeck for sail changes or anchoring duty. She took the adage, "one hand for the ship, one for yourself," to include arms, legs, feet, teeth, and any other body parts that could affix themselves to the boat. If she had awoken one morning as Spider Woman, she would not have been disappointed.

At the same time we began to meet fellow cruisers who had already been to the Bahamas that winter. Skip Clements, owner of an Alberg 30, was one. He was a former National Outdoor Leadership School instructor from Alaska. Whitewater kayaking, mountaineering, and fly-fishing were his specialties. Tall and lanky, with an untrimmed mustache that dangled below his chin like strings of yarn, he was fond of Roman sandals and Iditarod T-shirts. Dave Landmann brought him to breakfast one morning at the Olympiad, a Boca health club. He'd just flown back from George Town, Exuma, to see his girlfriend, and he painted a grim picture. Cold and windy northers, he advised, were running through the islands at the rate of two to three a week, pinning the cruising community down like marines on the beaches of Iwo Jima.

Andra and I conferred, ultimately deciding to postpone our Bahamas cruise until summertime, after the baby arrived. Native Floridians, we were told, fled across the Gulf Stream in July and August for the breezy, less humid island climate. In the interim we would dally in the Keys, investigate the vast and mysterious Everglades, sail up Florida's west coast as far as Tampa Bay, then return via the Okeechobee Waterway to Boca Raton by April 1 for the Big Wait.

Immediately she relaxed. Her mother sent maternity tops, her hips splayed, and she began to waddle with a newfound confidence. Her skin darkened, her lips moistened, and the radiant glow of motherhood—that indescribable quality she had so long envied—was now hers.

Our first mail since the Chesapeake caught up with us at the Greens, long-awaited letters from family, friends, and even a few from *Cruising World* readers. Many were heart-wrenching: "I cry for a kid I never knew." "How you can go on is beyond me." One reader sent an electronic transponder she hoped we would pin to the baby's diaper when it was born, so it would set off an alarm if it fell overboard—she didn't want us to lose another child. Another wrote, "Hopefully, when you get offshore again, and I feel that you must be longing for that unique comfort, as the stars rise and set and again you feel one with the powers that be, you will be able to enjoy what your son has taught you. I hope that you will find amongst the pain something that can explain all this. It hurts to think how you'll get on."

Then there was Kenn Miller's letter:

It is very hard for me to write any letter these days, and this one is particularly hard. I hope you will be indulgent if somehow I write anything insensitive or stupid.

Pete's personality and spirit — and a good part of his intelligence — hadn't been touched by the medical malpractice attendant to his birth. Think about it . . . if Pete weren't your son, but rather a kid we grew up with, we would have wanted him for our friend, just as his friends did. Pete was game for all the adventures, all the ideas boys his age have. Sure, his handicap killed him, but it never stopped him, did it? If he'd been growing up in Hannibal, Huck and Tom would have been tossing pebbles against his window, inviting him to sneak off to join their outlaw gang. The kid went out in the only classy way a kid can go out — dying on a forbidden adventure.

Fuck all the motherfuckers, fuck all the stumblecatchers, cut the harnesses, and go, my man! Live your life out to the end, and don't let them stop you! The boy caught your genes, and old Caesar [Pete's labrador that died a year earlier] always set a good example for him, and though I'll miss them both for the rest of my life, I don't see any cause to get too maudlin over either of them, when it's so much easier and more accurate just to honor them instead.

You knew Caesar, and you know Pete, and you know that when it's something as common to us male mammals as youthful, dangerous adventure, we got to deal in our brothers and uncles, at least among the carnivores, primates, and toothed whales, and maybe the elephants as well. Pete's old Uncle Caesar was a sure scout for genius, tolerated the friendly, spirited, clumsy pup, and saw the promise in him. Hwei-li [Kenn's Taiwanese wife] once commented on the fact that Pete would watch Caesar closely, and Caesar would pretend to ignore him, but always be glancing over, or surreptitiously nudging Pete's shoes with his nose. Pete studied Caesar, and learned from him. As you know, I am serious. I think Pete lived an absolutely complete life, and lived it to the end with modest courage and indomitable spirit, and I think we ought to give Caesar his due credit in forming Pete's character. And so, this male mammal solidarity is true.

Danny Keirns had said the same thing to me about adventuring the night of Pete's death. Sometimes you have to step back from your life and imagine it as a stage play. Have you got your role right? How do you look? Don't be a punk or a snitch, a stumble-catcher, or a Walter Mitty. Do the right thing. To think that Pete acted true to his nature was more comforting than accepting the rationalization of those who said he was better off dead than handicapped. And many did.

The parents of other CP kids wrote, some lucky, others pinned to the wall with their own grief. Parents who had lost perfectly normal children wrote. The father of a fourteen-year-old girl copied a poem found among her things:

> *Love is an image of how you feel and what you want to be,*
> *A reflection on the way you live and what you like to see,*
> *A picture you paint of yourself and the things you like to do,*
> *An impression left about the ones that mean so much to you.*

This set me to thinking about the importance placed on memories. More specifically, the dead, we are told, live on in our recollection of them. It is a poor substitute for the real corpus, or even the belief that they persist in a glorified and heavenly form, full-faced, radiating golden rays. I didn't find much comfort in memories, because when I die my memories will go with me, orphaning Pete to the blank universe. Who will think of him then? Berkeley's god?

You find yourself reduced to the simple notion that your thoughts of the deceased may yet bring some pleasure. After all, it is the condition of the living that causes the problem. It's no sweat to Peter, because he no longer exists. But as I replay my memories, is there nothing more complex or heroic going on than an attempt to salvage some happiness from loss? Have we nothing more to grasp than what philosophers call a motivational theory of pleasure?

Where is Pete? That's what we want to know. The answer: He is molecules of ash floating in the water and resting in the earth. He is an idea in my mind. This must suffice, and strangely, on figuring it out, it helps.

An old black-and-white photograph in my album: Pete, age three, sits on the hill below the house, his left arm raised to Caesar's sturdy neck. The guardian dog sits on his haunches, his large head poised over Pete's. Both look out toward the road, from whence I will never come driving home again, though Caesar's head is cocked a little, as if he sees something. And beyond the road and through the trees, there is the faint outline of the railroad berm and the empty tracks.

South Florida is hard to love, yet millions of people do. Most are over fifty-five and have bought condos on the coast on doctors' orders, their children's orders, or God's. We met a couple who cited directives from all three — "I have bursitis," the wife said, "in my elbow, see?" She showed it to me. "Doctor told me to move some place warm. My daughter said, 'Good idea. We'd love to visit.' I wasn't so sure they weren't trying to get rid of me!" She laughed. "For years I put it off. Then one Sunday I went to church and asked God. He said go, I'd suffered enough."

I was used to Newport's tourist season, heaviest during July and especially August, when the waterfront chokes and the locals never, ever go near it, but I was unprepared for their numbers in South Florida. A population of some six million swells twofold. They come from every corner of the United States, and many from Canada and Europe. And they arrive by every means: airplane, car, pickup truck, limousine, motorhome, and (how could I forget) boats, large and small, fast and slow. They fill the KOA campgrounds, fish camps, motels, hotels, houses, townhouses, garden homes, villas, condominiums, marinas, efficiencies, inefficiencies, unlocked cars, beach cabanas, and tiki bars. No vacancy. Make your reservation now for next year.

Andra and I arrived about the same time as several million other people. But never having spent a summer in Florida, when the bridge clubs, jewelry stores, and bagel shops fold up like stage props, we were unaware of this great transmigration. Dave Landmann loaned us his car for a week, and as we drove up and down the highway growth rings along the coast, Andy kept remarking at the crowds, "Doesn't anybody work?"

Six-month resident: "No."
Twelve-month resident: "As little as possible."

In South Florida there are no town centers, no pillared institutions or bricked banks, no commons or band shelters, nor any visible center of gravity to control the milieu that whirls about ungoverned by any natural law.

In fact, if there is a community order in South Florida, it is measured by how far you are from the coast, not by the miles north of Ft. Lauderdale or the proximity to Coconut Grove.

"Where did you say you live?"

"One block from the Intracoastal."

This is the way it works: The very richest live on the ocean—the Donald Trumps and Bebe Rebozos—which means beachside of the barrier islands. In descending order of wealth follow furniture tycoons and talk-show hosts on the waterway side of the islands, Cadillac dealers on the mainland shore of the waterway, and law partners and land developers on the hayfork pattern of canals. The rest of the sweltering masses are shoved far enough inland to be out of sight and out of mind.

Real-estate ads that say "East of 95" mean homes for the upwardly mobile close to the expressway. Nobody says "West of 95." Instead, confusing maps are printed in the newspapers and buyers' guides that attempt to hide the expressway and the fact you are now ten miles from the Atlantic Ocean. What an embarrassment!

Worse are the yuppie developments east of the Florida Turnpike, where builders have drained the unprotected portions of the Everglades. A large pit is dug, pumped full of water, and called a "lake." Cheaply constructed townhouses are erected seemingly overnight and termed "waterfront properties." Hundreds of units form concentric circles around the shallow, brown pond, and the community is called something enchantingly tropical like "Banyan Bayou" or "Pelican Harbour." "The Palms of Puerto del Mar—because you've earned it!"

*

Ken and Karyn Green chauffeured us one evening to the Christmas Boat Parade. The Cove Marina leans over the Intracoastal Waterway at the Boca Raton–Deerfield town line; two tiers of decks and a gas dock maximize waterside seating. Ten dollars parade cover, and no, the steel band won't be playing tonight.

Ken, a professional helicopter pilot and quick-escape artist from all formal and overpriced functions, led us around the entrance by way of the charter-boat docks to a vantage point near the bait shop. In the fragrant night sky hovered the Goodyear blimp, its supergraphic, digital message proclaiming, "Pompano Beach Christmas Boat Parade is nation's oldest."

A whoop and a cheer erupted from the crowd when the first sportfishermen idled past. The big diesels gave a throaty burble, and the miles of colored lights blinked. On the foredeck was a real palm tree, and underneath it sat a covey of bikini-clad girls waving at us. Bands, replete with amps and synthesizers, rocked out the night, and girls in leotards danced the boogaloo until the decks oilcanned and the skipper shouted *no mas!* More followed, some with ingenious designs rivaling the floats in the Rose Bowl parade. But the main attractions were the antics of owners and guests pouring champagne over each other as if their team had just won the World Series.

Later we met the professional captain of a fifty-foot motoryacht. It wasn't in the parade but had been decorated with fifteen thousand dollars worth of lights for the annual yacht-club party. The owner was president of a car dealership. At Christmastime he gave to his most valued friends and customers Buck knives containing the message: "God is chairman of the board of my company."

Just before Christmas we embarked for the Keys. We were two days in Miami, our progress slowed by seventeen highway bridges, many restricted during rush hour. This area is called the "Washing Machine" for the pandemonium of wakes that crash and reverberate between the concrete seawalls, or "Condo Canyon," where the biggest danger (or so the saying goes), is being hit by a potted geranium.

Near Hollywood we were overtaken by three thirty-foot sport-fishermen. They were trying to keep their wakes down, but I could sense an edginess in the throttles. Behind, a dinner-cruise boat sped forward and climbed up their sterns. When the skippers turned and noticed, to their collective horror, that the huge steel bow was nearly even with their tuna towers, they put their hammers down.

I saw it coming, a row of parallel wakes high as the seawall. The trick is to turn into them just before impact. No problem. But as I was about to whip the wheel over, the cruise boat passed. To cross courses would have been suicidal.

The first wave rolled *Adriana* deeply to starboard. In the trough she came back to port. It would have been a graceful recovery had she not been battered by the second and third waves. The mast spreaders swung precipitously close to the seawall, and when she crashed back the lockers below emptied. Dishes, silverware, skillets, pans, cans, coffee, bananas, rice pilaf, tiger sauce, garlic cloves, sprouting potatoes, and a gentle rain of dried onion skins covered the cabin sole. The only sentimental loss was a glass coffee pot, which shattered.

By the time *Adriana* settled, I felt like a cowboy thrown from an unbroken horse. My instinct was to unleash a row of obscenities, but the noise was deafening and we were lost in a cloud of filthy diesel smoke. Our helplessness angered me. I wanted to kick something out of sheer frustration. Then Andra calmly picked up the pieces and, by example, hushed me.

We skipped Miami, too anxious to slip under the Rickenbacker Causeway Highway Bridge at Mile 1091, kill the engine, and raise the sails. There wasn't much wind that day, and it took a long time to make the last miles to Hurricane Harbor on Key Biscayne. But we were in open water at last, free to turn left or right, with no pressing need to make ten miles or forty or none at all. For two days that's just what we did — none at all.

A priority was changing the propeller. The boat still shuddered from the bent blade. I'd bought a new one in Ft. Lauderdale, but hadn't wanted to dive in the murky canals.

At the entrance to Hurricane Harbor is a shallow sandbar, protected from wind and wave. The water is clear as lead crystal. Just after high tide I ran the boat gently aground. *Adriana* draws nearly 5 feet loaded for cruising; a 2½-foot tide would leave her radically heeled and the propeller just below the water.

But I was anxious to work with the sun high. I taped a five-foot length of clear vinyl hose to the end of my snorkel and slipped over the side, wrenches in hand. From the cockpit Andra held the hose end above water. My breathing was labored just two feet underwater, but it gave me enough time to remove the cotter pin and unscrew the retaining nut. Then I assembled the wheelpuller I'd bought in Elkton, Maryland, thinking smugly that its cost could now be amortized over two jobs. I dove again. A weight belt would have kept me from floating up under the hull, but I managed to wrap a leg around the rudder and work upright with both hands. As the propeller came off I dropped the square metal key that keeps it from spinning on the shaft. In vain I studied the bottom, which was shells and marl that blew up in soft, white clouds whenever I touched it. Fortunately, I had an oversize spare, and with a good hacksaw and file was able to make it fit.

By the time I had finished, the tide had dropped enough to expose the propeller shaft, and the boat sat heavily on its side. I had made the job more difficult than necessary but was glad I had proved the hose breathing system worked. A year later, however, a physician who had read my account of the episode in *Cruising World* chided my foolishness, warning that I could easily have ruptured some blood vessels, hemorrhaged, and died.

With the new propeller in place there was nothing to do but wait for the tide. The angle of heel made it difficult to get comfortable in the cockpit, so we climbed on deck and read books. At the harbor entrance two young men threw castnets for bait fish, and on shore several teenagers laughed at us, yelling "Land ahoy!" Gulls squawked on exposed sandbars, herons probed the shallows, and pelicans executed their crazy kamikaze dives. Three kids poled a raft across the flats, calling to passersby for a lift.

A retired gentleman named Fred rowed over from his big cruiser in the harbor to ask if we required assistance. He recommended a stop at Boca Chica Key, fifteen miles south. The island is part of the Biscayne Bay National Park and has a large basin where one can tie up free of charge. Fred told us how to pilot in through the many shallow bars, then left us to continue our wait alone.

The sun set in a blaze, and when the last light melted into darkness *Adriana* floated free. I started the engine, Andra retrieved the anchors with the electric windlass, and we headed into the safety of the harbor. Strangely, the boat did not seem to respond to the throttle. I revved the engine and slowly, almost imperceptibly, we inched forward. Then the awful truth dawned on me. I had given the propeller shop the wrong dimensions! I had specified a 13 × 9 wheel instead of 13 × 15. (I had remembered the prop dimensions that fit the old Westerbeke engine.) The pitch was way off, spinning madly, uselessly. Cursing my stupidity, we anchored in Hurricane Harbor. There was nothing to be done but live with the problem until I could get the old propeller straightened once again. At least, now, we had the option of sailing.

While Andra fixed dinner I got out the fishing rod and tried to work off my anger casting a finger mullet lure into the still water. Much to my surprise, I caught fish number three of the cruise — a catfish, which I had no desire to skin, and so threw it back.

The familiar Florida Keys slogan reads: "Better than the Bahamas!" Indeed, the two island chains are quite different — culturally, topographically, and, thanks to tourism and pollution, zoologically as well. What they have in common is near-tropical weather, clear water, and a mutual interest in American-tourist dollars.

A fundamental decision in cruising the Keys is whether to go "inside" or "outside." Boats drawing five feet or less may go inside, which is the west side, between the upper keys and the mainland tip of the Florida peninsula. The dredged channel descends through shallow Biscayne Bay, traverses sheltered sounds like Buttonwood and Blackwater, then follows the arcing chain southwest. Locals refer to the west side as "bayside," because it rims Florida Bay. Just several feet deep and dotted with tear-shaped mangrove islands, Florida Bay is great for wilderness cruising in extreme shoal-draft craft such as multihulls and sharpie-types with retractable leeboards.

The distance to Key West is 154 statute miles, for that is the system used on the Intracoastal Waterway that begins in Norfolk, Virginia, and ends in Key West at Mile 1240.

It is important to formulate a game plan before reaching the Keys, as there is only a handful of places to cross from one side to the other. After Key Biscayne, the first satisfactory channel is Angelfish Creek at the northern end of Key Largo. It is sometimes used as a departure point for Cat Cay, Bahamas, because the north-flowing current of the Gulf Stream can be used to better advantage here than when leaving from, say, Key Biscayne or Government Cut, Miami. At midtide five feet may be carried over the shoals at either entrance to Angelfish Creek. In the Keys, five to seven feet is considered deep water.

After studying the charts, my plan was to go inside as far as Angelfish, then outside the rest of the way to Key West. Despite Fred's directions into Boca Chica Key, we ran aground repeatedly and so continued on to Pumpkin Key, near the famous Ocean Reef Club at the northern end of Key Largo. There we anchored in the lee of the private island among several other cruisers.

The water was too deep for the dirtbaggers, who wash down to the Keys and catch in the mangroves like flotsam from the sea. Farther south, we would see them stuck in the shallows, erecting crude plywood shelters on derelict hulls. Unlike the mainland coast, there are few anchoring prohibitions in the Keys. And since a Florida state land-use act prohibits cutting mangroves because they are so important to keeping what little soil there is above water, these old, weathered boatmen are generally granted squatter's rights. They are escapees—from bad marriages and grunt jobs, from the tough reality of the "real world," which does not tolerate boozy breath, a dirty chin, or a man living out his days in debilitated laziness, eating only what he catches with a line and a trap.

In the morning we motored slowly through Angelfish Creek. Now we were running the engine faster and going more slowly than before—pitifully slowly! The only consolation was that we were no longer in the narrow waterway. And by crossing to the oceanside of the Keys, we could find plenty of room to sail, dodging the powerful sportfishermen that roar back and forth inside the reef.

Andra worked the helm while I dropped the hook on the Atlantic side of Key Largo. The boat swung lazily in the serene water, and I jumped overboard to cool off. It was my first recreational swim since August 18 at Horseshoe Cove, Maine. We took the dinghy ashore to buy groceries. Highway 1 runs the length of the Keys like an artery, delivering traffic north and south in one throbbing flow. The upper and middle keys are so narrow that one may walk from oceanside to bayside in minutes, assuming he doesn't become road kill while trying to negotiate the two-lane war zone.

On the way back to the boat we stopped at Sharkey's Bar. It sat directly above the water, near the charter boats. And of course stuffed fish festooned the barroom walls—grouper, yellowtail, hammerhead, and mako. Andra ordered a nonalcoholic beer.

The bartender, a woman, said, "You're pregnant, right? Years ago I was in the hospital for an appendectomy, and the only room they had was in OB/GYN. The woman next to me kept going into premature labor. So the doctors stuck an alcohol drip in her arm, and at night she could have any drink she wanted. I mean they kept her drunk! She always chose red wine. Today that kid is fourteen, and I mean to tell you she loves to drink!" The bartender turned to fill a mug, then winked over her shoulder, "Red wine, of course!"

Andra turned in early. As I read, the wind shifted and gained strength. The bow heaved up and down in the building waves. At midnight I climbed into the cockpit for my customary look around. To my horror, the beach was just yards behind *Adriana's* stern. Somehow we had dragged without my knowing it. I turned on the depthsounder—five feet! The boat was just inches from the bottom, and as I reached to start the engine, the keel hit. Thud!

I ran forward and shook Andra. "We're dragging," I said. "Better get up."

"Now?" Andra asked sleepily.

"Soon as you can."

She murmured assent.

I turned the switch for the electric windlass and climbed back into the cockpit. Minutes passed.

"Andra?"

There was no answer.

I ran back down and found her sleeping like a baby.

"Now!" I yelled.

She had an irritated look in her eye. "Why didn't you say so the first time?"

The rest was easy. The anchor came up smoothly, and we motored into the lee of Rodriguez Key, dropped the hook, and ran the engine in reverse to set it. I took bearings on several shore lights so we'd know if we dragged again, watched for twenty minutes, then retired.

"Happy birthday, Andra. Sorry I didn't get you anything." It was December 23.

My birthday is December 31, and we were planning no special activities for that night either. (Of course, being New Year's Eve, there is always a party.) Our combined birthday-Christmas treat was a night at the Holiday Isle Resort on Windley Key. We slept on the sandy beach, I had a rum runner at the tiki bar, and we ate dinner at the sixth-floor restaurant. Phil, the hotel's refrigeration maintenance man, said local wisdom recommends a sunrise breakfast on the oceanside and a sunset dinner on bayside. One has all day then to make it from the breakfast room to the lounge by way of the long, well-stocked bar. If you find yourself with a burger and brew at noontime, he said, with dead soldiers to your left and armed commandos waiting to your starboard, you'll have glimpsed the sinister, bloody-eyed, liver-riddling implications of the Keys Disease.

15

The End of the Road

As we sailed down the Keys, *Adriana* reveled in her newfound freedom. Following the Hawk Channel, the five-mile distance between islands and reef, gave us room to tack at will. Much of the time, however, the wind blew from the north, so we eased the sheets and rode the galloping waves closer to the bottom of America. Not since the rugged, rocky coast of Maine and the tumultuous sounds of Georgia had we felt the excitement of passing into new country, the oaks and elms supplanted by black mangroves and cabbage palms, the brown soil giving way to white sand, and the dark clouds of New England and the gray mid-Atlantic states blown away by balmy trade winds. The color of the water was the brilliant aqua featured in travel advertisements, and the sun, hot and white, a most regular fellow. You're not in the true Tropics, but it's close enough (though there is West Indian vegetation in South Florida, in the continental United States sixty-three miles is as close as you can get to the Tropic of Cancer).

I was anxious to see both sides of the Keys and, after studying the charts in great detail, decided to cross back over to bayside. Depths of just five and six feet were recorded, but there was a margin of safety if we sailed on a high tide. Channel Five is a deep-water cut under Highway 1 that would enable us to spend a day in the comparatively calm waters of Florida Bay. Twenty miles farther south it would be necessary to return to the Atlantic side, at Marathon on Vaca Key. We were scheduled to meet Adria in

Newfound Harbor, twenty-five miles east of Key West, where her boyfriend's parents owned a small plot of beachfront. After New Year's we'd sail together to Key West.

When Peter was six years old, he and I had sailed these same Keys on assignment for *Cruising World*. I had billed the cruise to him as "a week with the guys." He straightened his shoulders a little, puffed out his bony chest, and whispered, "Guess it wouldn't be much fun without me."

Crewing with us, from my near-forgotten life as a hospital administrator, was my old mentor Gene Correll. After my parole from prison, St. Joseph's Mercy Hospital was the only business that would hire me; the others said, "Our firm is proud of its civic involvement, its participation in federal youth programs, and its minority employment record. We will give your application serious consideration, but these things take time. . . . Don't call us, we'll call you."

For several years I languished in menial clerical capacities, and it was not until Gene Correll replaced the administrator in charge of my department that I had a chance to demonstrate my abilities. Equally important, he reintroduced me to sailing. He taught me basic navigation, the Rules of the Road, how to trim the sails, and how to pinch the bow in a gust to spill wind from the sails. In the chill of autumn he and I sailed his twenty-three-foot trailer-sailer across Lake Michigan. It was my first overnight cruise, and I felt as though I were treading on holy waters, partaking of some strange, mystical rite.

Now I had left Ann Arbor, a promising career in hospital administration, and was learning a new trade as a sailing-magazine editor. By inviting him to join Pete and me in the Keys I was making a first attempt to repay his many kindnesses.

Pete, Gene, and I anchored in the cove at Long Key. Around us were six other boats, part of the "flotilla charter" concept I was reporting on. New Zealander Barry and Canadian Lauren were the group leaders who each day shepherded us to the next anchorage. The cove water was shallow and clear, and the crews swam and snorkeled. Gene and I noted that the sun was below the proverbial yardarm and so kicked back in the cockpit with planters punches.

Suddenly Barry climbed up our stern ladder, flipped aside his face-mask, and thrust two spiny lobsters at Peter. "For you, mate!"

Pete just grinned. To him, Barry, with all his dive gear, must have looked as strange as the creature from the black lagoon.

As Andra and I sailed past Long Key, like a blind man fingering a knurled shell, my memory felt its way over all the tender details of that earlier cruise. Unsure of himself, Pete had sat on the lip of the companionway hatch, half inside the cabin and half out. He felt safe there, yet still part of the action. Aware that he was some-times in the way, his eyes would widen and he would say, "If you guys need a beer or something, just let me know."

After the cruise, Peter and I flew from Marathon to Miami. From there he would return to Michigan and I to Rhode Island. He was not afraid to fly alone; he had courage, or at the least face. When he flew with Adria, he never cried on leaving me, but this time his eyes reddened as I buckled his safety belt and playfully punched his shoulder. "I love you, Dad." Then he looked away, steeling himself, a sailor ready to go home.

That evening Andra and I anchored behind Fiesta Key. On shore was a KOA campground. The men pulled their jonboats up the launching ramp and gutted fish on the cleaning tables. Through binoculars I could see pelicans waiting for handouts, and anxious children watching as their fathers swept through the scaly bodies with long filleting knives. They threw the heads and skele-tons high in the air, and I could not distinguish between the chil-dren's shouts and the screams of hungry birds.

En route to Marathon the fish started to bite. The sage advice of a baitshop owner was this: "Forget trolling in Hawk Channel; there ain't nuthin' there. You gotta go out past the reef. But Flor-ida Bay, well sir, for whatever you got in that tackle box, there's a fish waitin'."

The problem was knowing which lure to use. I had no clue. I trailed a blue-and-silver spoon with a few scrawny feathers and in two hours had three fish. The first was a blue runner, or so I was told by a woman fishing with her family at Channel Key. I held it up as we glided by on autopilot—proudly—all eight inches of it.

The next was a yellowtail something-or-other, too small to

keep. And the last was either a lizard fish or snake fish. In any case, it had a decidedly reptilian look about it, all tail with a wide, flat head like a cottonmouth's. I had no proof it was poisonous, but I used gloves to free the hook. I lost the lure on the next cast, following a ferocious hit.

Months later Ken Green would show me how the drag knob works, letting the monofilament unwind rather than break.

"You got to let the fish run," he said. "Work him in, let him run, work him in, and so forth, until he tires." Setting the drag, of course, is a basic tenet of fishing, but it had escaped me for forty years.

Not only couldn't I think like a fish, I couldn't think like a fisherman either.

Newfound Harbor is several miles wide, bordered by Big Pine and Little Torch keys east and west, and by the smaller Newfound Harbor Keys to the south. One was the location for the film *PT 109*, the story of President John Kennedy's World War II adventures in the South Pacific. The other barrier islands are thick with mangroves on the harborside, partially cleared on the oceanside. None is connected to the big islands, and residents must commute by small boat.

I maneuvered as close as possible to Cook Island, once owned by a descendant of the famed Captain Cook. The greenish brown bottom was easily visible in the shadow of the hull. I dove to check the anchor. Drifting in the current, I watched the grasses waver, undulating softly like hula dancers, and played peekaboo with schools of small fish.

Later, Andra and I mounted the outboard motor and rode the dinghy through a shallow pass to the oceanside of Cook Island, where Adria and Aku waited for us on the Lahtis' dock. Adria had flown to Marathon the day before, and already her skin was burned pink. We hadn't seen each other since Peter's funeral and needed this time together.

Alexis and Bonnie Lahti had built their stilt home six years earlier as a winter getaway. It was rustic—a screened-in platform perched in the gumbo-limbos like a castaway's tree house. The Lahtis slept in tents on the ground, only eating meals inside. The

177

stove was fueled with propane, and a gravity-fed tank furnished water. Of Finnish descent, all of the Lahtis are industrial designers by profession and gifted artists by nature. Only Aku, the middle of three children, seemed about to swerve into another lane with his rock n' roll band.

Shyly, Aku made introductions, tossing his long blond hair out of his eyes at each name. I counted ten of them, including cousins and grandparents, all creeping and crawling from brightly colored nylon tents flung among the trees like beachballs.

Great Uncle Uolevi (" 'Wallaby' is close enough") threw tangerines at me faster than I could catch; cousin Tanya strutted about in a bronze-colored bikini with an eight-month-old baby strapped to her back; sister Aikia massaged her mother's back; and brother Taru stared boringly at the sea, thinking about boats.

The no-see-ums were just coming out when Alexis and his friend Dick Buckheim banged into the dock aboard an aluminum pontoon boat. A third, older man stood aft, arms folded, trying to keep his balance. Soon they were lugging buckets of stone crabs up the path, Alexis's share of the day's catch. Buckheim, once an advertising executive in Ann Arbor, had dropped out big time and was now living out his Robinson Crusoe fantasy in the Keys. On a nearby island he had built a fabulous home, and to it he had brought his attractive young wife, Susan, and his son, as if he were the knight errant running off with a Viking king's daughter. He also owned a fancy French restaurant in Key West called the Bagatelle, and twice a week he drove to town for menu meetings. Beyond that and the periodic inspection of his crab traps, his wife was pretty much stuck with him.

The three men turned the crabs over to Bonnie and poured themselves drinks. Alexis, his great Scandinavian gut bulging over a black bikini suit, popped a beer.

"Hey Buckheim, that's hard work! My hands are bleeding!"

Buckheim, balding, grinning with buck teeth: "I told you, I can't retire yet."

"Don't pull my leg, Buckheim, you've got life by the ass."

The old, white-haired man dropped his lanky frame on the wooden deck where the rest of the Lahtis sprawled on beach chairs and deck furniture. Suddenly I recognized him.

"Do you know Steve Spurr?" I asked.

He half turned, as if his venerable age excused him from facing me fully. "Very well."

"You're Reeve Bailey. I used to play water polo with you at the University of Michigan intramural pool."

He craned his neck a little farther. "You know Steve?"

"As best a son can."

The old man, Buckheim's father-in-law, turned away and said nothing more, letting the memory of my face sink in, trying to match it with the skinny twelve-year-old boy, who on school holidays used to follow his barrel-chested father through the university showers to the ancient pool. There, everyday at noon, the "Flounders" stripped naked and wrestled each other mercilessly, jamming the balls into the gutter, which was the goal net. Half wore caps, half were bald. The only rule was you had to let up a man pinching you. And he could only pinch if he were drowning. As a matter of pride, this repressed bunch of research scientists, academicians, and valedictorians would rather sink to the bottom than signal defeat. It was too rough for me, and I usually ended up practicing flip turns in the shallow end, thinking about the hamburger and ice cream lunch that followed in the men's union.

Andra and I spent nearly a week trying to keep up with the Lahtis. Like any overworked droid, each of them was determined to make the most of his two-week vacation. We declined offers to sleep in one of the communal tents, preferring the relative luxury of our boat. Several times each day Aku and Taru roared alongside in the family runabout, either to pick us up for dinner or en route to a shoreside excursion. Adria would stand next to the console in her swimsuit, her blond hair impossibly ratted by the wind, and her bright, blue eyes blazing with excitement.

"Sure you don't want to come, Dad?"

"No thanks."

"You going to be alright?"

"Sure. I can use the time to write."

After they tore off, leaving us gently rocking in their high-speed wake, I sank below, feeling like a fuddy-duddy. I thought I was pretty hip, letting her run off like that, but the truth was I couldn't crack my knuckles, bounce curbs on a skateboard, or name one member of the rap group Run DMC. Easy as it was to forget at times, I was somebody's dad, a "hundred-year-old fart."

Adriana, my precious baby girl, was nearly grown up, my son had beat me to the other side of the river, and I was about to start the same painfully delicious cycle all over again.

One night at dinner the conversation turned to Peter, and my heart quivered. Alexis spoke, his Nordic eyes twinkling and his big white teeth sparkling.

"Understand, I've never lost an immediate member of my family," he said, "but the three deaths that have affected me most are Ernie Kovacs's, John Kennedy's, and Peter Spurr's. He was that special." I nodded and smiled and felt the muscles in my stomach contract. I never asked how he had connected such an unlikely trio. I took for granted the heart-shock of their deaths on Alexis, knowing he spoke with sincerity.

After dinner, Alexis's father, Aarre, strolled among the palms playing his violin. The eerie sound of the strings serenading the beautiful night evoked two memories: the flute played by an unseen shepherd one night while I was anchored off St. Nicholas Island in Turkey, and a passage in the book *Eighty-eight Men and Two Women,* when the haunting strains of "Claire de Lune" played through the halls of San Quentin's death row, soothing a murderer's last night alive.

The Lahtis and Buckheims had bought their properties from a wonderful woman named Betty Brothers, who runs a small real-estate brokerage on Little Torch Key. Since 1962 she has kept pet dolphins in a man-made lagoon near her home on Newfound Harbor. Her experiences inspired a children's book and two local histories. The public is invited to the feedings, and one day I decided I must meet this woman who would live with dolphins.

She is old now, short, with a head of long white hair. There is a wisdom in her smile that I recognized, deriving, I felt, from an understanding of death. Our conversation corroborated that first impression. Dolphins, husbands, and parents in Ohio had all passed her by. After nursing her terminally ill mother, Betty turned to the sea.

"I no longer feared anything!" she wrote in her book, *Dolphins Love Our Florida Keys Home!* "I swam in the open sea every day. The ocean was my new mother; her creatures were my friends. In the wild sweep of the crystal-clear sea, I could forget the spiritual torment that I had endured for so many months. I devoured life, enjoying my swimming and skin diving. I studied and loved the wild dolphins that swam in front of our house. So, when someone told me about Milton and Virginia Santini and their pet dolphin, 'Mitzi,' I drove to Marathon to see the tame dolphin."

Mitzi had been the first star of the television show "Flipper," and Betty grew to know her intimately. Later, the Santinis caught Dal near Naples and trucked her to Betty's lagoon. Thus began a twenty-seven-year love affair, and according to Betty, the longest recorded "one person to one dolphin relationship." She taught Dal to eat dead fish and perform simple tricks, and ultimately learned how to talk to her with simple, high-pitched "Eek!" sounds. After several years a mate was found for Dal and brought to the lagoon on Little Torch Key. Dal helped Suwa adjust to this mild form of captivity, because, in fact, they were penned in by just a low, underwater fence. It was an emotional barrier rather than a physical one. The dolphins let children feed them, towed visitors around the lagoon in a dinghy, and played with Betty, who frequently donned mask and snorkel to swim with them.

Dal died at the ripe old age of twenty-seven, and though wild dolphins occasionally visit Suwa "to exchange sea tales," none has been able to lure him back to the open ocean. It seems he is a one-woman man. Once, when Suwa was sick, Dal comforted him. Betty wrote, "Like a loving wife, she worked her way in beside Suwa and placed a protective flipper over his trembling body. This gesture seemed to quiet him. Then, they slowly backed away from the beach, flipper-in-flipper like two humans arm-in-arm, and swam off together."

The next day we were having breakfast with the Lahtis at a small diner on Big Pine Key when Bonnie told us that Buckheim had shot his wife. She had heard it on the radio; police were investigating. There are no telephones on Cook Island, so she had been unable to reach either the hospital or the Buckheims' home.

Minutes later Dick burst in grinning, grabbed a chair, and sat down at our table. "Everything you've heard is untrue," he said. As Dick told it, he and Susan had heard strange noises in their yard. He suspected prowlers and loaded his .22 with ratshot. Susan preceded him out the door with a flashlight. He tripped on the sill and peppered her right shoulder. "If I'd wanted to kill her," he said, "I'd have loaded it with dumdums!"

The intruder turned out to be a raccoon. Alexis laughed and announced that henceforth, instead of Buckheim, Dick would be know as "Buckshot."

On New Year's Eve we all drove to Key West for dinner at the Bagatelle. Dick was already in town, and the plan called for Andra, Adria, and me to drive with Susan. The hospital had released her after one night, her right shoulder heavily bandaged. Halfway there, she and I realized we had gone to high school together. She was two years behind me and remembered me as a "hood." I protested, to no avail, that hippies or straights or good girls or whatever she was, mistook a person with mechanical aptitude (read: cars) for someone who hangs around soda fountains looking for nerds to bully. My rebuttals fell on deaf ears, and my best counterattack was saying that I didn't remember her at all.

The Bagatelle is one of Key West's grand old houses, built in 1884 by a sea captain named Frederick Roberts. Later, it was owned by a foreman of the Cortez Cigar Company, and in 1974 it was moved to its present location on Duval Street. Its expansive verandas were host to many parties, attended by local artists and luminaries such as Tennessee Williams. Just down the street is Sloppy Joe's, the bar made famous by Ernest Hemingway's two-fisted patronage. Dick ordered rounds of champagne, and we toasted in the New Year perched like parrots above the mayhem that swept the street below. Bearded sailors, leopard-skin tarts, neatnik gays, gypsy fortune tellers, beachcombers with skin as leathery and wrinkled as an iguana's, potato-faced college kids from Massachusetts and Illinois, one-eyed truck drivers, everyone moving in and out of the bars on a hyperhormonal mission, shouting, toasting the moon, drinking till they dropped.

The Buckheims let us borrow their van to meet my sister Jean at the Marathon airport. The Lahtis had already begun the long trek north to Michigan, and Adria was now aboard with us. We hadn't seen Jean since Ann Arbor, and she was anxious to see how we were coping. And as the director of a residential home for autistic adults, she sorely needed a vacation.

On January 2 we sailed out of Newfound Harbor for Key West. To starboard was "Big Al," the intelligence balloon tethered high above Little Torch Key. Its purpose is to spy on Cuba and, according to locals, it is so powerful it can read lips on the streets of Havana. We sailed past a big green schooner from Belize that was anchored in the harbor. Its crew had delivered a load of lumber to another resident of Cook Island and was helping the man build a similar inter-island trader. And at the harbor entrance we passed the *PT 109* island, where a luxury resort was abuilding, so it seemed all manner of construction was happening in these Keys, some primitive, some for the future, and all changing their plain faces forever.

Adria wrote in the log: "Cook Island Farewell: Bye-bye Barracuda." It is highly probable that her meaning escaped me, but I took it as a lament for the reef snorkeling, spearing needlefish at night in the shallows, setting shark bait with hooks big enough to hang a side of beef, sunbathing on the Cook Island beach, and for Aku and the family that in some ways, I feared, gave her a better sense of belonging than her own.

A light rain followed us partway down the coast. The water was a light green, at other times a metallic blue against a Confederate-gray sky. A large stingray leapt before us, its wingtips curled upward as if in joyous song. Then the sun returned as we anchored behind Wisteria Island out of the wakes of the boats and ships that ply the Key West harborfront. *Adriana* had carried us five months and 2,727 miles, from Newport to 24°28′ north latitude and 81°48′ west longitude, the westernmost and southernmost point of our cruise.

Key West seemed almost a sister city to Newport, though the Yankees haven't the Conch's secessionary spunk. After the U.S. Border Patrol shut down the Keys in April 1982, looking for drugs and illegal aliens and requiring proof of citizenship to pass, Key West declared independence, flew its own flag, and applied for foreign aid from the U.S. Government.

Still, Old Town is owned by the shopkeepers, who curtsy at the knees of tourists as though they were visiting royalty. Duval Street and environs is a dizzying row of shell shops, obscene T-

183

shirt shops, French boutiques, leather goods, not-so-goods, rowdy bars, Mexican restaurants, the Aquarium, Red Barn Theatre, and two-wheeled carts pumping popcorn and jewelry. The out-of-town traffic compresses bumper to bumper with trolley tours, the Conch Train, and cyclists upon whose backs ride red-and-blue parrots, coiled boa constrictors, and giant iguanas. Four dollars admission to Ernest Hemingway's house, where he wrote *For Whom the Bell Tolls, A Farewell to Arms,* and *The Snows of Kilimanjaro.* Rents are high and wages low, yet somehow the young and restless manage to filch a wage and sleep four-deep in attic apartments near the navy base.

At sunset, Mallory Square is a buskerfest of street performers and fast-food wagons. A stout German lad balances a shopping cart on his forehead, a Jamaican reggae contortionist fits himself into a two-by-two glass box, musicians hunched on ratty Persian carpets play sitars and zithers, unicyclists throw flaming torches at one another, and an escape artist unchains himself under the billing: "Only act to race against the sun. One show daily."

Adria had her palm read by a gypsy woman, who told her she'd have only one serious relationship in her life, and three kids. The tarot-card dealer told Andra she was divorced with two children. Andra shrugged and said, "Think you got me mixed up with my husband."

And when at last the sun makes its final rush beyond the liquid horizon, the crowd stops. On clear days it is possible to see the green flash, a rare phenomenon caused by the color-by-color eclipse of the spectrum; green is the last to go, and sometimes it winks where the last sliver of sun has vanished. The crowd claps, oohs and aahs, or simply checks for missing wallets and meanders back toward Duval Street.

Standing on the seawall I could see *Adriana* riding against the darkening curtain. Her anchor light danced like a firefly, and I felt a deep love for her. She had been my home for five years in cold and heat, fair weather and foul. In safety and relative comfort she had borne me down the entire Eastern Seaboard of the United States, from Canada to Key West—the proverbial and true end of the road.

16

My Dust to Where Some Flowers Grow

The resort beaches of Key West shrank to yellow slivers of light as *Adriana* worked her way slowly back toward Miami. I regretted having to leave before January 6, the date Roger Miller had hollered early that morning in Norfolk as he blasted out of the marina. Everyone, I suppose, dreams at least once in his life of chucking it all and escaping to the Tropics. Like his country-singer namesake, Roger Miller was "a man of means by no means—king of the road."

Adria fluffed up the sail bags on the foredeck and read her calculus text, a subject I had cunningly dodged through both high school and college. Andra and Jean read books in the cockpit, occasionally repositioning themselves for maximum sun exposure. And I sat behind the wheel, elbows on knees, chin in palm, dark sunglasses concealing the trancelike cloud that moved across my eyes as we bobbed and rocked in a lazy breeze.

For the second time we were retracing our steps. But unlike our passage back down the Maine coast, this time there wasn't the promise of new horizons. The Caribbean was definitely out, now or after the baby's birth. We'd be lucky to make it to the Bahamas with a newborn. The dream of open-ended cruising had been closed with the finality of a bank-vault door shutting out the light—airtight. In fact, all we were doing now was killing time.

At Looe Reef, a protected underwater park five miles south of Newfound Harbor, we tied the boat to one of the free state-owned moorings. Touching the reef with keel, propeller, or errant flipper is prohibited. A park ranger patrolled the several-acre reef like a mother hen, now and again turning on his blue police light to warn off approaching boats. The coral reefs along this coast are the only ones in the continental U.S. and are popular with divers, too many of whom break off pieces as mementos for bookshelves and end tables. A coral formation is delicate, easily damaged by a clumsy foot.

"Touch the coral and I'll have to write you a citation!" he would yell.

"Huh?"

"Four hundred dollars!"

"Yes, sir!"

With mask and snorkel, I dropped into the deep ocean side of the reef and in the distance saw the purple mountains of coral rising from the corrugated plain of sand. Jean and Adria followed as I worked my way carefully over the first shallow ridge. The fingers of reef reached toward the ocean depths like inert floes of hardened lava, and in between, in the valleys, dozens of barracuda hung motionless as if painted on a Japanese screen. The surge of water against the reef lifted both our bodies and the fish up and nearer the sharp coral, then on the outflow sucked us back toward the deeper open ocean, where the floor disappears in a murky distortion of shapes and faded colors.

The rhythmic pulse of the waves is soothing, and you feel yourself suspended in both space and time, eyeing these great, snaggle-fanged fish. If you move too close they might start at you, but if you stand your ground they veer off.

Still, a large barracuda is a lesson in intimidation. Later, relaxing in the cockpit, you might read a guide to reef fish and realize you had forgotten to remove your shiny silver ring; if he had gone for it, your response would have been to swing with your other hand. It is an inadequate defense, but it's all you've got. In reality, by the time you'd clenched your fist, he would have been gone, and so would have been your finger.

Brain coral the size of Toyotas grow from the center of the reef, and around them swim the smaller fish—the pucker-lipped sergeant major, the queen angelfish with eyes like licorice balls, Beau Gregory, grouper, rock hind, pencil-thin needlefish, and the queen triggerfish, a dowager empress with blue-lined lips and masked eyes.

And under the sculpted shape of the brain coral sleeps the nurse shark. He is mostly benign, and often just his tail shows. Until he is awoken and slithers silently for a less crowded bed.

After an hour we returned to the boat and set sail. Soon a dark-blue Cigarette circled in toward us. These are the boats that run huge payloads of cocaine and marijuana from offshore mother-ships into the shallow backwaters of South Florida. His intentions were clear; he wanted to check us out. It is the sight Bahama cruisers dread, fearing they may have accidentally witnessed a drug deal. More than one innocent bystander, outpaced and out-gunned, has come to a bloody end at the hands of ruthless drug traffickers.

The Cigarette slowed, squatting into its own wake as it came abreast. It was only then that I noticed the driver's shoulder patch—U.S. Customs.

"Where'd you come from?" he yelled.

"Looe Reef," I answered.

"Before that?"

"Key West."

He scanned my crew: all women, one teenager, another preg-nant. With a wave he was gone, and we breathed easier. In the Gulf Stream the eyes of the government are ever vigilant.

At Marathon we stopped for provisions. Boot Key Harbor is the best in the Keys, protected as it is from all directions. Both entrances are narrow, winding channels. A healthy fishing fleet operates from one end, and we were able to buy shrimp just hours off the boat. Unfortunately, there is only one approved dinghy landing, at the Dockside Restaurant, and there is a two dollars per day charge.

Cruisers seem to love it here, though we found their devotion difficult to understand. The town is an ugly strip of fast-food stores, the skyline blemished by condominiums, and the harbor so full there is scarcely room to swing a cat. Many of the dirtbaggers who have been kicked out of every mainland community settle in Marathon. They live on derelict craft of every sort—jonboats with crude plywood shelters, barges upon which the skeletal remains of a small aluminum travel-trailer have been dropped, and once-elegant motoryachts long ago abandoned by owner and engine. When the hulls rot out from under these victims of the Keys Disease they wade across the sandbars to set up camp in the mangroves. They are partly the spiritual ancestors of the nineteenth-century "wreckers" who salvaged—and sometimes looted—ships aground on the reefs, and partly the Keys version of hobos living under the railroad bridge. And they gave Andra the creeps, if only because, without jobs, she feared we too might terminate in the same compost heap.

Ever since our return to the Keys I had wanted to revisit Islamorada. Gene Correll, Pete, and I had spent a night there at the Lorelei Restaurant and Yacht Basin. The flotilla had tied to the wooden pier that runs along the inside of a mangrove-covered neck. The one-story restaurant was not greatly distinguished, but I had liked it. There were the usual fishnets and glass fisherman floats (coveted treasures from the Mediterranean carried westward by the ocean currents) draped across the walls, and the menu was standard: shrimp, grouper, steak. Outside, at the head of the basin, was a tiki bar that curved along the water's edge. In particular, I remembered Red, one of the old fellows who lived aboard houseboats jammed into the nearby mangroves. He spent a lot of time on a bar stool, and if you asked him what he was doing, he'd say, "Jus' waitin' for a beer front to come through."

Those twenty-eight-foot flotilla boats had drawn a lot less than *Adriana,* and we ran aground twice attempting the entrance. I was about to give up when a Cuban fisherman yelled from the deck of his boat and pointed toward a series of stakes. If there was a channel there, we didn't find it; the third time we hit I revved the engine and slid over the bar into a deeper channel. The bartender left his station to direct us in, motioning me to make a wide turn and berth next to the restaurant. The bow was ten feet from the patio when the keel hit for the fourth and final time. That caught everyone's attention. Including Red's, who was still sitting at the same bar stool he had held down six years earlier. The bartender caught a line, and Red made it fast to a four-by-four patio-roof support. I wrapped the other end around the electric windlass and dragged the boat in close enough to hop off the bow onto the concrete seawall. *Adriana* could not be coaxed farther, her stern cocked forty-five degrees. By the time I finished sorting lines, Red was gone.

The Cuban, I soon learned, was a Marielitos refugee named Pedro. When Fidel Castro opened the jails in 1978, Pedro and thousands of other criminals and political dissidents fled to South Florida. Somehow Pedro washed ashore at Lorelei, ran his boat into the mangroves as he saw Red and the others do, and began fishing. I would like to say he was adopted by the staff at Lorelei, but I think it was the other way around. Pedro began doing odd jobs — cutting the lawn, painting, carrying out garbage, and in return was allowed to run lines to the dock in bad weather and eat black beans and leftovers when the kitchen closed.

Our predicament seemed to agitate him; three times he came by frantically trying to explain how we should pull ourselves to deeper water. Once he motored his fishboat into the basin, threw a line, and tried to pull us off. To no avail. Only when Jean and I took Red's empty seat at the tiki bar did he give up and join us, grinning and toasting us with beer bottles.

The bartender collected a five-dollar deposit for the shower key, then settled to chat, apparently glad to have someone new to talk to. He was from Ireland and had been at Lorelei several years. "Red? Oh, he does a little stone crabs, some lobsters, this and that. It's nice here, off the main road more than some other places. Not much money, but it's quiet."

A man named Catboat Jim took a stool next to us. He had come down from Biloxi, Mississippi, and was living on a small boat near the basin.

"I come from gunrunnin' ancestors," he told Jean. "We're survivors. They used steam paddlers to sneak up the coast, then dart over to the Bahamas to trade rum for guns. They could outrun the side paddlers of the Yankees. We know how to lose. It should serve as a good lesson for the rest of the country. Even Vietnam didn't teach us much. We were too arrogant."

He liked to talk; his vital statistics were easy. Forty-seven years old. Ex-hippie. Marine illustrator. Used to own a Pearson Triton but it drew too much for the Gulf Coast. Bought a twenty-four-foot shoal-draft catboat, pumped his savings into it, and sunk his centerboard into Islamorada sand.

The bartender poured him another drink, and the last thing I heard Catboat Jim say, before the beer front enveloped him, was

"I'd rather have a free bottle in front of me than a pre-frontal lobotomy."

Later Jean and I moved to the inside bar. *Adriana* was canted now at low tide. The elderly woman manager, wearing a blue-and-yellow flower-print dress, said the next high tide would be at 11:30 A.M. The bartender, another old woman with wide eyes and a red wig, called the Coast Guard to make sure. "I asked the man," she said, "*What* is the best time for a *sailboat* stuck in our marina to get out? He said, 'Eleven fifty-five.' "

"But that's twenty-five minutes after high tide," the manager corrected.

"I didn't ask him *that*," the bartender returned. "I asked *what* is the best time. . . ."

The two women haggled over the meaning of the guardsman's advice another twenty minutes. I played with the swizzle stick in my coffee drink, trying to keep the melted whipped cream from separating and trying to remember at which table Pete and I had dined.

By the time the sun rose the next day *Adriana* had straightened herself and slumped again. The cook, Pedro, the Irish barkeep, and the two old ladies came out of the kitchen to see how we were progressing. As the tide started to fill in, I rowed an anchor into the middle of the lagoon and started the engine.

Adria and I spread some of Pete's ashes over the water. "Pete," I said, "we think of you every day."

The prop kicked up a lot of mud and did a good job of circulating Pete around the basin, but the anchor wouldn't hold.

A crowd gathered. Free advice flew from every quarter. Red was nowhere to be seen, probably sleeping off a beer front. However, some of the other liveaboards handed lines and waved directions. Most said we'd never get off.

"I seen a sailboat stuck here for weeks," one said fatally.

"Phoenix Towing is the only way," advised another.

"One guy brought in a crane, and it collapsed on his boat," warned a third.

A stringer for one of the local weekly papers was lying on the dock taking photographs. A couple in a Corvette pulled in and watched with arms folded. Apparently we were not bad entertainment for a Wednesday morning in Islamorada.

Finally I took a line from the masthead across the basin to a piling and winched the boat over sideways to increase its angle of heel. Pedro motored in on his fishboat and again tried futilely to pull us free. Then I raised the sails, assigned Adria the helm, and moved the rest of us to the bow. Slowly we inched forward, cast off our lines, and slid free. Polite applause.

In the furor I had forgotten to return the shower key. Jean tossed it onto the deck of a houseboat as we moved down the channel. It slid off into shallow water, and a couple of old live-aboards pointed to it lying on the bottom as if it were a gold doubloon.

"Whoever gets it," I yelled, "has five dollars of drinks on Spurr!"

For two days we motored slowly into stiff headwinds, unable to sail because of the narrow channel. Nearing Miami, we again tried to enter the basin at Boca Chica Key. Using binoculars I spotted two range markers half-hidden in the trees and followed them in without touching. Odd, I thought, that Fred, who had first given us directions, never mentioned them.

The manicured grounds of Boca Chica are maintained by rangers of the Biscayne Bay National Park. Adria hacked open a coconut, and we strolled under the palms and balmy skies until the mosquitoes drove us below.

After dinner I found Adria outside sitting on the boom, crying softly for Peter. We talked about her support group at school, and of a girl whose father, mother, and younger brother had been killed in a Wisconsin airplane accident.

"I've sort of forgotten Pete on this trip," she sniffed. "I should have some time for him. It doesn't seem fair that everything about my life is so good, and so much of Pete's life was bad. I want to believe his soul is somewhere—in the wind, water, stars. One night about a month ago it had been quite chilly. But suddenly I felt incredibly warm. I was coming home from a babysitting job, and I walked onto our deck. I stopped, looked around, and felt Peter all around me. He was behind the trees and bushes, at the front door, everywhere. I don't know; maybe the night air had strange effects, or I may be crazy. It was an odd feeling, but good.

The next day was gorgeous—seventy degrees, warm, and sunny. There was a spectacular change in weather from the usual. I woke that morning to find that someone had dropped a card off at the front door. It said 'We are with you on a very special day today.' There was no name. I didn't understand until Mom told me that it was a month that day since Pete's accident. That night there was a full moon, just as on the night of the accident. The sky was only clear near the moon, blurry, no stars anywhere else. But near the moon was a small star. It was very pretty. . . ."

I held her in my arms and rocked her like a baby. I couldn't tell her Peter was walking around on a heavenly cloud, his body emanating light as he played with other kids, rode bikes, and petted tame lions under the watchful eyes of white-robed angels. There wasn't much I could say. I remember spending a weekend on the boat alone with Adria when she was about six. She had asked me what happens when someone dies, and we had a frank conversation about religion. Later, just as we drove in the driveway, she said, "Well, if everything is made by something, then who made God?" Bertrand Russell would have been proud.

Tonight, however, the question wasn't quite so rhetorical. I knew she felt guilt. Despite the family's reassurance, it was only natural to expect that her doubts lingered. The right explanation could help her accept Pete's death—I took a chance and explained as gently as possible my own beliefs, insofar as I understood them: that everything that has ever lived is still here, in energy or matter. That the Earth is a great recycling plant. And that spirits are not invisible bubbles floating in space, but the memories the living have of those departed. The ideas of life after death and reincarnation probably had their origins in the very real physical truth that matter doesn't simply disappear. It may change form, some of it convert to energy, but it is all here and always will be. As in Joe Hill's poem, some of Pete's ashes may help fertilize a plant or feed a fish. Death defines life. It is part of life, the price we pay for the privilege of breathing and walking, laughing and loving. We all face it. Pete just got there a little ahead of us.

Adria wiped at her eyes and nodded. "I never thought of it that way," she murmured, but I wasn't sure she was buying it. When the wound still bleeds, nothing can staunch the flow, not a father's arm, sterile logic, or even a kiss from the pope himself.

The denouement of Jean and Adria's vacations was fraught with difficulty. The refrigerator quit. Inside were many dead, unidentifiable *things*. I gutted the contents, tossing the dark shrunken shapes of meat and vegetables overboard to squeals of disgust from my crew, each louder and higher pitched than the last. I ate a leftover shrimp and had stomach cramps the rest of the day.

We spent two days at Miamarina, the controversial city yacht basin in the heart of Miami's Bayside development—again designed by James Rouse. Half the piers were closed due to inadequate fire protection, the pilings wobbled under pedestrian traffic, and an uncomfortable surge from the ship channel kept the boats rearing and dunking night and day.

Nevertheless, we enjoyed an anniversary dinner at Bar Balu on Friday night. Below in the courtyard young men in three-piece suits and flat-top haircuts courted dark-haired Hispanic girls with glistening lips and four-inch pumps, their bottoms pushing wild dresses slit to the hip.

Andra looked over the railing, turned, and said, "Listen to the hormones scream."

Jean flew home one day and Adria, on standby, the next. When Andra and I returned to the boat from the airport there was a message in the marina office saying that Adria had been bumped in West Palm Beach. We arranged for Ken and Karyn Green to bring her to their home for the night, feed her, and take her back to the airport the next day. By the time she reached Ann Arbor three days had elapsed, and she had forsworn the tempting bargains of standby ticketry.

George Day had asked us to help run *Cruising World*'s booth at the Miami International Sailboat Show at the end of February, so we had a few weeks to kill. And since my childhood friend Jim Dunlap wanted to fly down from Michigan to visit, we tucked our tails between our legs and limped back up the waterway to Boca Raton. Tossed about as the mispitched propeller whirred ineffectively, we tied up at Dave Landmann's grandmother's dock, sighed, and waited.

✳

One day Dave took Ken, Karyn, Andra, and me to "do polo." The sport has a following in Newport, too—Mason Phelps, debutantes such as Cornelia Guest, friends of William F. Buckley—but we had little interest and never went.

The Royal Palm Polo Sports Club was equally pheffy, but as Dave had a reserved parking spot on the infield, and we were virtual prisoners of his grandmother "Ammy," his invitation was gladly accepted.

The ticket taker at the gate was new to the job.

"Hi," Dave said, handing her a list of his parking partners. "This is for you. They should get in free."

The woman squinted at the handwriting. "What's your name?"

"I'm *David Landmann*." He flashed his "Charter Member" card. "What's *your* name?"

The woman stuttered.

"As I said, I'm David Landmann. Good to meet you, and see you next week." We roared in.

Compared with American-style football, the rules of polo are simple. Each team comprises four men on horses. Each has a rating based on skill, and the team total determines its handicap—which means one team may start with a one-, two-, or three-goal lead. Play is divided into six chukkers, which are akin to innings in baseball. They last seven minutes, and occasionally there are timeouts. The field is ten acres, and at either end are goals into which the players try to hit the small, white ball with their long-handled mallets. The direction in which the ball is traveling is sacrosanct, and it is illegal to cross its imaginary path for fear of collision—a form of pass interference.

As I read *The Glenlivet Guide to Polo* Dave had handed me, he tugged at his white canvas Indiana Jones hat and said, "Basically, polo, like sailing, is an excuse to drink cocktails outdoors."

Team Michelob had spotted Fort Lauderdale two points at the start. At the end of the third chukker Anheuser Busch IV had tied the score. The play-by-play announcer invited the crowd to stomp down the divits while the players rested. Sort of a seventh-inning stretch.

Ken, Andra, and I strolled out just to get a feel for the magnitude of the field.

Far to the west, over the Everglades, the clouds were building, white with gray tops like burnt meringue.

Andra said, "We don't have a car, and they get fresh horses every seven minutes?" She stepped over a steaming pile of dung.

"Can you imagine," Ken mused, "running and taking a shit at the same time?"

Then the field was cleared for the game's sponsor. A candy-colored Donzi sportboat and trailer were dragged across the field by a snazzy convertible with the company president waving from the back seat. Play resumed, and all I recall is drinking Bloody Marys, eating fried chicken out of somebody's trunk, and hearing the announcer scream, "Tiebreaker!"

Jim Dunlap arrived at the end of January. He is a quiet sort, six-foot with a full face. His blond hair has dirtied just a little over the years. We have been friends since age five. Our paths diverged a long time ago, during high school perhaps, and we followed different stars. Mine led me to prison and his took him to Vietnam. Kenn Miller and Jim bolstered one another with the promise of the glory of going Airborne. Margaret and I drove them to Fort Wayne for induction. They completed basic training together, but there Jim was seduced into enrolling in Officer's Candidate School. While Kenn practiced jumping off tall scaffolding, Jim learned how to calculate the trajectory of a 105mm shell.

Kenn spent two tours in Vietnam doing Sneaky Pete reconnaissance behind enemy lines, investigating sinister tunnels and engaging in hand-to-hand combat with bayonets and knives. Killed a few and left virtually unscathed. In contrast, Jim lasted six months with the artillery, lobbing ordnance at unseen targets. Lasted until his unit came under mortar fire one fine day. He was helping evacuate wounded soldiers to helicopters when he caught shrapnel in his eye, wrist, and legs. And so began a seemingly endless tour of military hospitals—Saigon, Tokyo, Ft. Collins, Colorado. The army gave him lifetime disability but refused to discharge him; he spent his last year as a supply clerk at Fort Knox. The scars on his leg are savage, and on hot, humid days the hundreds of tiny shrapnel bits still embedded there start to crawl.

195

Once, a few years ago, a piece closed down a major artery, and he almost lost his left leg.

Today, Kenn spends a lot of time with veteran's groups, reveling in the dramatic memories. "It was the only job I was ever any good at," he says angrily.

Jim has moved on, in mind and spirit. "I can't live in the past," he says. His memories are not as good.

Jim rented a Voyager minivan, and we spent two weeks land-cruising South Florida. First we drove north to Stuart where Andra had a temporary job helping Pete and Gina Smyth paste up their last issue of *Florida Waterways*.

I asked Pete why he was killing the small, regional magazine. "Save the marriage," he said. "You know the saying—for better or for worse, but not for lunch?"

While Andra cut up little pieces of type and aligned them on boards, Jim and I got horizontal on Jensen Beach. The wind was sharp, and there were few sunbathers—no swimmers. For a time I watched an old man with knee boots casting into the surf. Curiosity got the better of me, and I walked over to ask him what he was after. Tom Mazur was his name. Retired.

"Hell, I don't know," he snorted. "I just like it. If I don't enjoy this, I might as well be dead. This is my *life!* The graphite rod cost a hundred thirty-five dollars, and so did the reel. I could catch fish with a board and string, but if that's the way I had to do it, I wouldn't."

"Part of the pleasure must be in the gear," I said. "That's the way it is with boats, anyway."

"Yer damn right," he said. "I like good equipment. If I'm gonna stand out here all day, I got to know I'm going about it right. My son is a commercial fisherman in Hyannisport on the Cape. If you're a dope—smoke dope—you ain't gonna do shit. But if you bust your stones, you can do alright. My son and his partner grossed a hundred sixty-eight thousand last year, with a thirty-one-footer. Six months work. They had to clear eighty-five. They got new houses, RVs, just returned from an elk-hunting trip in the Rockies."

I asked Tom to show me his rig. The rod was long, between twelve and fifteen feet, and the monofilament heavy, perhaps fifty-pound test. At the end was a lead pyramid weight that sits on the bottom as far out as he can get it. Behind it were three hooks, each baited with baby crabs. He was working two rods, and on the other he had decided to use a green plastic "worm."

"Don't know what it's supposed to resemble," he chuckled. "But if the fish thinks it looks good, who cares!"

"These lures confuse me," I confessed. "Seems what's important is that the *fisherman* thinks the *fish* thinks it looks good."

"Yeah?" he said, putting his left leg forward, cocking the rod back over his right shoulder and heaving the weight and worm thirty yards into the breakers. He had good follow-through, and I bet he played golf, too.

When Andra and the Smyths had put the issue to bed, we drove across the state, through the grazing land and sawgrass, around the rim of Lake Okeechobee. At the turn of the century the lake flooded frequently, hindering development to the south. The land is barely above sea level, flat, and the flood plain cocked a little to the west. When it rained the water seeped over the edge of the Lake and flowed slowly—about four miles an hour—through the sawgrass, covering thousands of square miles on its journey south to Flamingo and west to the Ten Thousand Islands. Now it is contained by earthworks, and one must climb up from the road for a view of the second-largest freshwater lake entirely within the border of the United States.

We made quick work of the fine-sand beaches at Sarasota and Naples, then shot east on Tamiami Trail. Paid six bucks for an air-boat ride at a Miccosukee Indian reservation, saw one alligator, and sat on a barely dry piece of turf during "intermission" while Indian seamstresses worked their sewing machines with doleful eyes and never said a word: Dresses $40. Skirts $30.

Jim drove as far south as Key Largo, then backtracked to Key Biscayne for the dolphin and killer-whale show at the Miami Sea Aquarium. It was a quick circumnavigation of South Florida, and for us, an interesting counterview to the Florida we had seen coastal sailing.

On Jim's last day he and I went to Deerfield Beach, found a free parking place, and threw our towels down between piles of dynamited coral. I watched as he waded knee-deep in the gentle surf, stiffening on his toes as each wave swept past. He turned and grinned like a kid. Despite the purple gash running down his leg,

Jim was still the faithful friend I remembered after thirty-five years.

As he pulled out of Ammy's driveway, he made our old Caramaba brothers' face and said, "Bet you'll miss the car more than me!"

Then he was gone. Andra and I climbed back aboard *Adriana* thinking how wrong Jim was. Later, sitting around the dinette and sinking into big pillows, we contemplated the next chapter in our odyssey, considered dinner, but fell asleep before we could make a decision.

17

What a Fool Believes

"Let me get a look at you!" Glennie's voice carried across the show grounds. Faces turned. Andra blushed. She had just waddled through the ticket gate at the Miami Beach Marina, and the last thing she wanted was to draw attention to herself.

Glennie worked in *Cruising World's* promotion department, and one of her jobs was coordinating the magazine's exhibits at boat shows. She was big boned, her face animated, and she wore her blond hair in a Dutch-boy cut. She squeezed Andra, then stood back to admire her bulge.

Other comrades from Newport gathered—easygoing, networking Jack Callahan, Florida ad rep; mischievous and handsome George Day, editor; Irish Madonna Bernadette Brennan, managing editor; and twenty-year-old Tania Aebi, the diminutive, dark-haired girl *Cruising World* had sponsored in her single-handed sail around the world. She was greeting readers at the booth, autographing specially bound editions of her articles. Shy at first, she soon showed her spunk.

"Hey, Glennie," she baited, "how'd you get so tan? You've only been in Florida twelve hours!"

Glennie, not to be outdone by a girl nearly half her age, wrinkled her nose and, invoking the name of a well-known Newport tanning salon, punned: "Tan-ya!"

The public dogged Tania around the show. Her fans—male and

female, young and old—approached the booth and stared. She lit a roll-your-own cigarette. No one seemed to know who should talk first. The fans studied her closely, as if to ask, "How could such a cute, petite thing sail around the world by herself?"

Tania seemed to be thinking, "How queer of these people to stare at *me*! Every one of them could have done what I did if they'd really wanted."

Perhaps that was the mystery, the invisible thing in her that said, "Yes, I will do this." Before the circumnavigation she was a bicycle messenger in New York City, quick-tongued, agile, pugnacious as James Cagney. It explains a lot.

"Would you do it again?" one woman blurted.

"Not in a twenty-six-footer," Tania answered flatly.

"What size boat would you want?"

"Fifty feet."

"Really? Could you handle such a big boat?"

She shrugged. "Sure, why not?"

"Do you have plans to buy a fifty-footer?"

She laughed. "Are you kidding? I don't have any money. Why do you think I'm here?"

Andra and I spent ten days at the Miami Boat Show working the booth, attending cocktail receptions, and testing boats for the magazine's "Down the Ways" column. *Adriana* was docked at the Crandon Park Marina on Key Biscayne, and we rented a car to commute back and forth. One evening we were surprised to see Carl Shoch, the skipper of *Sundog,* ambling down the dock. We hadn't seen him since Beaufort, South Carolina.

Sundog, he said, had been sold in Key Largo, and now he crewed on a Bristol 35.5 with a couple of dangerous beginners and their two dogs. They wanted his help traversing the "Thorny Path" upwind a thousand miles to Charlotte Amalie in the Virgin Islands, but he had doubts. Also, there was the possibility of a summer job as a backcountry ranger in Alaska's Brooks Range.

The next evening Carl accepted a dinner invitation. Sitting around *Adriana*'s dinette under the warm, yellow glow of the lantern and sharing a bottle of wine, he told us his story.

Once he worked for the U.S. Geological Survey in Anchorage.

The job paid well, and he owned a new car and a nice house with a big mortgage. But something wasn't right. And one day he quit, sold everything, and enrolled in the Apprenticeshop wooden boatbuilding school in Rockport, Maine. The students built a traditional working sloop called a Quoddy Pilot, and he learned how to swing an adze and handle a spokeshave. Yet he recognized the futile romanticism of filling his shoes with sawdust; the world no longer really needed wooden boats. And he wanted to test himself as an individual, not as a cog in a machine, however simple, however organic it might be. A team of men could spend years building a cruising boat. Alone it would take him ten. Besides, there were too many mountains to cross, too many seas to sail, and too little time. In some strange Zen way he wanted to be part of the world, yet remain outside it. He wanted the broad view from a windy peak as well as the more precise, empirical knowledge that comes from eating pokeberries and toothwort.

He bought a kayak and by train moved it north to Schefferville, Quebec. There he hired a bush pilot to drop him on the banks of the River George. "Good luck, jerk," was the pilot's parting shot.

He paddled north to Ungava Bay, where he met Cecile, ministering to the Inuit Indians who live on bannock and seals. Then he passed east to the Labrador coast, and in August was trapped in ice. His food ran out, and starvation seemed a grim certainty. He traveled eighty miles, focused on a thin plume of smoke from a construction site. The men working on the North American early defense system took him in from the wilderness.

"One minute I had nothing," he said, "the next, everything I could possibly wish for. Showers, steaks, you name it."

Eventually he made his way back to Rockport, bought *Sundog,* and fitted her out for a leisurely cruise. A tropical journey. Nothing strenuous. Let an outboard do the work of his weary arms.

"The ICW was a piece of cake," he said, tilting his coffee mug at midnight. "Comfort is relative to past experience. I am convinced that a small boat is the only way to do the waterway. I wouldn't have done it otherwise."

He was too polite to say that he had seen things the rest of us in larger boats never could have, yet I knew he had.

He stood to leave. "You're going to Flamingo in the Everglades, right? Do yourself a favor: Rent a canoe and spend a night on a chickee." Then he pulled his tall, lanky legs out through the hatch like a fireman pulling a hose up after himself. We did not see him again.

Chickee?

It was unexpected. It was mad. Reckless even. Then again, it was totally predictable. Danny Keirns, our irrepressible, indefatigable, redheaded friend from Newport was in Florida. And he wanted to go sailing. He'd driven down to paint a client's house in Fort Lauderdale, and yes, he would accept an invitation to cruise the Keys.

"Kernzy-boy" squealed into the marina parking lot, slammed the brakes of his white Ford pickup, turned off the Marshall Tucker tape blaring on the stereo, and hopped out. He looked like the fall guy in a Chevy Chase movie—dirty felt hillbilly hat, paint-speckled collarless shirt, khaki shorts, nine-inch workboots, and gray wool socks.

"Hey!" he bellowed, "It was the best I could do on short notice!"

"If you want to see short notice," Andra deadpanned, "take a look at our liquor locker."

After dinner, on the eve of our departure for the Keys and Florida's West Coast, Keirns and I set out to remedy the beverage deficiency. We stocked up at a package store then dipped inside Stefano's Italian restaurant next door.

"Just one, Danny boy."

"Sure."

We hit every bar on Key Biscayne, and when those were exhausted we drove over the Rickenbacker Causeway to Coconut Grove. Found a clean-looking joint surrounded by a white picket fence, veranda bar, and shade tree to peek at the moon. I opened my backpack and fumbled for a fresh pipe.

"Whad'ya keep in that bag?" Keirns snarled. "Your *brain*?"

He saw my notebook and grabbed it. When he handed it back, he had written on one of the pages, "Things are gonna be a little bit different from here on in."

He was right.

For starters, he caught three "eatin' fish" on the sail down Biscayne Bay. My rod, of course.

He drank rum for breakfast, snored in his sleep, belched and flatulated indiscriminately. Andra had an excuse to abstain—she was pregnant. But slowly I was being corrupted. Keirns had no excuse, he was The Corruptor, capable of destroying a man's New Year's resolutions faster than Arnold Schwarzenegger can stave in the skull of a marauding Visigoth.

One evening we anchored off the mainland shore, just south of the first bridge to Key Largo. On shore was the infamous dive called Alabama Jack's. Nestled in the mangroves, it was squeezed by the road on one side and a narrow, dredged channel leading into Barnes Sound on the other. The unpainted wood of the rickety structure was weathered gray, the planks split, the dock heaving like a roller-coaster track. A few cruising boats were tied up next to the open-air bar, and we could see a few men drinking under the thatched shelter.

"Looks like an outpost," Keirns said, "and that bridge toll-booth, the checkpoint to some foreign country."

"The Keys *are* foreign," I affirmed. "You'll see when we get ashore."

"Yeah?" Keirns yelled. He turned to Andra. "Grab yer lump and let's go!"

We ordered a round of spicy conch fritters and Cajun shrimp. The food was good and cheap, but as the bartender was also the cook, it slowed down the bar action. An impatient customer looked at me and said, "Why'd'ya have to order food? This here's a drinkin' bar!"

"Don't pay him no mind," said his wife. "We pulled in here on our boat for one night and haven't left yet. That was two weeks ago. I want to see Key West, but at this rate we'll never get there. The beer's too cheap at Alabama Jack's." When it came time to pay, Keirns sheepishly turned out his empty pockets. He'd paid for all the drinks our last night in Key Biscayne; "No problem," he'd said that night, "just got paid."

"I did get paid," he protested now. "Gosh, I guess I just spent it all."

The next morning I changed the propeller again. The original we'd had reconditioned in Fort Lauderdale, and though possibly weakened a mite, it had to be more efficient than the new mis-pitched prop. Again, I cheated death with the hose-taped-to-the-snorkel trick, and the entire job was completed in less than half an hour.

At Key Largo we tied the dinghy to the docks of the Upper Keys Sailing Club. There was a fish fry scheduled that evening, and we were invited to attend by one of the members we'd met at the dinghy landing. First, Andra wanted ice cream and Keirns another drink. At Baskin-Robbins we stood behind a girl wearing sequin- and rhinestone-studded shorts with white lace sewn to the cuffs. On her head was a weird paper hat that made her look like Spuds McKenzie, the pit bull who drinks Bud Lite on television commercials.

Keirns rolled his eyes.

I nudged his arm. "See what I mean about the Keys?"

Then we trundled across Highway I to a bar called Coconuts. A man with a guitar and synthesizer sang:
"On a night like this,
You can't help feelin',
Hot, hot, hot!"
Keirns ordered shots of banana liqueur and leered at the waitresses. By the time we made the fish fry he was also fried.

The next morning Keirns hitchhiked back to Key Biscayne. I gave him ten dollars in case a bus came by, and he found six more blowing down the side of the road. Andra and I sat in a nearby Wendy's restaurant, drinking coffee, watching him wave his thumb, but after half an hour we gave up and returned to the boat.

Weeks later we learned that two apocalyptic Cubans in a truck had eventually picked him up, preaching doom all the way to Miami: ". . . and the sea weel turn to fire and a great beast weel rise up and consume all the seenners. . . ." Keirns nodded and rested his head against the window, yearning for sleep.

Yes, he had consumed, too—mostly rum. He knew he didn't have to sin to have a good time; and he knew he didn't have to sin to get into trouble. The house he had come to paint was half finished, and he was already three days late returning to Rhode Island. I wanted to say to his wife, Diane, it would be a mistake to expect more of a redheaded Southern boy.

✳

The channel to Everglades National Park and the West Coast of Florida strikes off in a northwesterly direction from Long Key, about halfway between Miami and Key West. Much of Florida Bay lies within the boundaries of the park, marked by signs posted by steel girders sunk into the sand. You see them when sailing down the inside of the Keys; in the distance they may be confused for the red and green navigational markers of the Intracoastal Waterway, though they are neither triangular nor square, but white rectangles—an important distinction.

As on our first trip down the Keys in December, we anchored behind Fiesta Key and the KOA campground. In the middle of the night the wind veered northwest, and I awoke to find us aground on a lee shore. The anchor, fortunately, was firmly embedded, and by gunning the engine and hauling the rode with the electric windlass, we were able to pull ourselves into deeper water.

The sky was black, and there was no loom of city lights to silhouette the islands. The wind howled through the rigging, and as I motored away from shore the bow began to dip and buck in the whitecapped waves.

"I hate dragging anchor more than anything," Andra lamented. She was sitting under the canvas dodger at the head of the cockpit, gripping the companionway handholds. "Try to get some sleep," I said. "It'll be another hour."

"Hour! Where are we going?"

I handed her the chart and flashlight. "There," I pointed, "behind this mangrove island."

"Why so far?"

"Because it's the closest protection."

And it was, a low, unnamed spit of sand and mangroves about a mile west of Lower Matecumbe Key, three miles north of Fiesta Key. We were backtracking, and I cursed myself for having failed to anticipate the wind shift. Of course, the marine weather forecast hadn't predicted it either, but sailing eight unnecessary miles required a whipping boy, and I was it.

The cloud cover lifted long enough to reveal the bridge lights at Channel Five, and the radio beacon tower on Lower Matecumbe. A fix with the hand-bearing compass corroborated the position indicated by the Loran. Good enough. The only problem was an Everglades boundary marker; I could see it on the chart, and it lay smack on our course. I could swing left or right, but how far? I figured there was perhaps a maximum quarter-mile error possible in our position fix, which meant I'd have to swerve at least that far east or west of our course to feel comfortable. With the chart and parallel rules I computed a new course and pressed on. Occasionally I grabbed the flashlight and peered into the dark murk ahead. The least they could do, I prayed, was affix reflectors to the steel girders. Unsure of myself, I throttled back and steered a little wider. My senses were useless. Like Berkeley's rock, the boundary marker would exist only if we hit it.

When it seemed certain we'd passed the sign, I calculated a new course to our anchorage, and in another hour decided we had arrived. The bearings seemed right and so did the depth. It was, in effect, an instrument landing.

"Here?" Andra asked incredulously. There was no land to be seen anywhere, just a few distant lights along the Keys' shoreline.

"I guess." The waves did feel smaller.

Once the two anchors were down Andra fell into bed exhausted. Nerves mostly. I sat in the cockpit awhile and watched the new day dawn. Before the sun came up the clouds blew away, and a few stars shone. The eastern sky turned a watery rose color, then deepened. And a hundred yards before us was the silhouette of our mangrove island, exactly where I had supposed. A navigator needs a successful landfall once in awhile to keep his confidence. Smugly I congratulated myself and stepped below. We would kill another day here waiting for the wind to blow itself out, a day lost, but it didn't really matter. There was work we could both do, and in fact I rather liked the idea of anchoring far from the madding crowd. Out of sight, out of our minds. The world was, and we were.

According to an article in *Outside* magazine, the most species of birds sighted in one year is 726. Sandy Komito of Fair Lawn, New Jersey, set the record in 1987 at the age of fifty-six. For many of the visitors to Everglades National Park, he must be bigger than Babe Ruth.

I came hand to toe with my first birder while docking *Adriana* in the park marina. He was standing on the seawall, focusing a very large camera lens on a pelican that sat on top of a nearby piling. His tripod stood squarely over the cleat I needed to tie off our bow line.

Okay, I thought, it's only polite to wait. But this fellow wasn't shooting snapshots. As I crouched at his feet I had ample time to look him over, from the L.L. Bean gum boots and nylon camouflage suit to the brown-frame glasses and floppy canvas hat. He squinted and adjusted the focus ring, then stopped and scratched his ear. Again he peeked at his target, slowly turning the various tripod control handles.

Jesus, I thought, you'd think this geek had just spotted a rare spoon-billed sandpiper or an oriental cuckoo, something guys like Sandy Komito wait years for. But a pelican? We see them every day, rolling into those crazy kamikaze dives, hitting the water upside down, and coming up dazed-looking, shaking their long bills as if embarrassed to be seen.

"Ahem. Would you mind if I tied my line to this cleat?"

He looked down at me as if I were a pesky jay.

"Go ahead and shoot," I said. "But I can't hold off my boat too much longer."

Without a word he collapsed his tripod and stalked away.

"Sorry," I said.

Why he never shot is beyond me. Apparently I had disturbed some deep and silent communication between man and bird. Perhaps he was waiting for the right expression on the pelican's face, a beguiling tuck or twist of the beak like the thin smile of Mona Lisa. Or maybe birders are simply used to moving slowly, still as sunning reptiles, fading into the rock and brush like shadows on the Earth.

Everglades National Park does not belong in South Florida. Then again, it is the only unspoiled, unchanged land left. That is the problem; it is out of sync with the rest of the state—the new culture, rapid development, the mindset. It is hard to make the transition from blender sports to trail snacks, topless donut bars to granola bars, Vette shops to canoe liveries, tourist information booths to backcountry ranger stations, neon flamingos to real flamingos (or at the least roseate spoonbills). There are no high heels or lipstick in the national parks, no mag wheels, Magnums (speedboats, champagne, or handguns), banks, bikinis, crack, ice, cocaine, or rock n' roll. The birders may look like nerds next to a Fort Liquordale bartender, but they connect you with a part of America you haven't thought about since the last time you opened your high school yearbook.

The park staffers are mostly young men and women in their twenties who earn minimum wage.

"It's nothing," one of the marina hands told me, "but it's the only way I can live in the national parks. The park service hires concessionaires to manage the facilities, and the opportunities for advancement are limited, but when I get to look at *this* every day, who cares?" He swept his hand across a neat, uniform row of palmettos and out toward Florida Bay, framed by two banks of mangroves.

I said, "I know what you mean." And I wanted to tell him about cruising in a sailboat and how you can have this and more. But then I realized that in order to get the boat you have to pay dues somewhere else, dues much dearer than $3.35 an hour.

Alex and Julie had already paid those dues, and $3.35 kept them cruising. They were the young couple living on the twenty-seven-foot *Adios* next to us. After cruising around the Gulf from Texas, they'd stopped here at park headquarters in Flamingo to earn money. A wrinkle-faced bulldog named Bumper watched the boat while they worked. After deducting slip fees, they didn't take home very much. Alex worked in the store, and Julie was a hostess in the restaurant.

"At first it was hard taking general jobs," Alex said. "I'm an ironworker, and Julie is a CPA. But then I thought, shit, these people gotta go to work when they leave; I can pick up and blow out of here tomorrow!"

Andra and I portaged *For Pete's Sake* over the dam that regulates the flow of the Flamingo Canal, sidestepped a sleeping alligator on the banks, and shoved off. Our outboard motor prohibited us from engaging the most interesting trails—Homestead, Rowdy Bend, and Snake Bight, which are off-limits to powered craft. Instead we pushed north through Coot Bay and Tarpon Creek into Whitewater Bay. It is four feet shallow, miles wide, and dashed with innumerable clusters of mangroves. Strawberry-colored butterflies flitted about in the breeze, heron and ibis froze against the green-leafed banks. A solitary osprey flew overhead clutching a trout in its talons as if it were a B-52 carrying a cruise missile.

There isn't much room to stretch in a dinghy, and it's too tippy to stand in. After a few hours my bottom ached and my legs felt dead. I was reminded of old adventures on small boats—learning to synchronize my stroke in my grandmother's rowboat, kayaking down the Huron River when I was twelve, practicing draws and turns in my father's birchbark canoe. There was more than a simple lesson in physics to be learned on those basic craft, and somehow it was more arcane than riding a bicycle. It is more than the exhilaration of self-propulsion that delights a boy; perhaps it is the risk of gliding over dark, ominous depths and the unseen creatures that lurk beneath. Or the isolation of midlake, and fantasies of pygmies firing blow darts through the willows at the river bend. Or being upset and swallowed by a giant sturgeon. More, it is a feeling, knowable but ineffable, that would die on the tongue if ever uttered. Once experienced, the boy is drawn back to the water so that he may feel it again and again. The years pass, and he becomes a man, and still he cannot describe what it is that happens out there.

On the Little Joe River we found a chickee, one of the crude wooden platforms built by rangers for parkies like Carl Shoch. Chickee is an Indian word and concept forged by necessity; the Calusa were the first but certainly not the last Floridians to build their homes on stilts.

The Little Joe chickee sat just a few feet above the water. At one end was a square wooden platform for sleeping, at the other an outhouse. I lay down on the wide-spaced planks and closed my eyes. I saw Ursa Major and Minor, the bear constellations, saw mama lay down on the shores of the big lake, and Little Bear, whose tail is Polaris, a thousand light-years away, scrambling to keep up.

I felt as though I lay on a burial mound like some troubled Seminole youth deciphering the magic of his medicine man, and I felt nearer to my own youth, to manitou, and to the moment I had come so far to relearn.

18

The Land of the Newlyweds
and Nearly Deads

Gulf of Mexico water is a light brown color, and
when you swim in it you cannot see your hand in front of your
face. In some places, on some days, it is a milky jade green, but
still impossible to see through. Locals say it clears in an east wind
. . . sure, and Eskimos say the weather is warm when the air temperature rises above zero.

During 1978 I had joined the Texas Antiquities Committee's
search for two seventeenth-century ships sunk in Matagorda Bay.
The Committee's crewboat was positioned by four anchors over
the suspected site of one wreck. A large L-shaped aluminum tube
was bolted over the propeller, and divers directed it over the bottom; when the engines were revved the sand and silt blew up like
a pestilence. Even after the engines stopped you couldn't see the
man or woman next to you, just bump elbows and clang tanks as
you groped in the hole for a piece of timber or cannon. We never
did find Robert de La Salle's *La Belle* or *Aimable,* hampered as we
were by tricky "hits" on the magnetometer and the murky waters
of Big Brown. And I am sure if a man dived long enough in the
Gulf, evolution would transform him into a rare, sightless species
drifting like a manatee among the oyster-encrusted pilings of piers
and offshore oil rigs.

On March 1 Andra and I left Flamingo for the West Coast of
Florida. As we had all down the coast, we viewed each new area as

a potential place to live. The warmth and subtropical vegetation of South Florida, at least for a Northerner, is magical. But we'd already ruled out the Ft. Lauderdale–Miami corridor—too many people, too much crime. The West Coast, we were continually told, was different, more laid back, affordable, prettier. We aimed to find out for ourselves.

At the turn of the century, southwestern Florida was prime ground for plume hunters, who shot flamingo and ibis to supply the New York milliners—high fashion was a woman with a feather in her hat. A young man named Guy Bradley was hired by the Audubon Society to protect the birds. On July 8, 1905, the new warden spotted two men with birds in their hands, running from the shore to a waiting sailboat. He pursued them in his small boat and, pulling alongside the larger vessel, was shot in the face.

The captain, Walter Smith, fled to Key West, where he surrendered. However, Bradley's family refused to press charges, and Smith was freed. But his death was not in vain. The public was outraged, especially the environmentalists, and it was not long before legislation was passed protecting Florida's beautiful birds. Not, unfortunately, before the extinction of the pink American flamingo. Those you see today in the parks and apiaries are imported from Africa. And Guy Bradley's bones are buried in the Everglades, earning him the distinction as the only Audubon warden ever to die in the line of service.

We rounded Cape Sable in moderate headwinds and sunny skies. The park wilderness ran low and flat to the east, rimmed by a short girth of sandy beach. The north wind drove waves at oblique angles to the coast, and they curved around the cape with a thin sneer on their faces as they slapped *Adriana*'s bow.

At dusk we reached into the Little Shark River, which reminded us of the wooded streams of Georgia and South Carolina's Low Country, except that the trees here were not moss-draped oaks, but sixty-foot red mangroves braced in mud. At low tide we could see the vast intricate network of their roots, plunged like crooked canes into the muddy banks. In a hurricane there is no better protection for a boat than running into the thick of the mangroves, the hull cradled by the thousands of tiny, resilient arms.

The Little Shark follows a meandering path into the Everglades, and there is sufficient depth for large boats to follow it more than ten miles to the head of Whitewater Bay. Alex, who had been our neighbor at the Flamingo marina, told us he had spent weeks anchored up the river.

"I don't think I'd cruise if I couldn't fish," he said. "And I don't like using bait. Try spoons for redfish, but if you get desperate, get some bloodworms. I also drop a crab pot right away and bait it with a punctured tin of cat food. It's real peaceful in the Shark, but there isn't anything up there except mosquitoes and mangroves."

As we motored past the ten other boats anchored fore and aft along the banks, I could see that Alex was right. It was easy to fantasize that this was the Mekong or the Mae Nam Ping, the anchor lights marking a moored fleet of fishing junks, and we some twisted Conradian adventurers daring to confront our own hearts of darkness.

That night Andra dreamed she had returned to Newport to visit her former supervisor in *Cruising World*'s production department. In this fantasy, Joy "Cougar" Mellon-Scott worked in a crawl space under the old blue clapboard building on Thames Street and was delighted when Andra wriggled snakelike up to her desk. Andra said she'd like to stay and chat, but the space was too small. She needed to stand up.

Andra described the dream to me the next morning as we lay in the V-berth. At six months pregnant, there wasn't a lot of clearance between her tummy and the underside of the deck. She began the laborious process of turning herself around, exiting the bunk feet-first. Over her shoulder she quipped, "Can't imagine why I'm dreaming about crawl spaces."

One night, not long after, I had the first in a recurring series of disturbing dreams about Peter. The settings and situations varied, but the theme was unchanged: Peter had returned from the dead and was about to be killed again. I was always with him but helpless to intervene.

On this night, I dreamed I was climbing a snow-covered mountain. Men wearing skis were engaged in a fierce competition, trying to hit golf balls uphill through croquet hoops. At the summit, Pete was suddenly standing next to me, and I pushed him inside an underground hut where some other children were drinking hot chocolate. Then I was at the foot of the mountain, watching a kid's game of softball. At a critical juncture, I asked the coach, "Who do we have left?"

"Your son," he sighed.

I raced up the hill yelling for Pete. I poked my head inside the shelter, and a kid told me, "Pete's having his bottom washed."

I said, "C'mon Pete, you're up."

Then I started putting on his shoes and socks and crying, because I knew he was going to die.

I got him down the mountain and into the game. He hit a single up the middle and drove in two runs. I was yelling and smiling as he stood in the base path beaming back at me. He got picked off. And I kept crying and lamenting, "Why does he have to die?"

The drama woke me from a sound sleep, and I felt as though I had a fever, clenching the sheets and thrashing my head. Andra slept silently next to me. Outside was the gentle lapping of water against the hull. As I lay there, the image of him on the railroad tracks played before me. I saw him waving frantically at the engineer, his skinny, muscle-knotted legs buckled beneath him, and at the moment of impact I flinched, jerking my head. I was afraid to go back to sleep, afraid of reentering the world of dreams, a world where the unreal becomes real, and details too horrible to remember endlessly replay.

The Ten Thousand Islands dot the fifty-six-mile coast between the Little Shark River and Marco Island. The only refuge is Everglades City, located five miles up a channel that winds through the green mangrove islands. We tied up to the Rod and Gun Club and clambered ashore to inquire about fuel. It was dark and cool inside the stately building. The lobby seats were leather, the carpeting deep, and the wall paneling expensive. The club was once owned by Barron Gift Collier, who had made his fortune selling ad space in trolley cars "up north."

Everglades City was the hub of what he had envisioned as a private empire carved from the Florida wilderness. An avid sportsman, he hosted various dignitaries and several United States presidents on fishing trips. The club's genteel ambience began in the old, moist walls and on the shabby, gardened grounds, ending in the flowing moss, the slow-moving fans, the silence, and the shade.

213

The rest of the town—a couple of stores and a palm-lined boulevard—was sleepy and undernourished, and I had the feeling, as I swatted mosquitoes, that here the insects had subdued the grandest dreams of man and millionaire.

The club manager looked up. "What do you need?"

"Fuel."

"I'll try to have somebody down to the dock in fifteen minutes."

She must not have tried very hard, or whomever she was looking for must have gone fishing, because it wasn't until the next morning that a cranky fellow riding a golf cart rapped on the hull and yelled, "Gas or diesel?" It was 6:45 A.M.

The days that followed gave us fine sailing past Cape Romano, Marco Island, and Naples. Shell mounds are common in the area, some the sites of important archæological digs. The roving Indians who predated the Spanish conquistadores returned each season to the same places and built crude platforms shaded by palmetto fronds. The shell mounds they left behind, mixed with pieces of bone and pottery, were their refuse heaps. Archæologists call them "kitchen middens," which is a nice name for dunghills.

On the north side of Big Carlos Pass, just south of Fort Myers, is the former site of a strange, half-religious, half-scientific cult called the Koreshan Unity. The founder of the Koreshans, Dr. Cyrus Teed, moved his followers here from Chicago in the late 1890s. "New Jerusalem" was a voluntary cooperative community similar to those in Oneida, New York, Bethel, and Brook Farm. Teed's improbable doctrine posited a one-celled universe, of which the Earth's surface was the outer realm. He conducted elaborate experiments supposedly proving that the Earth curved upward or concavely, and that the planet was actually a hollow sphere with the sun and moon at its center.

Sailing past Fort Myers Beach we came upon a gathering of shrimp boats and pleasure craft assembled for the annual blessing of the fleet. The shrimpers had chosen the occasion to launch a loud protest against TEDs—Turtle Exclusive Devices, designed to let these fabulous reptiles free themselves. According to one fisherman, these mandatory holes in his nets made him lose up to thirty percent of his daily catch. And he wasn't happy about it. The sign on his boat read, "Save an Endangered Species. Support the American Fisherman. Stop Turtle Exclusive Devices."

214

The only dinghy landing on the town side of the harbor was at the home of Bob and Charlotte Wallace. Andra had been directed to them by her mother, who knew Charlotte by way of acquaintances in Rhode Island. Their dock and water were free so long as you signed their guest book and deposited trash in town. Bob invited us inside for drinks, reminiscing about the many cruisers who had come their way over the years.

"The Wallace Yacht Club," one guy called it. "The best yacht club in the world—no dues, no rules, and no meetings!"

The Gulf Intracoastal Waterway begins just north of Fort Myers Beach on the Caloosahatchee River and continues for 150 miles to Tarpon Springs. The first night we anchored inside Sanibel, an island famous for shell collecting. After a storm dozens of old women prowl the beach looking for coquinas, nautiluses, turkey wings, and whelks. The most ardent collectors love them as philatelists do stamps and numismatists coins. Others have a more pecuniary interest. Some, like the short Hispanic women, sell the better specimens to shops or glue them to button boxes and lamp shades. And they are abundant, swept in the millions from vast underwater deposits to the snow-white shore, where the sun quickly bleaches out the deep hues of blue, flecks of red and pink, stripes of yellow, black, and gold. Most are tiny and do not hold your eye. If, however, you stoop on the beach and narrow your field of vision to a square foot, the delicate swirls and lips come into focus, each empty chamber telling of æons spent underwater in some unimaginable community of mollusks.

Sanibel is also home to the J.J. "Ding" Darling National Wildlife Refuge. Darling was a Pulitzer Prize–winning political cartoonist. In 1934 he helped found the Migratory Bird Hunting Stamp Program to call attention to conservation issues.

The day we visited, a chalkboard titled "Recent Sightings" listed the following fauna: white pelican, pileated woodpecker, bald eagle, belted kingfisher, ruddy turnstone, magnificent frigate bird, yellow-crowned night heron, bobcat, and river otter.

I saw the eagle, soaring high above the trees, as fierce-eyed as our country's mascot. I watched for a long time as we dinghied back to *Adriana.* He never dived, and I couldn't help thinking that, on the whole, pelicans eat a whole lot better than rodent killers.

I had just ambled up to the bow to check our anchor rode when I heard a man yelling. *Adriana* was anchored in the lee of Punta Blanca Island near the mouth of Charlotte Harbor. I looked up at the one nearby boat, a thirty-six-foot sloop named *Lark*.

A man on the foredeck waved at me, repeating his call, which I failed to understand. His Spanish accent threw me off. At last he yelled, "Do you have *sixteen?*"

"Yes!" I called back, and climbed below to turn on our VHF ship-to-shore radio.

"*Adriana, Adriana,* this is *Lark*. Would you like to come for a dreenk?"

Before I could answer, some eavesdropping third party answered, "Hell, yes!"

I looked at Andra. "What do you think? This guy sounds a little crazy."

She shrugged. "If you like."

"When?" I answered.

"Now! Whenever you like!" His shrill voice gave me second thoughts. But we didn't often have other people to talk to, and what the heck, I thought, we can't live in a vacuum.

"Half an hour," I said.

Three unshaven men emerged from the cabin to help us aboard. Two took Andra by each hand and pulled her up the stern ladder into the cockpit, whereupon she promptly stepped through the top of their Styrofoam cooler.

"No matter," they chimed. "Have a seat. Have a drink."

Tim, Don, and George were doctors at a well-known southern hospital. Dr. Tim, the tall, handsome one, with a strong Davy Crockett chin, was the head of the *Lark* partnership. He and his son had sailed the boat down the Mississippi River several years ago and berthed her in Englewood so the partners' families could vacation in Florida. Dr. George, short, dark complected with black horn-rimmed glasses, was a native of Chile and the one with whom I had spoken. Dr. Don was fair and heavyset, of Norwegian descent.

Andra had juice while I accepted a beer. But stronger stuff was coming. As night fell we filed below and sat around the roomy dinette. Dr. Don poured me a drink of bourbon and Everclear, a white grain alcohol listed at 190 proof. The label read: "Danger. Flammable. Keep away from sparks, open flame, or heat. May ignite. Do not drink in large quantities. Mix with a nonalcoholic beverage."

"Jesus!" I cried. "This stuff is dangerous!"

"Yes," cackled Dr. Don. "But it's highly efficient!" He threw down a whack that sparked a mischievous glint in his eye.

Soon they were all pulling at the evil bottle, and their stories poured forth.

Once a pediatrician in the military, Dr. Tim was now an anesthesiologist for a famous heart-transplant specialist. So was Dr. George. Dr. Don's speciality was ENT—ears, nose, and throat. All listed credentials as high in octane as their taste in booze.

Time passed quickly. Dr. George insisted we stay for dinner and began boiling whole potatoes in hot oil. A month ago, he said, he and his wife and son had flown down for a week on *Lark*. In an east wind they had anchored off Redfish Creek, in the unprotected waters of the Gulf. By dawn the wind had shifted to the west, and the boat began to pound on the beach bottom. He radioed the Coast Guard, which refused to send assistance unless there was an immediate life-threatening danger. A fisherman in a small boat threw a line and attempted to tow them off. Dr. George's son broke his leg trying to belay the line, and then the fisherman's boat flipped. The man drowned, and later they saw his body wash ashore.

"It was incredible!" Dr. George screamed. "I could not *beleeve* it! I called the Coast Guard again and said, 'Well, a man has died trying to save us. Do you have enough reason to help us now?' "

Ultimately, a Coast Guard helicopter lifted the family from the deck in harnesses, and the boat was towed back to the marina.

Meanwhile, Dr. Tim, propped against a bulkhead, had fallen into a morose stupor in which he played over and over a tape of country-western songs recorded by a friend now dead. The most memorable tune was Walter Brennan's talk-song about a mule named "Old Rivers."

"We always talked about escaping," Dr. Tim ruminated, "and now he's dead, made the Big Escape."

He lit a cigarette.

"Not many doctors left who smoke," I said to change the subject.

Dr. Tim picked up his head, which had fallen back on the cushions. "Only smoke when I drink and only drink when I'm on vacation."

Dr. Don moved to fill my glass with Everclear, but I snatched it away in the nick of time. He looked hurt.

"Bonded moonshine, that's what this is," he said, tossing back another shot.

By now Dr. George was drinking too, and Andra, the only sober person left on board, was finishing cooking dinner.

Dr. Tim asked her when she was due.

"May twenty-fourth," she said, adding that she had a blood-sugar problem that required frequent testing. Some nights her eyes reddened at the thought there might be something wrong with our baby.

"Forget blood sugar!" he yelled, thrusting his fist into the air. "And get rid of your doctor! That shit doesn't mean anything. Just have the baby and be happy." He slumped back in his seat.

Dr. Don leaned forward. "So few babies are damaged," he said. "You'd have to drink this shit every day." He held up the Everclear bottle and studied its transparent contents, awed, apparently, by its remarkable power over him.

Dr. Tim hauled out a guitar from the forward cabin and played an accompaniment to Walter Brennan's sad tale of the companion mule. "Now I was raised on a Kentucky hill farm," he said softly, "and I know about the things in that song. I went to school in Kentucky, and I can play the guitar. . . ." He drifted off, borne by the memories of his dead friend.

Andra served dinner, and for a time things returned more or less to normal, until Dr. Don suddenly fell to his knees clutching the bottle of Everclear. "I'm *sooooo* plain," he moaned. "I'm so *plain!*"

Clearly, Andra said, it was time to leave. I rowed her back to *Adriana* and was fumbling around the cassette-tape box for my Doc Watson instrumentals to take back to Dr. Tim when the Everclear slammed me inside the head. There I made one of the wisest decisions of my life, humbly climbing into bed beside my wife. Sleep, had I known it was coming, would never have felt sweeter.

The next day *Lark* overtook us motorsailing up the waterway.

218

The doctors were cool to us, subdued, perhaps a little embarrassed. We waved and snapped a few pictures as they passed. For a time we followed in their wake, their transom diminishing in size as the distance between us lengthened. Then, as the sun fell low in the sky, we drew even with them as they waited for a bascule bridge to open.

Dr. Tim yelled over, "Why don't you follow us to our marina; we'll all go to dinner."

"This is our turnoff," I called back. "We were planning on anchoring inside the cut here."

"No," Dr. George interjected sharply. "You follow us, *pleeze.*"

I looked at Andra, then back at the three amigos. "How much will the dock cost?"

"You *weel* be our guests," said Dr. George. "*Deener,* too."

The bridge opened, and a decision had to be made. We really had enjoyed their company, so I kicked *Adriana* into gear and followed them through the span to Dion's Yacht Basin.

The doctors had made a strong recovery, evidenced by the bottle of Kentucky bourbon they brought aboard for cocktail hour. Later the five of us drove to the Ship's Lantern restaurant in Englewood for dinner.

Dr. Tim ordered three dozen oyster appetizers. As it happened, Dr. Tim and I were the only ones who liked oysters, and I can only guess that he was anxious to make amends, reverse our first impression of them as drunken fools.

During dinner I made the fatal error of confessing to a past life as a hospital administrator. I told them only to get their goats, knowing full well that doctors hated us "bean counters," ninety-day wonders unleashed by an overregulated industry to harry the faithful followers of Hippocrates. As expected, they were not impressed, preferring to remember me as a magazine editor and comrade of the high seas. They wouldn't debate health-care issues, not without a bottle of Everclear between us, and I remembered too late that a man with ten years of higher education takes his occupation *very* seriously.

Nevertheless, we departed amicably. Andra and I would not soon forget Dr. George's strident criticism of the Coast Guard, Dr. Tim's sentimental guitar playing, or Dr. Don's singular lament of the face that disappointed.

*

A stinging rain pelted us for several days as we crept up the waterway past Venice and Sarasota. Stopping just short of Tampa Bay, we anchored in a protected hook of Longboat Key. The waterway was far enough away so as not to disturb us with the wakes of fleeting Scarabs and Donzis. There was a pretty beach inside, and on its tidemark two restaurants — Moore's Stone Crab, with a pet dolphin frolicking in an outdoor tank, and the Pub. A sign inside the latter read: "Ponce de Leon, near this site, fired the first cannon heard in this country. 1513."

Here we rendezvoused with two of Andra's Newport friends. Jessica, tall and lithe, had brought her two young children to visit her sister-in-law's mother. Nan Prescott, now in her fifties, was once a navy wife in California. She had lived on the base, raised kids, and waited for her husband's ship to come home. One day she decided she'd had enough loneliness, and left. I guess you could call her a hippie. Certainly she was ethereal, gliding about her small apartment in flowing white gowns, her long gray hair tied off to one side, and speaking in breathy, sensual tones.

After lunch we followed her home. Her landlord, who lived in a house connected to the apartment by a breezeway, was a young woman whose husband had died from an allergic reaction to cocaine. The curative she sought for her grief was marijuana, which her new boyfriend brought to her in great quantities. Sometimes they lit two-ounce buds and all inhaled at once, leaning toward the smelly fireball with practiced synchronization. For a second the ball would flame, as if it were the burning bush of Yahweh, before being blown out; then it would smoke like a diesel-soaked rag, filling the house with the pungent odor of the herb.

Nan was a professional masseuse, and we were given to understand that her therapy was exceptional. But I couldn't afford thirty dollars for the minimum treatment and so must trust in the accolades of her clientele. Her bookshelves were full of guides to the human body, relaxation techniques, tomes on muscles, respiration, digestion, and feeling comfortable with one's anatomy. A holistic approach to health and sensuality.

I was not surprised when from the rafters a cockatiel flew about the room, lighting on our seatbacks, jumping to our shoulders and foreheads. Paying it no mind, Nan said that one day the bird had flown into her garden and just "hung out." They watched one another for a week, until one morning she saw it strutting up the sidewalk. Afraid for its safety she ran out, threw a towel over it, and brought the bird inside. Ever since, they have lived together in the tentative symbiosis of man and animal, the way I imagine Eve cared for the unicorn before Adam ate his damning apple.

At dusk Nan drove Jessica, her kids, Andra, and me to the beach. Every hundred feet or so a lovelorn, unrequited poet had written love letters in the sand, forgettable lines such as, "Your love smiles upon my face, And fills up that very empty space."

While the rest of us picked through the seashells and stared at the setting sun, Nan and the children ran down the beach scaring up great flocks of birds. Andra, unable to find a comfortable position in the sand, watched her carefully and said, "How can she run? How can *anyone* run?"

The trip "home" to Boca Raton was executed quickly and timed to the day. Andra's obstetrician had advised her not to travel after April 1, and I had promised to meet the deadline. The route retraced our course south on the Gulf Intracoastal Waterway to Fort Myers, east through the Okeechobee Waterway that bisects the state, and south again along the Atlantic Intracoastal Waterway. Two weeks to cover 290 miles, which meant a leisurely pace of just more than 20 miles a day.

I ran *Adriana* aground in Venice, trying to find the free city dock. Men shouted advice from shore, which I steadfastly ignored. After all, I'd had plenty of practice making and correcting my mistakes. A violent thunderstorm rocked the harbor and buried us in rain. I rowed out the anchor at least a dozen times, only to have the windlass pull it free of the soft bottom. Once I even wrapped it around a steel channel marker, but the keel was irrevocably stuck and there was so much tension on the line that when I turned off the windlass, the bitter end unraveled from the drum and flew off into the rain and darkness. A makeshift grappling hook retrieved it.

I gave up and began fixing dinner. Inexplicably, the boat suddenly and quietly floated free, as if it had purposely resisted my will, relenting only when I had forgotten about it. There is wisdom in letting the tide do your work for you.

That evening I dreamed of Pete again. This time we were riding on top of a train like outlaws in the Wild West. Other kids were lying with us, cheek to the metal, hoping to make it safely through the tunnel that had abruptly appeared from around the bend. Then I was on the ground watching helplessly as Pete stood up. "Get down!" I yelled. "For Christ's sake, get down!" I waved my hands in desperation, screaming until I was hoarse, and awoke with the sheets knotted in my fists, sitting up as suddenly as if we'd been run over by a freighter. A light, sweet rain was falling on the deck. When it stopped, I opened the hatch and watched the stars revolve around Polaris, but of course it is we who are moving, spinning smoothly through the night.

At the mouth of the Caloosahatchee River we turned east toward Fort Myers. We spent a few days at the city marina while Andra rode a bus to Boca Raton for a scheduled blood-sugar test. I took the opportunity to finish sanding the boom Danny Keirns had started a month earlier. Virginians George and Martha ("as in Washington") Haycox babysat me evenings on their trawler, berthed on the other side of the dock. When Andra returned we toured Thomas Edison's winter home, laboratory, and botanical gardens where, fearful of rubber shortages in the event of another world war, he developed the material from hybrid goldenrod.

That marked the end of our brief cruise to Florida's West Coast. It was unquestionably lovelier than the East Coast, and slower paced. Numerous islands such as Captiva, Gasparilla, and Useppa add variety and interest. It is no secret, however, that the West Coast is a retirement coast; even at forty I felt out of place. Andra asked a young store clerk on Sanibel if there were many young people on the island. "There are a few," he said, "but we all seem to be working *real* hard."

That remark helped us decipher what was different about the West Coast. While men and women over fifty-five outnumbered the young a hundred to one, only the latter appeared to be working. It was the waiters and bankers and mechanics who owned homes, moving out for a few months each winter to rent their properties to vacationing geriatrics at fifteen hundred dollars per month. The old people who found work necessary were forced to take "kids' jobs" pumping gas and bagging groceries. We saw nothing wrong with this, just that it was a sometimes confusing reversal of traditional roles. In fact, the retirees appeared to enjoy life immensely. Everywhere we saw them playing tennis, fishing, or engaging in a quiet game of English bowls. But like them, we felt an increasing need to be with people our own age, and we realized, somewhat reluctantly, that it would take another twenty years before we could consider the West Coast as a permanent home.

The Okeechobee Waterway can be broken into three subsections: the Caloosahatchee River becomes Lake Okeechobee becomes a rather boring dredged channel becomes the Intracoastal all over again. There are five locks and a number of bridges, miles of citrus orchards, a few ranch homes on the banks, launch ramps, redneck fishermen in bassboats, and long straightaways that can numb your mind.

After the hamlets of Olga and Alva, there is a series of oxbows where the Army Corps of Engineers has straightened the Caloosahatchee. We anchored in one behind a small spoil island. The depth of the tea-colored water dropped from twenty-four to seventeen feet at the mouth, to five where we stopped and with much labor turned around in the narrow channel. The water was choked with reeds and yellow-petaled lilies. Mullet jumped to get a look at us. On the shores were cypress, bamboo, mangroves, and live oak draped in Spanish moss that fell softly to the water.

A brown-spotted heron lit on a nearby branch. An unseen bird called, "Psow, da-da-da!" A frog's flatulent voice echoed across the still, brown waters. The air was thick with the intense, soapy fragrance of orange blossoms. This was the lushness we had expected of the Everglades and only now had found.

At La Belle we looked up Uolevi Lahti, who had retired here from Michigan some years ago. He lived on a wild oxbow in an old "cracker" house built by cattle drivers in the last century. In his early seventies and living alone, he kept the place a shambles, every room an "office" of papers, gadgets, instruments, and utensils. Like his brother Aarre and nephew Alexis, he was trained as an industrial designer, an artist whose overriding drive was eccentric pragmatism. The family photo album shows Uolevi demonstrating to a group of Ford Motor Company engineers an upside down fiberglass dinghy molded as a removable headpiece to a '58 Fairlane.

To pay the bills in Florida he ran a small company manufacturing outdoor hi-fi speakers; about his pool and yard hung the cone-shaped devices wired to a master control panel so he could play his favorite operas at full volume, in company with the cacophony of the jungle.

We spent a day touring La Belle with Uolevi. The town's great claim to fame is the annual Swamp Cabbage Festival, a marketing twist to make "hearts of palm" seem less pretentious. We visited waitresses, pizza bakers, real-estate agents, and a gunsmith, all friends of Uolevi who were enchanted with (and to a degree patronized by) his eccentricity.

As we neared the eastern terminus of the Okeechobee Waterway, I began to realize our journey was nearing its end. Nervously, I broached the possibility of taking the baby to the Bahamas for the summer. "You two could even fly over and meet me," I suggested hopefully. "We'll find a nice, peaceful anchorage, not too far from a settlement, and just hang out on the beach. It'll be great."

Andra looked at me without expression. "I don't think so, Pook."

"Why?" I asked, more shocked than I had a right to be.

She grimaced. "I'm not taking a newborn to some Third World country. What if something happens to it?" She let that sink in for a moment, then added, "Besides, trying to care for a baby in a small boat isn't my idea of fun."

There, she'd gone and said it. I was crushed. Her feelings and logic were irrefutable. But why, I wondered, couldn't she throw caution to the wind, say, "Yeah! Let's do it!"? After all, we knew couples who had raised babies on boats, and from what we knew they'd suffered no ill effects. Where was Andra's spirit of adventure?

"You want to end up in a cramped cape with a white picket fence?" I asked peevishly.

"Yes," she said with surprising certainty. "Yes, I do. I know you don't, and I think that's fine. We're just different, that's all."

And so we motored on in silence, each wondering why we had married someone with such different goals. A year ago we hadn't seemed so estranged. But who could have foretold Peter's death?

Or Andra's pregnancy? For a moment—not the first in recent months—there shimmered over the bow the raw-nerved, electrically charged field of divorce, a snare from which it takes years to extricate yourself.

"I think you should take Adria to the Bahamas with you," she said at long last.

"What will you do?" I asked.

"Go back to Rhode Island."

"But why?" I was nothing if not obtuse.

"Well, I'm certainly not going to wait for you in Florida. What would I do? Live with Ken and Karyn?"

The rest of that day I wrestled with my choices. By the time we docked for the night near Indian Town, I had made up my mind. I would go. Adria was counting on it, and so was I. The plans were already in place. And hadn't Andra let me believe these past months that she would go, even with the baby? I'd call myself a quitter if I didn't go, even for a few weeks. It seemed this was my one chance, and I was determined to make the most of it.

At the same time I knew I was justifying a selfish decision. There was still a trace of the same bull-headed ignorance that led me to jail and divorce. Leaving Andra and the baby standing on the dock was leaving Pete and Adria all over again.

From nowhere, or so it seemed, Andra suddenly said, "Who knows, you might even like him."

"Who's that?"

"The baby."

"Why did you say 'him'?"

"Because I know it's a boy."

"For real?"

"Just a feeling. But I know."

19
Birth Day

The phone rang.

"Hi, Dad!" It was Adria calling from Michigan.

"How's it going, Sweetie?"

"Great. Listen, I want to fly down when the baby's born."

"Well, he's due May twenty-fourth."

"He? I had a dream the other night it was a girl."

"Hard to say. But Andra's convinced it's a boy. Mother's intuition, I guess."

Just about everybody who knew us—who knew Pete—predicted a boy. There were doubters, like the French woman at the pâtisserie we frequented in Deerfield Beach. "You will have a girl," she told us confidently. "I am *never* wrong."

Andra began to have doubts, too. She had had a lot of time to think about such nebulous issues. And a lot of time to nourish the baby growing in her belly. Last summer she had weighed 105 pounds, today fifty percent more. There was no air conditioning in Dave Landmann's investment house, and it was hot.

"I feel like some kind of canal mammal," she lamented.

Adriana was docked in the backyard canal, and each morning when I threw back the hatches to air out the cabins I could feel the dead burning air bursting to escape. Sleeping aboard was out of the question. Dave's Boca Raton house wasn't much better, so we purchased a couple of large fans—as much to blow off the no-see-ums and mosquitoes as to cool our sticky flesh. Welcome to summertime in Florida.

"Just wait," said our friends. "You ain't seen nothin' yet."

In exchange for dockage and use of the bedrooms, which were excluded from the ambitious renovation plan, I gave Dave three hours of labor daily. Skip Clements, the singlehanded cruiser we'd met last winter through Dave, signed on too for carpentry and general construction. Together we built a kitchen addition to the house on the canal side, tiled floors, tore out walls and built new ones, scraped, painted, and generally made mayhem.

Andra ran errands to the building-supply stores, priced windows and awnings, and weeded the overgrown lawn. The front yard, neglected for more than a year, was a veritable botanical garden. Palmettos and giant schefflera trees shaded the lower hibiscus and bougainvillaea bushes, and when the wind blew the air filled with blossoms as in a scene from Gabriel Garcia Marquez's *One Hundred Years of Solitude*. In the backyard were orange, tangerine, and grapefruit trees burgeoning with succulent fruits. To us, they represented the real beauty of Florida, falling faster than we could eat them.

Among the weeds a black racer hunted chameleons, which hunted roaches and palmetto bugs, which hunted our food kept in makeshift cabinets. If we had to get up in the middle of the night and turn on a light, there was always a surprise crawling on the ceiling or counter.

"It's a goddamned science lab," Andra said one day in disgust. She was watching an army of tiny ants carrying off the dead body of a wasp. "We could host field trips for the Boca Raton High School biology class."

On the worst days, I shoveled gravel from the driveway to level it for paving, jackhammered concrete, and smashed cinder blocks with a sledgehammer, ready to "run rabbit" with Cool Hand Luke. Some days, when I grew tired of the prison theme, I fantasized I was a Chinese intellectual relocated to the countryside during Mao's Cultural Revolution, assigned to menial labor as punishment for my bourgeois tendencies. I wrapped gauze around my blistered hands, let the sweat run down my face, and wheeled my barrow across a yard lumpy with decaying fruit.

"One child," I mumbled to Andra. "That's all the government will allow us."

Adriana, which rested miserably in the mud at low tide, tugged at her mooring lines and at my heart. The nearest safe inlet was

Port Everglades, three hours south on the waterway, which made daysailing impractical. Between housework and writing I began to dismantle her interior parts. It had been nearly a year since she'd been properly cleaned. Andra and I were sleeping on berth cushions in the house, so I took the opportunity to paint the boards underneath. We emptied the food lockers for fear of attracting bugs, and I presented Andra with a few label-less cans that, recalling the inky mulch of fruit cocktail I'd opened last September in Maine, made her skin crawl. Many of my good tools were rusted, some of the cabin-light wiring had inexplicably gone dead between the deck and overhead liner, the waterline was fouled, and there were sticky deposits of dirt everywhere. I remembered sitting in Tiny Clark's boatyard a year ago and feeling overwhelmed by the same mess, the same multitude of chores, the same infernal list. But as the weeks passed, I began to anticipate a summer's cruise of the Bahamas, and my spirits perked.

Quietly, Andra began setting up the nursery, which by necessity was in our bedroom. We bought a used crib for twenty-five dollars, Dave gave us a high chair, and Andra's mother shipped down a changing table.

"You know," Andra would say. "This really is Pete's baby."

How could I not embrace this new child with all the love in me? As the May due date drew nearer I found myself more resigned to sharing our lives and to the concomitant responsibility. At the same time I began to experience a strange sense of dread, different from any so-called loss of freedom or forced change of plans. This caught me deeper, like an intravascular probe looking for blockage. I couldn't put my finger on it at first, and the only way I could put it to rest was by more or less ignoring the imminence of the baby's birth. If Andra asked for my help in the nursery, I freely gave it. Otherwise, I lost myself in pounding nails, troweling cement, and following the blinking cursor on the gray screen of my computer. To Andra it must have seemed I was still pouting. I wasn't, not now. Something new had moved in, shapeless and foreboding. When I knew what was bothering me I would tell her.

While I ripped lumber and scraped ceilings there was much time for reflection. Andra and I still talked about the places we'd visited and where, if we had our druthers, we would like to settle. Maine was certainly the most beautiful, its fir-lined peninsulas and rocky outcroppings jutting into the whitecapped ocean, the purposeful lobstermen tending traps, and the crisp clear nights, unblemished by the loom of city lights, telling the perfect bedtime story when viewed from our berth through the forward hatch.

We remembered sailing down the East River past the skyscrapers of Manhattan on a sunny fall day, swept by the current under the great Brooklyn Bridge. At last I told Andra of the drowned dachshund with the red collar I'd seen floating by the 42nd Street heliport. "And you thought I was a fool to fear floating bodies in New York City!" She was vindicated.

Lennie Zazzarino. Cell mate. Soul brother. Kept us company that long night passing the Jersey coast when unlit barges and desperate Coast Guardsmen moved in and out of our sphere of vision like faces seen through a subway window. And the neon of Atlantic City, splashing the black night with an arc of wild red colors as if the casinos had caught fire inside an underwater bubble. The Destruction of Atlantis. Lennie and I were different, but a bond forever joined us. 26245 and 26292. Milan, Michigan.

Chesapeake City held good memories for us, despite the hassles of repairing the bent propeller. In times of need you learn who your friends are. Author/cruiser Wayne Carpenter. Bob Green and his boatyard staff. Tom and Jackie Karkos, who gave us use of their dock to recoup. The cruising code was real: What goes 'round comes around.

The bitter cold that frosted Virginia seemed to have rearranged our genetic code, for it was a long, long time before we complained of heat and humidity. The unusual snowstorm on the Great Dismal Swamp Canal, banding the cypress like forester's paint for some great lumbering operation, was as close as I wanted to get to another Michigan winter. And who better to share it with than Wolverines Robert and Mary Gibson, basic as peas and porridge, country folk who never have and—the spirit of Captain Tommie Drake willing—never will set foot in a yacht club.

The endless miles motoring through the Carolinas are practically lost in the cellar of my memory, and for those two states we harbored the greatest regret. Never did we have the chance to follow Mark Balough home to Cedar Island and sail the shallow bay waters in his small homemade boats. Or meet the blacks who speak a sort of pidgin English called Gullah, derived from their African roots.

Vivid are the miles of yellow and green sawgrass, wavering like Kansas prairie grain in the afternoon breezes. And the shrimp boats with booms outstretched and nets flowing, chugging slowly along the side channels as if they were toys directed by the hand of a child on a basement plywood board. Put on your waders, stand hip-deep in the brine, and sing a song of America. There are catfish that would smell good in the breakfast pan. And in the sky noisy flocks of ducks and geese fly over the Cape Romain Wildlife Refuge, patterned according to an order incomprehensible to man. I remembered watching a disarray of birds turn east and west, north and south before settling on a leader and falling into their customary V shape, one arm longer than the other, and feeling glad I do not live in an age when all the mysteries of Nature have been unraveled. I do not want to know *why* a particular bird points the chevron; I would rather *wonder* why, and marvel that he does.

Georgia showed us a different side of its face, not the poor homesteads settled among the pines and dry, red earth I had seen so many years ago driving to Fort Gordon, but the wild and turbulent waters of the rivers and sounds pounding down to the sea. How odd it was to see the miles of grass and islands, yet no sign of man. I had not expected wilderness.

Florida, I loved and hated. Disparaged, because of the perverse blight man has built on its inhospitable coast. Unique, because there is no seismic record of volcanic activity under its thin limestone crust, and no moraines left by retreating glaciers to entertain amateur geologists. Learning to see beauty in the flat and mosquito-ridden Everglades requires the same inward-opening eye as discovering beauty in the desert: Sometimes you have to walk out at night and see a cactus bloom.

Florida is always prettier at night, when the dew moistens the fantastic vegetation, billowing banks of clouds pile high in thunderheads creating the illusion of mountains, and the myriad species of insects sing their cosmic refrain, "I exist!"

Andra and I recalculated her due date, counting 266 days from our third night in Lubec, Maine, and arriving at May 22. Two days before the doctor's prediction. The evening of the 21st, Ken and Karyn Green brought Ken Love to dinner. Ken Love, tall and balding, was captain of a large motoryacht and once operated a charter-boat company in the Bahamas. We had first met at a beachfront bar called the Whale's Rib, owned by Rhode Islanders. His knowledge of the islands impressed me, and I wanted to go over the charts with him. He brought a bottle of rum and fresh mangoes, which he held out for my inspection.

"Fresh mangoes," he said in his measured Southern accent, "are highly prized by the Bahamians. You cannot give a better gift. If you want to make a lasting friend in the Family Islands, give fresh mangoes. If I were you, I'd take a bag."

Our guests left around 1 A.M. Andra woke me at 3.

"I just felt a contraction," she said. "I think it's happening."

My head was groggy. I looked at the clock. "Go back to sleep," I said. "I'll time them in the morning." Having been down this road before, it was hard not to be a know-it-all.

"No. Time them now," she said emphatically. "I'm not having this baby on a car seat."

During the next half hour I sat in bed studying the tiny Casio watch we'd bought just yesterday for this very purpose.

"How far apart?" she asked anxiously.

"Not sure," I said. By the time one contraction had ended, I'd forgotten the time it had begun. I pulled myself off the bunk cushion on the floor and found a pad of paper. After another half hour we determined that the contractions were about three minutes apart. Our Lamaze instructors had told us to go to the hospital when they got down to five!

At daybreak we checked into the labor room at Bethesda Memorial Hospital in Boynton Beach. Andra was indeed in labor—just two centimeters dilated, but in true labor nonetheless. Together we walked the hallway, trying to speed up the process. When Andra grew tired she lay in bed and watched television. Jimmy Swaggart announced his return to the pulpit following his prurient affair with a prostitute. An 800 telephone number, flanked by blinking Visa and MasterCard logos, solicited donations.

Later, when her labor intensified, and the fetal heart monitor showed the baby's pulse coupled to the strength of its mother's contractions, I snuck glimpses of the Detroit Pistons–Boston Celtics basketball game. I was glad Herb McCormick wasn't there to hear me root for the Motor City; eight years in New England, he said, should have instilled at least a small spark of Celtic Pride.

By late afternoon Andra was nearly fully dilated, and we were both exhausted. Never had I seen her concentrate so hard. Seldom did she break the rhythm of her practiced breathing, and when she showed signs of losing the beat, I got in her face and breathed with her, advising and encouraging as best I could.

Then the pushing commenced, and the baby's head began its slow, tight journey down the birth canal. I asked the labor nurse for the doctor.

"He left," she said. "I called him half an hour ago; he *should* be back."

I felt a pang of anxiety, and suddenly I knew why I had dreaded this moment.

The nurse shrugged. "Listen," I said, "I just. . . ." I couldn't finish the sentence.

"We've got two C-sections going," she called on her way out of the room. "Back in a sec."

I bit my lip and looked at Andra. Another contraction was coming. She braced her feet against my hands and pushed. Her face was contorted, red with effort, and when it was over she fell back against the pillow. When her strength came around she asked, "What were you saying to the nurse?"

I didn't answer, just studied the monitor graph. "Here comes another one."

Suddenly the doctor was standing beside me, and I felt a tremendous giving way of relief. Now I wouldn't have to go searching for an arrogant doctor, find the white-coated millionaire chuckling with colleagues in the staff dining room, lift him by the collar, and scream in his face, "Listen, I just lost a son because he had cerebral palsy, and he had cerebral palsy because the goddamn doctor wasn't in the room when he was born! For twenty-seven hundred dollars the least you can do is help my wife through the last hour!" I had been wrong. I could be hurt again. The toughness exacted by prison life and the loss of Peter had created a seemingly invincible layer of scar tissue, but this unborn child was my Achilles heel.

"How long has she been pushing?" the doctor asked.

"Two hours," I snapped.

"That's enough," he said calmly. "Let's go have a baby."

232

The nurse and I wheeled Andra down the hall to the delivery room and transferred her to the table and stirrups. Then the nurse cut all the lights except the big moonlike disc behind the doctor. Several shots anesthetized Andra's perineum, and an episiotomy was performed. Then forceps were inserted one at a time, like separate halves of egg tongs.

"You push and I'll pull," the doctor told her.

Slowly the baby's head emerged—purple, wet, hair matted, a line of blood across its scalp. The doctor turned the head clockwise, and the shoulders began to follow it out.

"Looks like it has the features of a girl," he said.

"You guys are always blowing it," I said.

"At least fifty percent of the time," he joked.

Andra squeezed my hand. Our muscles tensed.

As I watched the doctor pull the baby completely free and gently turn it over, I thought again about the metempsychosis of souls. In truth, I didn't believe any of it. But I thought about Peter and how I had cradled his head for fear he would fall onto the floor. And I thought, if this is a boy, in some strange way my son has come back to me.

The doctor pulled aside the umbilical cord and announced, "You have a boy!"

Andra and I looked at each other through a veil of tears. For Andra, it was the first son born on her mother's side of the family in more than one hundred years. The first son on her father's side in two generations. And for me, well, Stephen is Stephen, named for my father. Eight pounds, five ounces. Big, pink, alert, and healthy. And that was that. I had a son again.

I was released from prison on February 5, 1967. Two years had passed behind bars. The day before my release, a trusty had driven Robertson and me to a mall to buy clothes. There was another inmate with us, a likeable hillbilly named Trogden. We got stuck in traffic on the freeway, and Robbie got drunk at a truck stop. Wanted to buy everybody vodka and tonics. The driver refused to come inside, but Trogden said he'd take a beer. Robbie called him a "no-class motherfucker." I couldn't get them to leave, and so we drank. I turned twenty-one in prison, and it was my first legal drink, though I didn't have even a driver's license to prove it. The driver was outside honking, desperately honking.

The next morning I couldn't remember how we had made it back to the prison. And when the guards took me to pick up my parole certificate, the chief pulled me inside his office and asked if Robbie had been drunk. Threatened to hold up my parole papers if I didn't tell. "Take 'em," I said. "Only reason we were late was the traffic."

There was little point in denying my papers. Robertson got out the next week, and I saw a lot of him during the few months before he was arrested again and disappeared. Lennie stopped by briefly before catching the bus to New Jersey. Ten years would pass before I would see him again. Robertson, as I have related, vanished in the system.

But on this day my thoughts were focused squarely in front of me. Agoraphobia brought on a kind of queasiness that swept over me as the last gate opened, and I made my way nervously down the main corridor. The buffed tiles reflected the light at the end. Here was the warden's office and a reception area for visitors. For two years I had languished within spitting distance of the administrative wing, yet had *never* seen it. Were they really letting me go? Yes, it appeared they were quite serious. I paused at the door. So many inmates I'd known had subconsciously subverted their release plan; the caseworkers blamed it on "institutionalization," and the Freudians called it a fear of leaving the womb. Gunter Grass's Oskar, the dwarf protagonist of *The Tin Drum,* would have refused for psychopolitical reasons. Me? I had every reason to go and never look back.

A guard opened the door, and suddenly I stood *outside* the brick walls. The air was cold and dry, and there was light in the sky from horizon to horizon. Nothing impeded my view. As far as I could see were the cornfields of the prison farm. Above me to either side were the guard towers, and looking back I saw the roof and fence where they'd shot an escaping inmate, his body falling past the visitor's-room window. Not every prisoner left Milan on his feet. I was alive, though my kidneys were full of stones and my teeth full of cavities; like Pete, I was a little damaged coming out.

Space. There was so much of it! And it ran in all directions. And then Margaret's car pulled out of the driveway, and I stared in wonder out the window at the passing rows of withered corn and the dusting of snow in the furrows. Cars hurtled to and fro on the freeway; each driver, I thought paranoiacally, knows I'm an ex-con.

I didn't think of buying a boat that day and escaping this madness, but the impulse would come soon.

The day I was released from prison was the happiest day of my life. It was the day I started living again. But the experience changed me forever. The day Peter died was the saddest day of my life. It was the day I started dying again.

The sneering locomotive steams inexorably at my heels. I've been trying to outrun the train ever since. As fast as I can. Here, on the water, where there are no tracks, it feels safe, for my family, my son.

Who, studying his billowing white sails, cannot for a time forget his shortcomings, his mistakes, and the futility and insignificance of his menial endeavors, and, looking at the night sky, not find comfort in the falling stars?

EPILOGUE

The irony of the sign above the custom agent's desk was not lost on me, not after having waited an hour outside the tiny government office in West End, Grand Bahama, in ninety-degree heat. It read: "The pace of events is moving so fast that unless we keep our sights on tomorrow, we cannot expect to be in touch with today." — Dean Rusk

Worse, I hadn't slept a wink during the Gulf Stream crossing from Hillsboro Inlet, Florida, and the engine had quit thirty feet from the Jack Tar Marina fuel dock. The only thing that was moving fast was my temper.

"What time did you arrive in West End?" the agent demanded.

I had no idea, what with the engine quitting, tying up to the seawall, changing filters, and the subsequent tow to a marina dock. "Oh, about twelve-thirty," I guessed.

The agent looked at his watch. "It is three now. You realize you have been in this country illegally?"

I nodded.

He studied my forms. "You are Daniel?"

"Yes."

"You realize I almost put you in the lion's den?"

"Mmm."

"What do you do?"

"I'm a writer."

"You are going to write about your *engine?*"

"No. I'm going to write about *you*."

He burst into laughter. "Fair enough!" he said, stamping my passport, handing me my cruising permit, and waving me out the door.

Roland "Bones" Pinder and his apprentice "Fishnet" repaired the diesel the next day. My replacement fuel filters, he said, were all bad. "I, Bones," he pronounced solemnly, "tell you it is safe to run without one. You won't roll much on the bank. And you've still got the secondary filter, but you should buy a replacement for the primary when you get to Marsh Harbour."

Thus blessed, Herb McCormick, Danny Keirns, Jeff Schipritt, and I set out across the Little Bahama Bank, fifty-six miles to Great Sale Cay. They'd flown from Rhode Island to Florida the day before to help me sail across the Gulf Stream to the Bahamas. I hadn't seen Herb since the night he had come aboard *Adriana* in Newport Harbor with news of Peter. So many times I had replayed that stormy night and thought of Herb commandeering a fishing boat, determined to do what he had to do. And I loved him for it.

Stephen was just six weeks old, already pulling himself across the carpet by his fingernails. It was hard saying good-bye, watching him and Andra waving from Dave Landmann's dock as we motored out of the canal toward the Intracoastal. In a few days they would fly to Rhode Island and drive on to the Vermont summer home of Andra's childhood friends. I think she was a little shocked I was actually going. So was I.

We left the deep purple of the Gulf Stream at Sandy Cay, where the depths drop to ten and twelve feet and the color of the warm water turns a brilliant green.

We worked our way south through the Abacos, stopping at Great Guana and Green Turtle cays, the latter host to an annual summer regatta that brings nearly a hundred boats from the States. We trailed lures to catch barracuda, dove for conch and grouper, hid from the fierce sun under *Adriana*'s awning, and vainly tried to dodge the thunderstorms that we could see building over the islands like bomb clouds over Dresden.

At Marsh Harbour my buddies flew home, and Adria flew in. She stepped off the small Aero Coach commuter wearing baggy flannel shorts, pointed black shoes, a straw hat, and Madonna sunglasses. At seventeen, she was a desert flower, incongruously fresh and colorful against the drab landscape of the island's interior flatland.

Adria and I sailed first to Man O' War Cay, then Hope Town, and down the east side of Great Abaco to the Land and Sea Park just above Little Harbour. This was perhaps the most impressive reef we saw in all of the Bahamas. Great golden topiaries of elkhorn coral branched to the surface, the intricate lace of purple sea fans wavered in the currents, and the huge sulcate brain corals that sprang from the sandy bottom appeared as ancient fossils of a dead race. Among them swam rainbow parrotfish, blue tangs, angelfish, queen triggers, French grunts, yellowtail snapper, mejorra, and Nassau grouper. Near the surface hovered the translucent needlefish, and in the distance lurked a solitary nurse shark which, despite its benign demeanor, still cast a malevolent shadow across the undersea gardens.

Our plan called for us to meet Adria's friend Aku in George Town, Exuma, a week hence. So at first light we made the initial leap southward by tackling the deep-water passage across the Northeast Providence Channel to Eleuthera. Freighters large and small steamed the lanes to and from Nassau, and several times we were forced to slow or alter course. We passed a day in Spanish Wells, swimming off the beach and sidestepping towheaded teenagers racing down the narrow streets in brand-new Subarus and Isuzus. There are a lot of Alburys and Pinders in the islands, all descendants of the Loyalists who settled here during the Revolutionary War.

The winds blew southeast the entire month of July, and the cruise down Eleuthera and Cat islands was no exception, our slow progress exacerbated by squalls and thunderstorms above and the black, well-defined coral heads below. The steady diet of headwinds ended when we turned southwest, beam-reaching from Hawk's Nest Creek to George Town at better than six knots.

We crossed the Tropic of Cancer, 23½ degrees north, the northernmost latitude reached by the overhead sun and the beginning of the true Tropics. It was a small victory, considering how our original plans had been subverted, and I promised myself that someday Andra, Stephen, and I would return, pressing deeper into this band of equatorial trade winds, following the arc of somnambulant islands to meditate in the wilting heat.

Walking the streets that night we came upon a revival in the town park. The religious—old women wearing straw derbylike hats and young men in pressed white shirts—sang hymns to the accompaniment of an electric keyboard, swaying and stamping their feet as they rocked long into the night, professing their love for Jesus. The not-so-religious lay about the park walls like musing cats, observing the congregation from a distance. Boys whispered to girls in the shadows of the trees, and across the street even the patrons of the Two Turtles Inn seemed to slow their drinking, fixed by the incessant call and refrain.

Aku flew into the small airport on a commuter plane, and to celebrate we ate dinner at the Peace & Plenty Hotel, a popular hangout for cruisers. While Adria and Aku danced to the calypso music of the steel band, I made the acquaintance of a tall American wearing a Caterpillar diesel cap. He seemed the average working stiff, in the islands to mend a heart or spend lottery money. He parted with a thick roll of cash, purchasing three bottles of Dom Perignon at $125 per, which he generously passed around the bar. In the Family Islands, strangers are not strangers for long, and we toasted him until he dropped, which he did at about two in the morning.

Aku soon proved his worth aboard *Adriana*. The tall lad with a mop of long blond hair always in his eyes found four conch at Lansing Cay, then spent the next hour and a half cleaning them, plus the four fish we'd speared. He was up to his elbows in slime and viscera but seemed to enjoy it.

Slowly, we worked our way up the Exumas, snorkeled in the shallow, pastel waters, endured a boarding by U.S. drug agents in Nassau, shot across the Great Bahama Bank to Gun Cay, and returned to Florida in a rollicking broad reach.

Once again we berthed at the Landmanns' dock in Boca Raton. We relaxed in air-conditioned comfort, indulged ourselves with hot showers, and slathered cool balms over our sunburnt bodies. The cruise I had dreamed of and planned for fifteen years was over.

Adria and I drove Aku to the Fort Lauderdale airport, then drove north to meet Andra and Stephen in Rhode Island. The little tyke had lost all his hair, his pointed ears giving him the look of a comic-book Martian. Adria returned to Michigan for her last year of high school, and Andra grudgingly agreed to return to Boca Raton for the winter so I could complete the research I had begun on several books.

By January, however, we'd had it with the crime, the crack houses, the dull landscape, and the dim prospects of gainful employment. We loaded our old Chevy wagon with everything we owned, and feeling like Steinbeck's Joad family, drove back to Rhode Island for the last time. Stephen hated the car, and to amuse him we sang every song we knew, improvising hundreds of ridiculous verses to Old McDonald's Farm. We rented a hundred-year-old house, new by Newport standards, Andra was re-hired at *Cruising World,* and I free-lanced.

Realizing that we wouldn't be cruising again soon and that it was impractical to maintain *Adriana* for daysailing, we put her on the market. In May an English couple purchased her sight unseen. I flew to Boca Raton to meet John Schofield and his crew, Wayne Yohn. The three of us delivered the boat to Annapolis, sailing off-shore, borne by the Gulf Stream.

Matthew Maury called it "a river in the ocean." Jacques Piccard called it "the sun beneath the sea." Benjamin Franklin called it the "gulph stream." And author William MacLeish, awed by the powerful, arcane forces of the North Atlantic subtropical gyre that to this day still baffles scientific inquiry, called the stream "the blue god."

MacLeish is a former editor of *Oceanus* at the Woods Hole Oceanographic Institution and the author of an engaging book, *The Gulf Stream: Encounters with the Blue God.* To hear MacLeish tell it, the young scientists turn on their CRTs and build computer models while the old masters cringe. "I can't do my work with equations!" cries Woods Hole oceanographer Val Worthington. "I have to catch water."

MacLeish's Gulf Stream is something of a blind man's elephant, a changeling who flashes different looks at different people. Paul Richardson tries to get a handle on the surface loops and eddies by plotting the recorded sightings of derelict nineteenth-century sailing ships. Worthing and John Swallow invent a "tubular metal device that could be made to float with the current at desired depths," to prove Henry Stommel's hypothesis that a 1,600-meter-deep current runs counter to and under the stream. Lawrence Madin tethers a team of divers together and arms them with glass jars to capture salpae, the transparent tunicates that are lifelong residents of the stream.

Like the blind man touching the various parts of the elephant in a vain attempt at identification, MacLeish has approached his subject from every angle: first aboard the chemical carrier *Exxon Wilmington,* steaming down the meandering Mississippi — "the brown god"; sliding down the Florida Keys aboard a U.S. Coast Guard cutter toward the Yucatán Pass, pulled "back inside the choke point at night, running without lights, a seaborne stakeout," ultimately seizing from the *Daisy Marivel* ten tons of marijuana despite the crew's frantic dumping efforts; and sailing aboard the topsail schooner *Welcome* from Portugal to the Canaries and the West Indies, swept along by the Canary and North Equatorial Currents, all the while reading accounts of Columbus's passage of discovery — "spirit escorts," MacLeish calls the admiral, crew, *Nina,* and sisters.

After years of searching, one day while diving at the western edge of the Great Bahama Bank, MacLeish free-falls below the 100-foot-deep lip into the Florida Strait, flirting with nitrogen narcosis before hearing Debussy's "La Cathedrale Engloutie" and declaring, "This, for me, could be the way in to the blue god."

Before leaving Florida I obtained from the National Hurricane Center the latest Gulf Stream Flow Chart. This and additional sea-surface thermal-analysis charts are available free of charge from the Miami NOAA office. Studying them, it comes as no surprise that the eighty-degree water of the stream sweeps north practically within a stone's throw of South Florida's beaches, squeezed as it is between the mainland and the Bahamas.

East of Daytona the first eddies were depicted, spinning off east and west of the core. Farther north, off the coast of the Carolinas, they grew larger and more erratic, increasing the chance of our being slowed by the south-flowing side of a subgyre. But with even the slightest attention to navigation, I figured we should be able to stay within the mainstream and take advantage of the two- to three-knot boost.

We left the ICW at Palm Beach and guided *Adriana* into the stream, the same current that so fascinated the curious mind of Benjamin Franklin more than two hundred years ago. Noting that the mail packets took two weeks longer crossing the Atlantic than the merchant ships, he apprised the secretary of the British Post Office of the northeast-flowing current. Franklin's cousin, Captain Timothy Folger, had written: "We have informed them [the mail packet captains] that they were stemming a current that was against them to the value of three miles an hour and advised them to cross it, but they were too wise to be counselled by simple American fishermen."

Franklin's letter was largely ignored, too, which perhaps explains why during the American Revolution he proposed altering the Gulf Stream to throw Great Britain into a new ice age.

During the voyage to France, Franklin endeavored to study the stream with sea thermometers as far east as the Bay of Biscay. Not only did he take surface readings, but he also sampled to the depth of one hundred feet using bottles and casks. Together with Folger he recorded and plotted the findings. The reports represented original scientific observation and resulted in the first known map of the Gulf Stream, printed in London, England, around 1770.

Equipped with Loran C, it was not difficult for us to calculate the speed of the current in which we rode. Comparing our speed through the water, as measured by the paddlewheel log, with our speed over the bottom, as measured by the Loran, we isolated the difference, which could only be attributed to the Gulf Stream. It is like walking on a moving sidewalk between airport concourses without any newsstand landmarks or other references to gauge speed. The beauty of it for the northbound sailor is that practically no matter what he does — pinch into a gale or heave-to — the stream still gives some progress.

At 1800 hours we raised the mainsail and #1 genoa and pointed into a light breeze. By 1900 the log read 2.0 knots and the Loran 3.3. At midnight, boat speed remained a paltry 2.0, but speed over the bottom had zoomed to 5.2! The next day, sailing near the Stream's core, we picked up 3.5 free knots — not bad for a boat whose maximum speed is 6.4 knots.

Following the west wall about 130 miles offshore we curved gently to the northeast, and, as darkness fell on our second night at sea, the wind rose until it blew twenty knots, gusting higher.

We took a reef in the mainsail and switched down to the #2 genoa. Of course, the wind was smack on the nose. Starboard tacks took us inshore, more or less toward Savannah, Georgia, and out of the stream, while port tacks carried us eastward toward the core.

William Reidenbeck, writing in Fort Lauderdale, Florida's *Waterfront News,* posited a formula that predicts 3½-foot waves for every ten knots of wind in the open ocean. In the Gulf Stream, he suggests subtracting twenty-five percent for southerly winds and adding twenty-five percent for northerly winds, meaning that in twenty-knot winds we could expect waves of almost 9 feet. With this caveat: "Do not use this rule-of-thumb in deteriorating conditions. A thirty-knot northerly can build seas far greater than the 12 or 13 feet predicted by the formula. When news services predict significant seas, remember that about once per hour a wave roughly twice the average height is going to rumble through."

Our choice, then, was to stay out of the stream and its potentially square waves but risk getting caught in an eddy or inshore countercurrent, or accept the above-normal waves as the price of a free ride. Unable to make up our minds, we took six hours on one board and a half-dozen on the other until dawn when the wind died and left us slatting on a placid sea.

On we motored through the day and into the next night. *Adriana* rolled gently through the quilted waters, the main sheeted tightly and the waxing moon luminescent in the eastern sky. The foam earpads of Wayne's Sony Walkman warmed my ears, wooing my wanderlust ("Let's just keep going!") with the haunting insolence of Sade's "Never As Good As the First Time."

The sea was a pool of quicksilver. In the moonlight two dolphins broke the surface, arched in a perfectly symmetrical ballet, their silhouettes surfacing and sounding as though orchestrated by the linkage of an underwater carousel. I could have cared less about wind or time or destination.

Low on fuel, we left the wondrous habitat of the stream and headed for Charlestown, South Carolina, passing as we went a line of fishermen rumbling to and from these rich feeding grounds. There followed a day laboring in the waterway before we exited again and, like pilgrims obsessed with reaching Mecca, pointed offshore to find our small piece of the vast, clockwise-circulating gyre of the North Atlantic.

On my watch that night, I plugged in Jean-Luc Ponty's "Cosmic Messenger," and when my mind shifted from the stars it tried to imagine the five hundred years it takes for deep layers of the stream to come full circle, on a path shaped by the Coriolis force of the Earth's rotation and the secondary effects of global wind patterns and ocean-bottom topography. You cannot see the stream, but it can be sensed by instruments to assure its existence. If you had been a crewman aboard the U.S.C.G. *Tampa,* which once measured a twenty-two-degree Fahrenheit difference in sea temperature between bow and stern (where the Labrador Current and Gulf Stream meet), you could have felt the blue god on the palm of your hand.

Alas, our flirtation with the stream was cut short by a dire forecast of thunderstorms, high winds, and steep seas—we had thought we'd take a shot at rounding the redoubtable Cape Hatteras. Discretion is the better part of valor, and we grunted into Beaufort, North Carolina, then steamed north in the tame and tideless bay waters. The predicted storm failed to materialize that night, but the next, while we were anchored in an elbow of the Alligator River, dark clouds marched across the sky, illuminated by devastating ground strikes and a brilliant cloud-to-cloud latticework of white lightning. The weather reports that night told of huge seas off the Cape, and we slept smug in the smartness of our decision.

A frisky southerly breeze propelled us up the Chesapeake Bay on a dead run toward our Annapolis berth, blowing itself out by dawn. The rise and fall of the estuarine tides produce modest currents—a knot or so max—but unless you're racing they're not enough to get excited about. Not like the arterial flow of the blue god that makes its rounds with the dependability of a town crier, bearing news and history, dolphins and tuna, salpae, and all manner of sea life that thrive in its warm breath, helping a few small boats complete the journey they started so many months and tides ago.

On a Saturday morning, berthed just south of Annapolis where John Schofield and his family intended to refurbish *Adriana,* I collected my personal belongings, drenched by the humidity. There were toolboxes, compasses and dividers, books and charts, and years worth of dubious "treasures" to pack and move ashore. John, I think, was astounded to watch the waterline rise a full three inches as I off-loaded.

In a bin under the forward berth I found a deflated red lobster air mattress that was a gift from a friend to Pete, a wooden rubberband gun, a miniature plastic soldier, and a wad of duct tape that he used to trail behind the boat, watching the "waterbug" skip and skitter in our wake. Not allowing myself to fall into sentimentality, I threw them into a box and kept packing.

Only when I had said my good-byes to John and Wayne and started down the dock did I look back and let the memories flood the emotional voids. I was closing the book not only on a stately old boat, but on a personal history as well, and I confess to a tear or two as I turned to the waiting car and drove away.

As it stands today, my memories are clear if imperfect in their understanding of all that happened. I remember taking command of *Adriana* and thinking how big and able she was, standing up to the gusts like a stalwart oak; and how pretty the sheerline Philip Rhodes had given her, and wondering what the old master thought of his paperwork spread out on the drafting table; he must, I think, have dropped his pencil, leaned back, and mused, "Yes, that's it."

Most of all I remember the cruises, those summer-long adventures along the New England coast with Peter and Adriana, how the boat nurtured their love of the sea, and what the sea taught them about wildlife and the water, other cultures, however close, and of valued human qualities such as patience, vision, and sound judgment.

When our cruise of the East Coast was interrupted by news of Pete's death, I was surprised to learn from his friends in Michigan how much he had talked to them about boats and the ocean. He had considered sailing central to his life. Odd for a Midwestern twelve-year-old, I thought, especially one with cerebral palsy who must have had far graver matters to worry about. But maybe that's the point: Like the rest of us, Pete forgot his troubles when sailing.

And when I was told that the Dexter Public Library had purchased and dedicated a handsome volume on sailing in his name, I knew without any doubt that all those days of listening to, "Dad, when are we gonna get there?" had not been in vain.

*

Four years later, time has changed both Andra and me and the places we visited. Eastport, Maine, is no longer a moribund town of empty houses but the state's second-largest port, handling cargo of timber and salmon. Charleston, the belle of the South, was whipped by Hurricane Hugo, its nearby waterway crushed with falling trees, impassable to the cruisers who in autumn lock trunks and tails and head south. The Florida key we saw under construction near the Lahtis' camp is now a famous resort, featured in *Travel & Leisure,* the sort of place actors go to vacation. Newport is still Newport, an overcrowded fudgery in summertime and an empty, windy waterfront in the winter. During our absence we made a peace with the town, forgiving it its excesses and admiring it for its many beauties — the resplendent beech trees filling the spaces between the white church spires and the rocky, tumbledown shore, boldly squared to the open ocean.

I don't dream much about prison anymore. But there is the memory of one dream that has been with me for a long time. Federal marshals drove me from the prison in Kentucky back to Michigan. We stopped for the night at an unremembered penal institution, and while the marshals went to their motel, I was locked up in a large cell with many other inmates, all in leg irons and manacles, rattling and clamoring as if we were all ghosts from Christmas past. There was a small window, and in the morning you could see the mist hanging in the draws and stream beds that bisected the fields surrounding the grounds. The juxtaposition of the two worlds was unreal, so unreal that now I can't remember if this vignette of the netherworld was dreamed or actually experienced. It makes me wonder if something happened there that can only find expression through the subconscious. More than twenty years later, time still defines itself as the continuum of consciousness, which, like a boat's wake, begins strong, white, and frothy, each drop in perfect focus, and ends in a simulacrum, smoothing itself into the unimaginable vastness and blur of the sea.

Adria is a junior at the Rhode Island School of Design in Providence, gearing up for her senior year in Rome. Sculpture is her major — this term. Like most twenty-year-olds, she's trying to figure out what she wants to do with her life, which values she holds as important, and what she believes about the meaning of life and death.

She occasionally comes down to Newport for a weekend.

There's not much time to catch up. Stephen usually spirits her into the playroom for blocks and videos. He's crazy about his sister, though he doesn't quite understand why she's so much older and doesn't live with us.

For Adria, time with Steve is special, for reasons that everyone understands except him.

Every so often he points to a photo of Pete on my office wall and says, "That's Peter."

And I say, "Yes, he was your brother."

"I wish he'd come back," Steve says. "I miss him."

"Yes, Steve," I say. "So do I."

When she's visiting, Adria gets up at six with me to walk Tango, the wolf hybrid she, Steve, and I brought home a year ago. Usually we go down to the beach, which lies just over the hill from our house. On Pete's birthday, Andra and I throw a few flowers into the surf from the rocks at Purgatory Chasm. There, in what a French poet called the hour between the wolf and the dog, Adria and I talk about what she's doing—her sculpture, her mother, Aku, the future. Sometimes Pete's name comes up. It's not something either of us is ready for every day. Beyond the quick aside—"Pete would have liked this"—it is still too big for us. If you grasp him, you've got to hold him, and when you're trying to stay on track with the rest of your life, the weight can be too much. But every so often we let ourselves in to him, open our breasts and talk . . . about the way he smiled, the things he said ("So I was wrong!"), and how much we wish he were here with us, running into the surf with that awkward lope, kicking the waves with no more worries than Tango as she gallops after the sandpipers flying above the foam. I cannot imagine Pete without cerebral palsy. If he hadn't had CP, he wouldn't have been Peter. To wish otherwise would be to reject him.

There are, I realize now, differences between intellectual and emotional truths. Peter was a piece of artwork, and as such his life and death cannot be reduced to nothingness by the mere invocation of science. To apprehend him requires another language.

Returning home, I watch Steve closely as he plays with his blocks or tears around the kitchen on his tricycle. Occasionally I notice an odd movement in his legs, a look in his eye, or an expression that reminds me of Pete. It is a fleeting sensation to which I try not to attach too much significance. I say to myself, well, they have the same father . . . but it is almost as if Peter is winking at me through a window between two worlds, and Steve is that portal, a medium of communication. It goes beyond the temporality of memory and the cold truth of genetics to the supernatural, and that is where I wish to leave it — without explanation.

Andra and I are back where we started. But only in a geographical sense. We both work at home doing things we enjoy. Despite our differences, we have found we make a pretty good match. Most importantly, we are still in love. We returned only to an arbitrary point on the circle of our lives. For me, the real beginning lies buried with my seafaring ancestors, and the end lies in the seed of the unborn. Coming home was not a fessing up to reality, simply a pause between the end of one chapter and the beginning of the next. This book is one of those, the fulfillment of a promise I made to myself a long time ago when I first held Peter's ashes in my hands.

Life tilts on the axis of death, Nature adds where it has subtracted, and the older but wiser mariner is more careful where he throws his anchor. Mindful of the past, expectant of the future, what's important is that he still goes to sea, where the wind still blows and the waves still break, and shakes hands with the old outlaw he thought he'd left behind. I threw my anchor to the wind, and the wind blew.